The Value of Hawai'i 3

BIOGRAPHY MONOGRAPHS

The Center for Biographical Research of the University of Hawai'i at Mānoa is dedicated to the interdisciplinary and multicultural study of life writing through teaching, publication, and outreach activities.

In addition to *Biography: An Interdisciplinary Quarterly*, published since 1978, the Center sponsors the Biography Monograph series; a chronological list of previous monographs follows.

For further information about the Center or its publications, contact the Center for Biographical Research, University of Hawai'i at Mānoa, Honolulu, Hawai'i 96822 USA; biograph@hawaii.edu; http://blog.hawaii.edu/cbrhawaii/.

The Value of Hawai'i 3

Hulihia, the Turning

Edited by

**Noelani Goodyear-Ka'ōpua,
Craig Howes,
Jonathan Kay Kamakawiwo'ole Osorio,
and Aiko Yamashiro**

A Biography Monograph
Published for the George and Marguerite Simson Biographical Research Center
by the University of Hawai'i Press
Honolulu

26 25 24 23 22 21   6 5 4 3 2 1

Library of Congress Control Number: 2020946984

University of Hawai'i Press books are printed on
acid-free paper and meet the guidelines for permanence
and durability of the Council on Library Resources.

Print-ready files provided by Center for Biographical Research.

Cover art: *Liko Honua* by Kapili'ula Naehu-Ramos. Used with permission.

CONTENTS

III. Community Building—Turning Toward Each Other

IV. Emerging Futures—Turning Anew

ACKNOWLEDGMENTS

The editors would like to thank Joel Cosseboom, Interim Director of the University of Hawai'i Press, and its professional and supportive staff, who have done so much to make this book possible—Emma Ching, Noah Perales-Estoesta, Santos Barbasa, Mardee Melton, Cheryl Loe, Debra Tang, Carol Abe, and Alicia Upano.

At the Center for Biographical Research, Managing Editor Paige Rasmussen was integral to all stages of editing, design, and preparation for publication. This is her book too. Graduate Assistant Zoë Sprott's careful eye and public relations skills have been greatly appreciated.

N. Mahina Tuteur was invaluable in contacting and making arrangements with many contributors.

Special thanks to Kapili'ula Naehu-Ramos for her beautiful painting that graces the cover, and to Maile Naehu for making the space for Kapili's art to flourish.

We have been constantly inspired and strengthened by Auntie Terri Keko'olani and Haunani-Kay Trask, nā wāhine koa.

Some who have passed have never left us as sources of encouragement and support—Kekuni Blaisdell, Kanalu Young, Phyllis Turnbull, Paul Lyons, and Jojo Peter.

Noe thanks 'Īmaikalani Winchester for listening. Aiko is very thankful for her co-editors. And we are all profoundly grateful to the contributors for the love and commitment with which they create the value of Hawai'i.

A Prayer, Lifting

Kuʻulani Muise

Hulihia is an integral energy in our cosmologies, a natural cycle in our land/sea/sky/dreamscapes, and manifests, again and again, in our histories. In looking at these cycles, there is always a reciprocal and inherent energy that works in consort with hulihia, which is the kūlia energy. So entwined are the two that we cannot speak to one without beginning to name the other. Implicit in every upheaval is the rising, is the flowering up of something new.

We began in a turning,
over and over,
in the night before night.
A friction, enkindled.
A heat.

O ke au i kahuli wela ka honua.

Turned out of this turning,
out of the lipo-black, the lipo-blue,
rolling, roiling—
the shape of an island
heaped and hissing
from the sea.
A steam rising.

A prayer, lifting—
a prayer for rain.

A conjuring of cloud—
of dog clouds, blue and red, running on the sea,
of the short cloud, the tall cloud, the long,
finding, finally, the face of the new mountain.
A place to bring their carried waters.

Ua ka ua, kahe ka wai.

Then a torrent,
a rending of squall across the ridge.
Rivulets, streams, rivers.
Water settling into courses.
A weathering of rock.
The long work of softening.
The thick quiet of soil
and up out of the new earth —
an unfurling, green.

'Ōkupu.

A promise of forest.

—

How many turnings went after?

The first sound of footfall under the trees.
A flurry of wings.
Millennia of hands turning soil, moving stones,
invoking all the forms.

Kini, lau, mano, lehu.

Then big ships in the bay.
Mouths, of men and of women, together eating.
An un-naming of all the forms.
A toppling of all the stones.
Disease and a great dividing of ground.
Overthrowing, overturning.
A vast and devised forgetting
of the stories and their words.

—

We began, again, in a turning,
over and over,
of bombs rupturing earth,
of stone-dust and ash.

Turned out of this turning,
out of the lipo-black, the lipo-blue
their boats sliding on the dark water,
reflecting the stars.

O ke au o Makaliʻi i ka pō.

And up onto the dark shape of the island,
a procession of nine,
the ʻāina, Kanaloa, their aliʻi nui.
The coconut broken open,
the stars fed.

A prayer, lifting—
a prayer for rain.

A conjuring of cloud—
of the Nāulu, flying furious across the water.
Of thick clouds, of bomb-blocking clouds.
And everywhere a new rain pouring down.

Ua ka ua, kahe ka wai.

A rain for remembering,
for washing away the thick net of forgetting.
Rain filling mouths
turning them lush with ʻōlelo.
An adze-head rain opening the earth
finding generations of buried seeds.

ʻO ʻimiʻimi o nalowale o loaʻa ē.

Up out of the newly turned ground,
multitudes of fronds greenly lifting,
together standing,
growing, building.

ʻŌkupukupu.

A promise of forest.

Na ke aloha e kono akula.
Hele maila,
hele maila ē.

Kuʻulani Muise is a mother, a writer, and an illustrator. Mauna a Wākea is her mauna, Mahakea her wai, and Kahua her ʻāina where she resides with her husband, Jake, and their three children—Palikū, Leiʻohu, and Laniua.

Kūʻokoʻa

Independence

Noelani Goodyear-Kaʻōpua

I am writing in a time of hulihia. We are living in a time of hulihia.

An overturning. A massive upheaval, so great that when the churning eventually slows, our lives will be permanently altered.

> As I write this, Hawaiʻi has seen triple digit growth in COVID-19 daily
> for a month. Almost one in ten tests are coming back positive.
> On Oʻahu, we are beginning a second stay-at-home order.
> We cannot gather in groups of more than five people.
> Trails, beaches, dine-in restaurants, and all non-essential businesses
> have been closed.

Hurricane Laura has just torn off roofs, shattered windows, and flooded the Gulf Coast. In May 2020, Typhoon Vongfong destroyed the city of San Policarpo in the Philippines, forcing more than 91,000 from their homes. Six days later, Super Cyclone Amphan ravaged Kolkata in India. Two and a half millon people were evacuated in Bangladesh.

Worldwide, storms are intensifying, as the extraction and burning of fossil fuels changes our climate.

In 2019, Hurricane Dorian was the worst natural disaster the Bahamas have ever seen. The year before, Hurricane Michael devastated the Florida Panhandle.

The year before that, the "unprecedented" category 5 hurricane Irma brought catastrophe to several Leeward islands of the Caribbean. Two weeks later, Hurricane Maria ravaged Puerto Rico.

The US President made light of their hardships, failing to provide urgently needed resources for the recovery. Thousands died.

Harvey in Texas in 2017. Winston in Fiji and Tonga in 2016. Patricia in Mexico in 2015.

In *Ka Honua Ola*, Dr. Pualani Kanakaʻole Kanahele writes of a distinct group of "Hulihia" chants, describing eruptions so drastic that they make the landscape unrecognizable.

A few days ago, on the US continent, Wisconsin police shot Jacob Blake
seven times in the back, in front of his children—
the most recent instance of state violence against Black lives.
We say their names . . .
George Floyd, Breonna Taylor, Tony McDade, Ahmaud Arbery, David McAtee.

So many names to say.

New iterations of the white supremacy and systemic racism *endemic*
to the founding and expansion of the US continue to deem some
less worthy of life, freedom, and happiness.
A summer of protest that has rocked cities,
the largest social movement in US history,
is not over.

Hulihia phases are explosive—filled with heat and movement—
both devastating and generative.

The US government has not mounted a cohesive public health response
to COVID-19. To date, almost 190,000 Americans have died.

I open my Twitter feed to see videos of self-proclaimed American patriots
verbally and physically attacking clerks, salespeople, and other workers
just for being asked to wear a simple face mask.
A few square inches of cloth could save lives,
but hyper-individualism must not be inconvenienced.

When new case counts spiked in Hawaiʻi
and the public demanded answers about contact tracing,
the head of the State Department of Health deflected criticism by opening
a press briefing with what he called "good news."
The daily numbers were higher because they included over 56 inmates at OCCC.
Were we supposed to be less alarmed?
Are incarcerated folks somehow less deserving of care?
Over 40 percent of OCCC inmates tested positive.
Where is the good news in that?

This summer in DC, US President Trump had peaceful protestors teargassed,
all for a photo-op in front of St. John's Episcopal Church.
Instead of defending free speech, he called demonstrators disgraceful.
He said the National Guard should "dominate the streets."
He said America was "the greatest country in the world."
He couldn't even hold his Bible prop right side up.
We see more than incompetence.
We see an empire made brittle by its own supposed exceptionalism.

The US spends more on defense than China, India, Russia, Saudi Arabia, France,
Germany, United Kingdom, Japan, South Korea, and Brazil combined.
The 2020 appropriations bill contained $738 billion for military spending.
If dollars were seconds, that would be 23,401 years.
All for "national security,"
though most folks in and under US empire are far from secure.

The number of incarcerated US citizens and houseless folks
has mushroomed over the last few decades.
This is not a policing and military problem. It's an inequality problem.
Injustice creates precarity and insecurity.

Quaking earth. Rivers of lava. Leaping fire and ash. Clouds of steam.
Whole sections of land rising, falling, extending, disappearing.

Hulihia, a transformative change. Things do not go back to normal.

It is my first day teaching fall classes on Zoom at UH Mānoa.
I ask the students to share where they are, and what they are grappling with
in this time. The first one introduces themself, then—
"What am I grappling with? I don't want to go back.
I'm asking myself, what can I do with these next few months of lockdown
so we don't have to go back to the old '*normal*'?"

Dr. Kanahele tells us hulihia chants are inspired by continuous cycles of the living
'āina's own renewal. Overturning the assumed normal makes way for new life.

We are writing in a time of hulihia. We are living in a time of hulihia.

* * *

Nothing lives forever. Empires are not permanent fixtures. A time will come—like it or not—when US empire recedes, crumbles, and transforms. Or collapses. In my lifetime, the deterioration of US empire has never been more plainly observable.

No matter how we feel about the US occupation of Hawaiʻi, or whether we celebrate or mourn the Amerian empire's decline, the people of Hawaiʻi must prepare to be more independent. Such preparation will be good for us, regardless of our future relationships with foreign powers across the ocean.

Many take for granted that Hawaiʻi is the "50th state." It's all most adults living in the islands today have ever known. But the Kānaka who came before exercised political independence here, long before the dawn of American empire.

And these islands will be independent again.

In 2014, I watched the Scottish independence referendum with great interest. As the historic vote unfolded, I was intrigued by how different the debates were from those regarding Hawaiian sovereignty in the past thirty years.

In a nutshell—

Instead of focusing on historical or legal justifications, the Scottish National Party explained how independence could make the lives of everyday people better. The Party offered a vision of "a greener Scotland," which would provide rural areas with greater support. Of "a smarter Scotland," with free, high-quality public education from pre-school through university.

Parliamentary representives in London were seen as too distant to be accountable, and out of step with Scottish values held dear. Smaller but well-networked groups such as the Radical Independence Campaign saw independence as a way to oppose UK wars, social austerity, and privatization that benefits corporations rather than everyday people. Such groups called for an end to poverty-level wages. They also urged Scots to raise their expectations, and exercise their imaginations. The possibility of independent government opened space to envision the kind of society they wanted to build.

The referendum's result did not lead to Scotland's departure from the United Kingdom. But as advocate Adam Ramsay put it, "the possibility of independence, and the ensuing debates, brought about a popular mobilisation for radical social change unlike anything we have seen in these islands for a generation."

* * *

What I propose is straighforwardly simple and infinitely complex. Let us talk regularly and vigorously about enacting *Hawaiian political independence* once again. E hoʻokūʻokoʻa, e ko Hawaiʻi. This tumultuous phase of hulihia, when what is above is falling and what is below is upwelling, is the perfect time to generate as many ideas as possible about what twenty-first century Hawaiian independence could look like.

How could independence improve the health of our waters and lands? How could it help us adapt to a changing climate and kick fossil fuel addiction? We need to regularly discuss and debate how Hawai'i could function more successfully as an independent country, once again.

Kanak leader Jean Marie Tjibaou once said that independence is about having the power to negotiate one's interdependencies. How could Hawaiian independence make ordinary people's lives better? What could independence mean for folks working low-paying service jobs in the tourism industry? What could it mean for UH students who want to apply their degrees to restoring and maintaining Indigenous and local food systems? What could it mean for families dealing with substance abuse and houselessness? What could it mean for multilingual kids and their families? Or for retired kūpuna who need regular care and support to stay healthy?

How can we craft visions for independence that *start* with these people?

Inspired by the natural process of a hulihia, imagining new possibilities can be the best consequence of this undeniable phase of massive disruption and overturning of the assumed normal.

Before the rock begins to harden once again,
may four hundred,
four thousand,
forty thousand,
four hundred thousand visions
for Hawaiian independence
burst forth.

Works Cited

Kanahele, Pualani Kanaka'ole. *Ka Honua Ola: 'Eli'eli Kau Mai*. Kamehameha, 2011.
Ramsay, Adam. *Forty Two Reasons to Support Scottish Independence*. Commonwealth, 2014.

Noelani Goodyear-Ka'ōpua is a professor in the political science department at the University of Hawai'i at Mānoa, where she teaches Hawaiian and Indigenous politics. Her books include *The Seeds We Planted*, *A Nation Rising*, and *Nā Wāhine Koa*.

Introduction

Craig Howes

Jon Osorio and I had the idea for the first *Value of Hawai'i: Knowing the Past, Shaping the Future* on October 29, 2009, while jogging and talking in Mānoa. I had arrived twenty-nine years before as a young assistant professor of English who knew nothing about where I now lived. Over the years I became part of Hawai'i's literary and theatre scenes, its young adult library programs, and eventually the university's Center for Biographical Research, which I still direct. Since its mission includes telling the stories of Hawai'i's people, I had also become a co-producer of the *Biography Hawai'i* television documentary series, and the principal scholar for several Living History programs, which meant identifying and getting the best informed people involved in public projects. Over time, my belief in the power of Hawai'i's stories and testimonies, and my wish to contribute what I could to creating a future shaped by such visions, steadily grew. In the process, I came to know many interesting and inspiring people. And Jon knew many more.

Published in 2010, the first volume had its contributors identify the origins of the troubled state of affairs at that time, and offer points of departure for a Hawai'i-wide discussion on the future. We organized over sixty events after the book appeared to have those discussions. Four years later, *The Value of Hawai'i 2: Ancestral Roots, Oceanic Visions* continued the conversation, gathering fresh voices together to share their inspiring work and ideas for creating waiwai—value—for ourselves, and coming generations. Among those voices were the editors, Aiko Yamashiro and Noelani Goodyear Ka'ōpua, who urged all of us to turn our gaze "to the watery world of Oceania" and "to commit truly to imagine and practice less fearful or judgmental ways of being together." They too made sure that many conversations inspired by their volume's contents took place.

On April 3, 2020, Jon and I were wearing masks, walking in the lower campus parking structure of a locked-down University of Hawai'i at Mānoa. When Jon said it was time for a third *Value of Hawai'i*, my immediate though unspoken response was that this was a terrible idea. We then tried to figure out how we might do it.

We decided two things that morning. The collection had to be online and free, and we needed Aiko Yamashiro and Noelani Goodyear-Ka'ōpua to join us as co-editors. In his invitation email to them, Jon described the project as "an update of the *Value of Hawai'i* series in which the authors would write shorter assessments of where we are in this new decade and in the throes of the virus." As we Zoomed over the next few weeks, we thought about who we wanted to hear—former contributors to the first two volumes, thinkers and doers, new and different voices. Hundreds came to mind. We also sought out poets, who have their own compelling ways of offering and celebrating value, and whose contributions appear at key points throughout the collection. Though this volume has twenty more contributors than either of the first two, we still didn't have enough space for all the people we wanted to ask.

Guidelines went out on June 1. We offered our writers a number of possible options and points of departure. Look to the future. Make it personal. Think about "value" or "waiwai"—what do we need, respect, cherish? Tell stories. Write for everybody. And make sure it is about Hawai'i. Because we wanted the pieces to survey an issue and create sparks rather than provide comprehensive coverage, 1,500 words was the limit—though we doubled it for a few specific jointly-written pieces. This proved a challenge. People had so much they wanted to say! But the length also provided focus. Aiko's concluding piece for this volume suggests how intense and productive the conversations between editors and writers could be.

Production matters were also being resolved. After a meeting with Interim Director Joel Cosseboom, we could tell our contributors that the University of Hawai'i Press would publish the collection, making it freely available locally and internationally on a range of online platforms. At the Center for Biographical Research, Managing Editor Paige Rasmussen took charge of the copyediting, proofreading, and interior design. By the first week of September, the collection was complete—five months from the idea to what you are now reading.

With regard to the editing, although we aimed for internal consistency in the individual essays, we left some latitude overall. For example, some people call the mauna so important to so many essays "Mauna Kea." For others it is "Maunakea," and for still others, "Mauna a Wākea." Some writers want "Moloka'i," others insist on "Molokai." We've respected their wishes.

As for the Hawaiian language, we are following common contemporary editorial practice. Except for emphasis, we do not italicize it—'ōlelo Hawai'i is not foreign to this place. We also let the writers decide how much or how little they would translate Hawaiian words, phrases, and paragraphs—not translating can also make a point.

Though the volume came together quickly, events unfolded even faster. Because some essays refer to the number of infections and deaths due to COVID-19, one of our grimmer editorial tasks was updating those numbers right before going to press. As you read this now, those numbers are higher. Other essays should be read as snapshots of when they were composed—June of 2020. Their subjects guaranteed they could not avoid seeming dated in certain ways. Yet they still channel the energy of change, courage, and clarity that can take us into a better future.

* * *

In one of our May editorial meetings, Noelani suggested "Hulihia" should be the volume's theme. We embraced the idea immediately, and the beautiful and power-ful poem by Kuʻulani Muise and Noelani's own meditation on Kūʻokoa that open this collection both demonstrate why "Hulihia" is such an apt term for its contents.

We are also profoundly grateful for the striking and perfect cover image. The creation of Kapiliʻula Naehu-Ramos, "Liko Honua" captures the feeling of extreme, profound, destructive, and creative turning and change.

The green darkening toward blue at the edges invokes the ocean always surrounding us, extending for thousands of miles in every direction.

Water. Moana. Kai.

The white swirling where the green meets the dark yet glowing central shape is steam, rising in billows from where the lava meets the sea. Fire becomes earth, water becomes air. But the swirling also represents the waves, always approaching and retreating from the shore, hurling themselves into the air, then falling.

ʻEhukai.

The central red and black form's surface is pebbled, each piece a different size and shape. But pōhaku by pōhaku, they come together into a bud. A sparkling raindrop. A tear. A mosaic.

And also a paradox. Is the surface being broken into pieces by the fierce glowing heat and liquid fire surging up from below, or are the fragments forming, turning dark as the lava cools, preparing to gather into ʻāina? Or both?

Hulihia.

At the center, lying still in a rising yellow aura, is a fetus, a keiki—and not just of a person, but of all living things. Hāloa. Then Hāloa.

The future, certainly. A womb, certainly. But also a kīpuka—a place where life is protected from harm during necessary times of convulsion, devastation, and transformation. Life waiting to emerge, to return, to flourish.

ʻĀina momona.

A settler to these islands, I had to learn these things. They are valuable to me, and affect how I live here. But they are not mine, and much of what pulses on the cover remains invisible to me.

Kaona.

I can say with confidence, however, that all the essays in this collection respond to this time of hulihia. Here you will find people turning to face threats to our health, safety, and sense of right. People turning to new possibilities—different economic models, changed relations to ʻāina, solutions to problems that have plagued Hawaiʻi for generations. People are turning to each other, knowing that only sharing the burdens will make lifting them possible. And we are all turning to the future, knowing that what is already truly valuable here—recognized, nurtured, preserved, and generously bestowed by the first and current kiaʻi—will be essential to our efforts to improve the quality of our lives, and to save the lives of those for whom we will be the ancestors.

A proud 2020 graduate of Molokai High, cover artist Kapiliʻula Naehu-Ramos is eighteen years old. She offers to us her vision of Hawaiʻi's waiwai, and its future.

Hulihia. The turning.

Craig Howes is the Director of the Center for Biographical Research and a Professor of English at the University of Hawaiʻi at Mānoa.

I
Overlapping Emergencies—
(Over)Turnings

What will it take to begin again now, in ways that open futures, rather than continue to foreclose them?

Want to get on board?

Grounded

Kathy Jetñil-Kijiner

Im eor jet rej buromoj im rej ettor im armej rej jibwe er mokta jan aer ekkake.
*And, there were some who were buromoj [afflicted by melancholia or grief], and they
run, and people seize them, before they can fly away.*

"Bwebwenato in Lōrro"/"Story about Lōrro,"
Stories from the Marshall Islands

Anchor yourself outside her room. A jaki
to sleep on, a cooler for drinks. Hands flexed
and prepared to ground her in this life.

There are some who grieve—
the weight there heavier than lead but you
grab hold of their ankles before

they can depart. Offer remedies—
a gloved hand against their face.
A mask-spoken word. Sadness pulls

us all beneath the waves. *Endrein*
you say when your mother enters
the hospital. Life is like this. You accept

so many years pulling others from flight,
harsh hospital ward alight but who
grounds you?

If I follow the family line to the sand below
which ancestors will still be anchored there
beside someone healing, someone asleep?

Offer remedies for grief. Instructions
for which leaf to boil, soft hands to soothe
the right chant to whisper into their ear

Would you have needed
to demand your safety then too?
Would we have listened to you?

* * *

My cousin has been a caretaker for much of her life, and is also a nurse who regularly works in both the hospital and the outer islands. The poem is about my fear for her, and so many in her field of work, especially after seeing the rise of deaths and even suicides of nurses and doctors around the world, being sent to the front lines without any protective gear, without the institutional support they so need.

My aunt, my cousin's mother, recently entered the hospital. I admired the way my cousin shifted from nurse to caretaker immediately. It's not just a job or occupation for her. It's who she is. There's a very specific way in which Marshallese family members support and nurse—"ri-kau" will sleep around the clock at the hospital. They'll take shifts, bring with them coolers of drinks and food so that they never leave the side of the patients. They'll massage their family members. They'll bring mats, or jaki, and pillows and blankets to sleep next to patients' beds on the hospital floors.

Confession: I've never been a great ri-kau. This is why I have nothing but admiration for caretakers and nurses. I have yet to fully embrace or understand that role, but for most Marshallese women, it's second nature. I'm uncomfortable, and frankly afraid, of hospitals. So for now, until I can begin to practice this role, I offer a poem. A small token.

Another source of inspiration was the lōrro. I thought I was done writing about the lōrro, the Marshallese legend character of the woman who flies from island to island from grief over a lost love and broken heart. But the line that inspired the poem I wrote came from a legend about the lōrro.

For rimajel reading this post, I've done a lot of writing about both the lōrro and the mejenkwaad. Most of that writing has been to reimagine these characters, humanize and understand them as more than a villain or a ghost. For this poem, I reimagined the grief that makes the lōrro fly. Instead of grief over a lost love or a cheating spouse, I reimagined the grief that must come for every person clinging between life and death, grief over leaving their loved ones behind, a grief so powerful it makes them fly.

Originally published on Kathy Jetñil-Kijiner's website on May 28, 2020, at https://www.kathyjetnilkijiner.com/a-poem-grounded/.

Kathy Jetñil-Kijiner is a poet and performance artist of Marshallese ancestry. She also serves as Climate Envoy for the Marshall Islands Ministry of Environment, and Director of the nonprofit Jo-Jikum.

Catastrophic Failure of the Planet

Chip Fletcher

In 2013, when the carbon dioxide content of the atmosphere passed 400 parts per million (ppm) for the first time in fifty-five years of measurement—and probably more than 3 million years of Earth history—a TV political drama marked the event by staging an interview on the evening news with an EPA scientist. The anchor asked the scientist about how dangerous 400 ppm would be for humanity. "If you were the doctor and we were the patient, what's your prognosis—a thousand years, two thousand years?" The scientist's answer stops everyone in the newsroom in their tracks.

"The person has already been born who will die due to catastrophic failure of the planet."

Wow. I was stunned—not by the content, but that somebody in Hollywood was actually paying attention to the reality of climate change. "Yea, that's about right, and it's already started," I thought. The scientist described what this would look like: "mass migrations, food and water shortages, spread of deadly disease, endless wildfires—way too many to keep under control, storms that have the power to level cities . . . ."

With that warmup, let's consider climate change, based on peer-reviewed scientific literature.[1] And let's not sugar-coat it.

In 2015, the United Nations passed the Paris Agreement to keep the rise of global temperatures "well-below 2°C (3.6°F)" above preindustrial levels, and to "pursue efforts" to stay within 1.5°C (2.7°F). But as the UN Environment Programme and others have repeatedly noted, there is a yawning gap between countries' actions and what is required to meet the Paris targets.

The release of carbon dioxide and other greenhouse gases is causing the climate to change 170 times faster than natural forces, and even after declarations of a global warming emergency, and twenty-six years of efforts by world governments, the scientific community, and citizens groups, average temperatures and fossil fuel emissions are still rising. Renewable energy use has risen and costs have fallen, but at far too slow a rate to offset the growth in fossil fuel consumption. Coal remains the single largest source of power generation, accounting for 36% of global power, while renewable energy provides only 10% of global power. In fact, the top fossil fuel producing nations are on track, and have announced plans to produce, about 50% more fossil fuels by 2030 than is compatible with stopping warming at 2°C.

Carbon dioxide emissions increased about 0.6% in 2019, driven by a 5% increase in land-use emissions, including fire deforestation—the fastest rate in five years. While land use represented around 14% of total emissions, it contributed more than half of the 2019 increase.

Economic indicators and trends in global natural gas and oil use suggest that emissions will continue to rise over the next three decades. Concentrations of carbon dioxide in the atmosphere will increase. The 410 parts per million average in 2019 was 47% above preindustrial levels, a concentration not seen since the Pliocene Epoch, 2.6 to 5.3 million years ago. Global warming has increased air temperature by 1.2°C (2°F), a rate that has more than doubled in the past forty years. However, land regions have seen nearly 1.8°C warming, and the oceans only 0.8°C.

The likely global temperature increase this century will be a median 3.2°C (5.8°F). There is only a 5% chance that it will be less than 2°C, and only 1% less than 1.5°C. The year 2019 was the second warmest in recorded history; the five-year period 2015–2019 has been the hottest on record; and 2010 to 2019 was the hottest decade lived through by any man, woman, or child . . . ever. Climate change risk is much greater than what the media usually portrays. The current release of carbon dioxide is affecting us ten times faster than any climate change event of the previous 66 million years. That's when an asteroid killed the dinosaurs.

Intolerable heat, extreme weather, animal and plant extinctions, and wildfires are all on the rise. Glaciers are melting, the oceans are warmer, and sea level is rising. Globally, a 12% increase in extreme rainfall is matched by a 10% increase in land area under drought. Due to current emissions, 70% of the world's population and gross domestic product face a 500% increase in flood impact. In the US, the number of weather disasters is up 14% since 1995–2004, doubling since the previous decade. In 2019, there were fourteen weather and climate disaster events—three floods, eight severe storms, two tropical cyclones, and a wildfire, with losses exceeding $1 billion for each. The 1980–2019 annual average is 6.5 events; but between 2015 and 2019, it was 13.8. Scientists have assessed more than 355 extreme weather events ranging from Hurricane Katrina to Russia's 2010 heatwave. Results indicate that human-caused climate change made 78% of them more likely or severe. Heatwaves account for 47%, droughts 15%, and heavy rainfall or floods for 15%. The evidence is mounting that human activity is raising the risk of extreme weather, and especially weather linked to heat.

Thanks to today's levels of carbon dioxide in the air, staples such as rice, wheat, maize, and soy have as much as 13% less protein, zinc, vitamin B complex, and iron. By 2050, an additional 300 million people will be malnourished, and 1.4 billion women and children will have iron deficiency. Let's look at wheat. Today it provides 20% of all protein for humans. By 2050, the world's nine billion people will increase wheat demand by 60%. But given anticipated droughts, floods, and higher CO_2, actual wheat yield is projected to decline by 15%—a recipe for food shortages, desperation, and violent conflict.

As for our freshwater crisis, 66% of all humans face water shortages at least one month each year. Seventeen nations are under extremely high water stress, meaning that every year, they are using almost all the water they have. Freshwater withdrawals are already exceeding sources. US withdrawals exceed natural recharge by 17%, China by 22%, India by 52%, and North Africa and the Middle East by more than 1000% each year. By 2030, global water requirements are expected to exceed sustainable water supplies by 40%. If warming continues at this rate, water supply deficits could increase five-fold, with once-in-a-hundred years droughts occurring every two to five years for most of Africa, Australia, southern Europe, southern and central US, Central America, the Caribbean, northwest China, and parts of South America.

With 1.2°C (2°F) global warming today, nearly one-third of the world's population is exposed to deadly heat waves. For every 1°C (1.8°F) increase, one billion people will have to adapt or migrate to stay within the climate conditions best suited for crops, livestock, and a sustainable outdoor work environment. As unlivable climate conditions spread, the already massive human migration problem will get much worse.

In the summer of 2019, two European heat waves just weeks apart shattered hundreds of all-time records—both linked to human-caused climate change. The one in late June 2019 reached 115°F in France, eclipsing its all-time record by more than 3°F. A World Weather Attribution study concluded that its core was around 7°F warmer than it would have been a century ago, and that heat waves of this magnitude are ten times more likely now. The heat wave in late July reached all-time record highs in the UK, Belgium, the Netherlands, Germany, and Luxembourg. Paris reached nearly 109 °F, breaking the former record by 4°F. Researchers determined that such a heat wave was ten to one hundred times more likely to occur now than before the Industrial Revolution. When it built north into the Arctic, that same heat wave caused the biggest melt day of the Greenland Ice Sheet in measured history.

In 2016, a quarter of the planet's ocean surface had its longest or most intense heat wave on record. In two regions—the Bering Sea of Alaska and waters off northern Australia—such an event was up to fifty times more likely due to human-caused climate change. The abnormally hot water triggered the worst mass coral-bleaching event on record for the Great Barrier Reef.

Unless warming is reduced, researchers estimate climate change could cause the extinction of more than one-third to one-half of all animal and plant species in only fifty years. The key variable driving these losses is maximum annual temperature—the hottest daily highs in summer. Extinctions will be two to four times more common in the tropics than in temperate regions—a big problem, since most plants and animals live in the tropics.

Although emissions have only warmed the surface 1.2°C, the impacts are severe and widespread, because they magnify the stress that communities already place on natural systems. Across 65% of the terrestrial surface, land use and related pressures have led biotic intactness to decline beyond 10%, a "safe" planetary boundary, with changes most pronounced in biodiversity hotspots. One recent paper concluded "the unparalleled appropriation of nature is causing the fabric of life on which humanity depends to fray and unravel" (Díaz et al.).

When the anchor in our TV scene asked the EPA scientist if this was the administration's official position, the scientist answered, "There isn't a *position* on this any more than there is a position on the temperature at which water boils." To those paying attention, it's been clear for years that climate change threatens the stability of civilization and the security of human communities. We are in the first stages of catastrophic planetary failure.

Note

1.   See Xu et al.; Hofste et al.; Jones et al.; and Abatzoglou and Williams.

Works Cited

Abatzoglou, John T., and A. Park Williams. "Impact of anthropogenic climate change on wildfire across western US forests." *PNAS*, vol. 113, no. 42, 2016, pp. 11770–75.

Díaz, Sandra, et al. "Pervasive human-driven decline of life on Earth points to the need for transformative change." *Science*, vol. 366, no. 6471, 2019, p. eaax3100.

Hofste, Rutger Willem, et al. "17 Countries, Home to One-Quarter of the World's Population, Face Extremely High Water Stress." World Resources Institute, 6 Aug. 2019, https://www.wri.org/blog/2019/08/17-countries-home-one-quarter-world-population-face-extremely-high-water-stress.

Jones, Kate E., et al. "Global trends in emerging infectious diseases." *Nature*, vol. 451, 2008, pp. 990–93.

World Weather Attribution. "Human contribution to the record-breaking July 2019 heatwave in Western Europe." 2 Aug. 2019, https://www.worldweatherattribution.org/human-contribution-to-the-record-breaking-july-2019-heat-wave-in-western-europe/.

Xu, Chi, et al. "Future of the human climate niche." *PNAS*, vol. 117, no. 21, 2020, pp. 11350–55.

Chip Fletcher is Associate Dean of Academic Affairs and a Professor in the School of Ocean and Earth Science and Technology, University of Hawai'i at Mānoa.

This Is Just the Beginning

Climate Change, Positive Peace, and the "New Normal"

Maxine Burkett and Naima Moore

The COVID-19 pandemic has upended daily life as we once knew it, and tested our capacity to respond effectively and "bounce forward" from catastrophe. Many have likened the pandemic to a trial run for the disastrous climate events to come. Some may believe that the end is nigh. What we are seeing, however, is just the beginning.

Reopening businesses and loosening restrictions may appear to be a cautious and protracted return to normal. However, from a climate perspective, "normal" was already a crisis—a time when climate crises were manifest throughout the islands and world. According to climate experts, this persistent state of crisis will continue as long as our leaders fail to drastically curb our emissions. While the pandemic-induced slowdown of industrialized economies has provided the world with a perceptible respite from pollution, our return to perceived normalcy should renew cause for concern.

As we embark on a new beginning, Hawaiʻi's precarity in the face of nested crises in governance, disease, healthcare, and a rapidly changing climate underscores the critical need for financial, political, and social investment in resilient recovery—a recalibration of policy and economic models that prioritizes the needs of our communities and natural environment over offshore profits. Hawaiʻi thus stands at a pivotal and promising embarkation point, one with the potential to determine our collective climate future and way of life for decades to come.

Transformation through Peace, Peace through Transformation

As opposed to depictions of collapse, we hold to visioning and effectuating "preferred futures." Hawaiʻi's successful recovery from COVID-19 depends largely on cultivating "positive peace," which could lay the groundwork for strong, equitable, resilient communities. "Negative peace" describes only the absence of conflict. Positive peace is the measurable presence of attitudes, institutions, and systems that help humans flourish and prevent conflict from arising. When conflicts do arise, they are transformed to enhance cooperation and understanding, yielding ever stronger communities. The research is clear: as a community's positive peace increases—signaled by accountable governments, equitable economies, access to health care, and more[1]—so too does its ability to mitigate emergent threats and protect vulnerable populations. Positive peace protects more lives and livelihoods exponentially.

The impacts of the climate crisis will vary across communities, as will the risks to peace and stability at the local level. We understand that when problems arise, local and sustainable solutions work best. Peacebuilding therefore requires and initiates a holistic approach to discerning the full ecosystem—human and non-human—in response to community needs. This is achieved through a proto-col of ethical communication, listening first, and honoring and elevating community-based wisdom to guide us toward a just and sustainable future.

Hawaiʻi is particularly well-situated to address peacebuilding in a time of emerging climate crisis and its convergence with such acute crises as COVID-19 and the movement to eradicate racial hierarchy and anti-black racism. Equidistant from populous and diverse countries and economies, the islands sit at the center of our Earth's climate crossroads and at the forefront of the perils—and possibilities— that environmental change presents. Hawaiʻi has fostered productive, place-based, and interdisciplinary climate policy endeavors. Though by no means free of racial hierarchy and discrimination, we have also forged a relative peace in culturally and ethnically diverse communities. Our rules of engagement differ from counterparts on the continent, suggesting greater possibility for healing and transformational change. Hawaiʻi continues to pioneer in peacebuilding and peace education.

Along with other Pacific Island nations, Hawaiʻi's cultural legacy can provide a foundation for stronger policies that will protect the spiritual, reciprocal, and famil-ial relationship between people and land, thereby enhancing human capital, right relations, and an equitable distribution of resources—all vital for positive peace. Hawaiʻi's state motto makes this explicit: "Ua mau ke ea o ka ʻāina i ka pono," or "The life of the land is perpetuated in righteousness." Climate change not only threatens the physical environment, but also endangers an essential component— the genealogical quintessence—of Native Hawaiian, Pacific Islander, and Aloha ʻĀina cultural and spiritual identity, imperiling these communities' cultural legacies and the wellbeing of future Indigenous generations. As George Huʻeu Sanford Kanahele writes, "In the Hawaiian mind . . . a sense of place [is] inseparably linked with self-identity and self-esteem. . . . Being without a place . . . mean[s] uprooted-ness in every sense of the word: being cut off from the most vital physical, psycho-logical, social, and spiritual values of one's existence" (175, 182). Climate change is often discussed as impacting our material or economic health. However, it will have negative psychological impacts on communities that regard the land, seas, and mountains as members of their own family and genealogy. In pursuing lasting peace and resilience, Hawaiʻi's post-COVID rebuild must strive to preserve the identity and sense of wellbeing for our communities—and particularly our youth, who risk a short-changed life by living in a world completely altered in landscape and environmental quality.

A Way Forward

While COVID-19 and the climate crisis appear to signal societal collapse, these are fertile grounds for growth. Those in the Pacific facing threats to their lands through no fault of their own know all too well the consequences of inaction. To date, most Pacific nations have avoided COVID-19's decimating impact by shutting them-selves off from the world. They can close their borders, but they cannot stem rising temperature and tides. Translating climate resilience and peacebuilding into tangible, culturally-responsive processes allows us to recover from this crisis, and to mitigate and prepare adequately for the next.

Food security is a potent example. Empty supermarket shelves and headlines about food and household and medical supplies raise serious concerns among government officials, healthcare providers, and residents about our extreme reliance on imported goods. Across the community, distinguishing between food security and food sovereignty has shifted from a marginal to a more central concern. Hawai'i's near absolute dependence on external food sources maintains a perpetual state of instability and vulnerability. Small Island States with limited capacity for food production due to rising sea levels, lack of freshwater, and soil salinization are at the mercy of imports, which makes this concern even more poignant. Climate forecasts indicate that rising temperature and CO2 concentrations will make food more expensive and less nutritious—and with varying availability. Hawai'i, however, has great capacity for self-reliance in terms of food and nutritional securi-ty, which in turn would make us more resilient, and perhaps even a food source for our Pacific Island neighbors. Implementing policy that gives communities agency to grow and access locally-sourced food is just one way of promoting a sound busi-ness environment and ensuring equitable distribution of resources. This also pro-motes peace.

That Hawai'i has one of the highest unemployment rates in the US due to COVID-19 also demonstrates a critical need for a more resilient economy that pro-vides more economic equity (that preserves our peace) and durability (that pro-tects our climate and our livelihoods). Several Hawai'i-based initiatives are working to achieve this, such as the 'Āina Aloha Economic Futures Declaration, dedicated to building a sustainable, *pono* economy based on Native Hawaiian cultural values, and the feminist economic recovery plan for Hawai'i, released by the Hawai'i State Commission on the Status of Women, which advocates for a more sustainable and diverse economy. Indeed, Hawai'i's dependency on imports and lopsided fiscal reli-ance on tourism and the US military present an immediate roadblock to resiliency efforts.

This moment of departure is an opportunity to usher in new, equitable, and regenerative communities, for which "normal" is defined by our resilience and cohesion in the face of change. Our islands cannot afford to revert back to the pre-COVID normal: a state of being initiated by over a century of Western models of modernization (and globalization) and most recently defined by a creeping climate emergency. Creating pathways to a preferred future for our children and grandchildren simply requires that we take the first step.

Note

1.   The eight pillars of peace are a well-functioning government, free flow of information, a sound business environment, acceptance of the rights of others, high levels of human capital, low levels of corruption, good relations with neighbors, and an equitable distribution of resources.

Work Cited

Kanahele, George Hu'eu Sanford. *Kū Kanaka, Stand Tall: A Search for Hawaiian Values.* U of Hawai'i P, 1993.

Maxine Burkett is the Co-Founder and Senior Advisor of the Institute for Climate and Peace, a Professor of Law at the University of Hawai'i, and a Global Fellow at the Wilson Center.

Naima Moore is an Intern at the Institute for Climate and Peace.

The COVID-19 Crisis

Josh Green

Sitting on a hotel lanai on Kauaʻi in early 2020, I watched a cruise ship make its way into harbor with hundreds of visitors from all corners of the world. This very normal ritual for the beautiful Garden Isle, welcoming tourists for a day or two, was about to become an existential threat.

I couldn't help but view this moment through my more practiced role of local emergency room physician, as opposed to the lens of Lieutenant Governor. It had been only six or eight weeks since we had first heard about a novel coronavirus coming out of Wuhan, China. We had few if any cases of COVID in Hawaiʻi at that point, but we were vulnerable. I thought to myself, Kauaʻi only has eight intensive care unit beds and fifteen ventilators. What happens if this ship is full of pre-symptomatic passengers infected by the virus? If Kauaʻi has an outbreak, can we handle it?

As acting Governor in the early days of the outbreak (Governor Ige was on a brief diplomatic mission to Japan) I pushed hard to set up a joint information center to help us sort through the reports that were exploding globally. There was a lot of misinformation to manage, and there were incredible unknowns. To that point, Hawaiʻi's Department of Health was minimizing the potential impact of COVID in Hawaiʻi, and most planning revolved around the inevitable need to push for social distancing. No one was wearing masks yet, and there seemed to be a feeling in the air that we wouldn't get hit like they were in China and Europe.

In fairness, despite what others might say, there simply was no roadmap to follow for Hawaiʻi for COVID-19. The department had only a handful of contact tracers should the disease reach our shores (SARS and MERS, other legendary coronaviruses, had had little impact on Hawaiʻi in previous decades), and the department remained severely understaffed for such rare emergencies. We were aware that the state lab could only process a total of 250 tests a week, and they were holding onto those tests for extremely ill patients should they reach the ICU.

What would happen if a cruise ship with 1200 passengers had hundreds of cases and spread the virus on one of our vulnerable neighbor islands? Or for that matter, how would large numbers of international travelers flying to Hawaiʻi spread the disease? Hawaiʻi has a severe healthcare provider shortage—22 percent statewide, and up to 40 percent on the Big Island and Maui. We were headed for a disaster.

To me, the question was not if this outbreak was headed our way, but when. In fact, I suspected it had already been among us before the reports started to come out of China. I heard innumerable stories from patients that they had a nasty "flu" in December and January, but had just ridden it out. Many reported a bad cough and fever, but had tested negative for the flu. Had they all been COVID patients?

A Japanese married couple had traveled to Maui, and the husband turned up sick and positive for COVID as they headed to O'ahu to see an old friend. By the time they returned to Japan, the wife also was sick with COVID. The Department of Health scrambled to contract trace this couple, but was reluctant to test their close contacts. Was this the beginning of things to come?

In early February, the White House decided to ban travel from China to the US, but many Chinese travelers could still go to Japan, then fly to Hawai'i. Reports of Chinese visitors continued to come to me as LG, and I knew we were starting to see cases clinically. But it was a war to convince our own epidemiologists to test widely. They preferred to quarantine suspected but unconfirmed cases at home. We were literally blind without testing. By March 5, a group of us confronted our own public health officials and demanded an increase in testing. They pushed back, citing shortages of swabs, reagents, and personal protective gear, all made more difficult by early challenges emanating from a CDC (Centers for Disease Control and Prevention) that was navigating Washington politics as it tried to address a global pandemic and a virus that didn't care whether you lived in a red state or a blue state.

The crisis would be managed with social distancing and self-quarantine, our department said. University leaders and the medical community pushed back fiercely. Had the Department of Health position prevailed, we would have had mass fatalities in our islands. One model showed that without immediate changes to our approach, we were facing an epic surge of COVID and 4779 deaths by April 20. The medical community's position prevailed, and we launched forty-two testing sites statewide. Some independent providers began drive-through clinics to meet both the medical and psychological need of Hawai'i's people. It was not a moment too soon.

Results of confirmed cases began to come in from the private statewide testing efforts, and the gravity of the situation became evident. This testing, while critical and extremely welcome, was still less than two percent of the population, and suggested an undercount of actual cases. Hawai'i was about to be overrun with COVID-19. We had to lock it down, or face a surge so awful that Hawaii's 244 hospital intensive care unit beds and 459 ventilators would be filled in a few short weeks, and we would be forced to make the same death sentence clinical decisions that places like Italy and Spain were now making. In these nations they could only provide enough critical care support for those in their sixties and younger. Our kūpuna were going to die.

Testing grew and Hawai'i's case count started to rise. First ten, then fifteen cases a day, then in March we started to see counts in the twenties. It was coming.

So we shut it down.

On March 17, I reached out to our lead in the administration, General Ken Hara, a thoughtful and nimble Adjutant General who had been appointed by the Governor to lead the COVID response, and asked him to impose a stay-at-home order (a mandatory quarantine on all of our residents who didn't work essential jobs) and a 14-day quarantine on all travelers who came into Hawai'i by sea or air. Eight days later the Governor made this lifesaving order official, and Hawai'i was spared an event so horrible that it couldn't be contemplated by anyone who hadn't seen behind the curtain. We in healthcare knew we were only days away from an outbreak that could not be contained.

In the subsequent weeks, Hawai'i's arrivals dropped a shocking but necessary 99.6 percent, and we saw a steady decrease in cases across the state to single digits. We also experienced legendary unemployment that peaked in late May. It was an impossible decision that had to be made, and one which would set the stage for how Hawai'i will view itself going forward for decades. We placed life above politics or profits. We placed 'ohana ahead of self-interest.

Federal aid and unemployment subsidies brought the state necessary life support, but its limitations began to become evident as the summer began. People's willingness to continue to socially distance waned, and the local kama'aina economy began to reopen in early May. Intermittent surges of COVID returned, but fatalities were avoided almost completely. Hawai'i's mortality rate remained the lowest in all of the fifty states, but our unemployment was the highest in the nation.

By June, most of the country began to open again and experience large spikes of COVID. Again we were put to the question, how long could we remain almost completely locked down with no economic activity? Domestic violence and suicides were rising. Children were not getting immunizations and their education was severely compromised. One out of five people had issues with food security, and almost half of our people worried they couldn't afford basic necessities. We had to begin to consider how to reopen Hawai'i safely.

Opening up to tourism meant allowing for the risk of spreading COVID and looking like the rest of America. Staying closed meant eventual economic ruin. So only one possibility remained. Test everyone who travelled to Hawai'i, and quarantine all who refused that commitment to health and safety. On June 24, after three weeks of exhaustive debate between dozens of Hawai'i leaders, a decision was made. We announced the plan to require pre-testing of anyone who wanted to come to Hawai'i and avoid a 14-day quarantine, beginning August 1, 2020, thus restoring tourism and an economic future for Hawai'i.

We had survived the first wave of COVID, and our community's unprecedented and brave sacrifice was recognized globally.

What would happen next, with comprehensive screening and testing for all who chose to come to paradise? Only time would tell.

Josh Green, MD, is the Lieutenant Governor of the State of Hawai'i.

COVID-19, the Disease that Has Shined a Light on Health Equity

Joseph Keaweʻaimoku Kaholokula

Not even Hollywood could dream up a more fantastic plot for a movie.

A global plague causes economic turmoil. The United States, a superpower once envied by other nations, is now mocked because of an egomaniacal president. A third of its citizens are unemployed. People on the right and left of the political spectrum take to the streets in protest. Major US cities are set afire. Domestic supplants international terrorism as a national security concern.

This plot seems too unbelievable to be true. Yet, it is our reality.

The coronavirus disease 2019 (COVID-19) pandemic, and the events surrounding it, have changed our reality, and exposed the cracks in our political, economic, and social systems. Before I get to these broken systems, let me go back to my pre-COVID-19 reality for a moment.

I have spent the last twenty years researching, teaching, and advocating to address how inequities in the *social* determinants of health are root causes for health inequities across ethnic groups in Hawaiʻi. I have shared that our health and wellbeing are strongly linked to our socioeconomic and educational status, physical environment, social support networks, access to health care, and race/ethnicity. I have shared that the decisions of policymakers and business leaders strongly influence these social determinants of health.

I borrowed catchy one-liners to make my points, such as "It is more about your zip code than your genetic code." Or "It is about what matters to people, not what's the matter with people." Or "The conditions under which we live, play, learn, work, and age affect how well and long we live." I shared these thoughts—notions with robust scientific backing—with policymakers, clinicians, healthcare administrators, other scientists, and the public.

These catchy one-liners did not impress all.

Policymakers, clinicians, and other scientists often asked me—

"Aren't these disparities due to bad genes and lifestyle choices?"

"If they ate better and got more exercise, wouldn't they avoid these health problems?"

"If they comply with medical advice, wouldn't they do better?"

These questions exemplify a myopic view of a bigger, more complex picture surrounding health equity. They also blame the individual—as if people choose to live unhealthy lives and die prematurely.

When I shared the same ideas about social determinants of health with the public, instead of asking questions, they shared with me their life stories—real examples of how their economic, work, and social circumstances get in the way of them living healthier. They also shared their experiences, good and bad, with medical insurers and the healthcare system. An Aunty struggling to manage her diabetes once told me—

"If I could, I would, but I cannot, 'as why hard."

She was saying that her ability to live a healthier life was not under her direct control. If her life circumstances were better, her health would be better.

The prevailing mindset among many leaders in politics, science, and healthcare stresses the genetic and biological over the social determinants of health. In fairness to my colleagues, many of them do recognize the social determinants of health, but feel ill-equipped to address these issues in their work. Some believe that these issues are too large and complex to change. Even public health funders seem to favor scientific investigations that discover new drugs or genes over those that discover how social conditions influence health, or how innovative community-driven solutions can prevent disease. I felt like a fish swimming against the current.

Enter COVID-19, a disease that spread rapidly around the entire world. A disease that government leaders proclaimed was colorblind and income-blind— that everyone was equally vulnerable. As it turns out, they were wrong. COVID-19 does discriminate—not based on lifestyle choices, but on life circumstances. The social determinants of health (Abrams and Szefler).

We see inequities in the risk of contracting COVID-19, in the severity of symptoms, and in the frequency of hospitalizations and death when infected. Essential workers, who are among the lowest paid in our society, have a greater exposure risk to COVID-19 and of exposing their families and neighbors. These inequities follow ethnic lines and socioeconomic conditions. Pacific Islanders have the most positive COVID-19 cases of all ethnic groups in Hawai'i (Kaholokula et al.). It is the same in other states, such as California, Oregon, Washington, and Utah, where Pacific Islanders are prevalent.

We are also seeing an uneven distribution of the financial burden and behavioral health problems caused by the COVID-19 containment and mitigation efforts across different populations. Those living under dire socioeconomic conditions before COVID-19 have taken the biggest hits. They are experiencing more severe financial deprivation and drastic increases in depression, interpersonal violence, and substance use during this crisis—problems likely to remain long after the discovery of a COVID-19 vaccine. These vulnerable populations—Native Hawaiians, Pacific Islanders, and Filipinos—are more likely to live in poorer socioeconomic conditions, denser homes and neighborhoods, and to be overrepresented among the homeless, incarcerated, and essential workforce than other ethnic groups.

COVID-19 has shined a light through the cracks of our systems, spotlighting the social determinants of health for me. It has awakened our understanding that inequities beget inequities, that our systems are actually broken, and that our old values and assumptions are flawed.

How will we emerge from this COVID-19 crisis? Will we maintain status quo, or make profound changes to our political, economic, and social systems? Will we continue to make decisions based on consumption and acquisition, or conservation and cooperation? Will we go back to our overreliance on tourism, or diversify and localize our economic base? Will we invest in our public education system the same way we vigorously have invested in tourism and development? Will we respect Indigenous rights and knowledge and preserve our natural and cultural resources, or will we continue exploiting them?

Here are some ripe ideas for systemic transformation:

- Make public-private investments in our public school system, from pre-primary to tertiary education. There should be no inequities in the value of education between private and publicly administered schools, or all social groups in Hawai'i. We also need to invest in our university system to strengthen our workforce and promote innovation. Education strongly impacts our health (Braveman and Gottlieb).
- Provide livable wages, in part through a higher minimum wage. A person should not need to work multiple jobs to make ends meet. States that have moved to higher minimum wages found that people were spending more, which strengthened the overall economy. Also, the more we earn, the longer we live (Neumayer and Plumper).
- Diversify and localize our economic base. As we diversify our economy and move toward lifting up local businesses, innovation, and entrepreneurship, we increase opportunities at home for our young people.
- Make Hawai'i affordable for kama'aina. We have seen an exodus of people due to the cost of living in paradise (Peterkin).
- Invest in those neighborhoods and communities where health promotion makes the most sense. People who live in communities with strong government investment live longer (Neumayer and Plumper).
- Ensure equitable access to educational, financial, and occupational opportunities, regardless of ethnicity or social condition. Tear down the walls of structural racism.
- Use Native Hawaiian values and perspectives to preserve our cultural and natural resources. Our natural resources are finite and fragile. Our cultural resources make us resilient and diverse, and our Native Hawaiian culture makes us exceptional and unified.

At the time of writing, Hawaiʻi had the lowest number of people who contracted COVID-19 and the second-fewest deaths of any state in the US. In that first wave, our value of aloha helped to contain the spread of COVID-19. While people elsewhere were worried about losing their rights due to the physical distancing and mask-wearing requirements, the people of Hawaiʻi readily complied with these necessary public health measures. We suspended our rights for the collective good because of our aloha for each other and our collective island values. We immediately turned our attention to protecting our ʻohana and kūpuna and the homeless and incarcerated. We were able to flatten the curve in that first wave.

Now, Hawaiʻi is near the top of all states where COVID-19 cases have grown the fastest. We need to once again show our aloha for each other and comply with all COVID-19 containment and mitigation measures.

After this crisis is over, let aloha also be the unifying value of Hawaiʻi that will be the catalyst for this Hulihia!

Works Cited

Abrams, Elissa M., and Stanley J. Szefler. "COVID-19 and the Impact of Social Determinants of Health." *Lancet Respiratory Medicine*, vol. 8, no. 7, 2020, pp. 659–61.

Braveman, Paula, and Laura Gottlieb. "The Social Determinants of Health: It's Time to Consider the Causes of the Causes." *Public Health Reports*, vol. 129, suppl. 2, 2014, pp. 19–31.

Kaholokula, Joseph Keaweʻaimoku, et al. "COVID-19 Special Column: COVID-19 Hits Native Hawaiian and Pacific Islander Communities the Hardest." *Hawaiʻi Journal of Health & Social Welfare*, vol. 79, no. 5, 2020, pp. 144–46.

Neumayer, Eric, and Thomas Plumper. "Inequalities of Income and Inequalities of Longevity: A Cross-Country Study." *American Journal of Public Health*, vol. 106, no. 1, 2016, pp. 160–65.

Peterkin, Olivia. "Hawaii Loses Nearly 5,000 Residents Amid Slowest US Population Growth in Decades." *Pacific Business News*, 31 Dec. 2019.

Joseph Keaweʻaimoku Kaholokula, PhD, is Professor and Chair of Native Hawaiian Health, John A. Burns School of Medicine, University of Hawaiʻi at Mānoa.

Local Foods Through Crisis

Hunter Heaivilin

One night in early April, I dreamt I was perusing the kalo shelf in a neighborhood market. A grocer ambled up and told me the flavor, color, and uses, of each corm in the array. Moi, Mana 'Ulu, 'Ula'ula Kumu, Haokea, Lehua Maoli, Lauloa 'Ele'ele-'ula and so on—all were organized by variety. When I woke, the night had ended, but this common dream has not.

Hawai'i's farms are often motivated by the desire to reduce imports and feed communities, and consumer demand for many local products is greater than supply. However, increasing production doesn't necessarily decrease food insecurity in our communities, as fair farm gate prices too rarely meet the budget of the family down the street. The COVID-19 pandemic has demonstrated the economic precarity of farms and families. To build a more resilient Hawai'i, we must address long-standing structural inequalities and systemic vulnerabilities in our food system. Fortunately, in this time of crisis, the opportunities for food system change are finding new purchase in the world that can be.

My adult life has been consumed with Hawai'i's food system, but when growing up in the islands it was mostly invisible to me. Outside of a middle school afternoon trying poi with sugar or the occasional lū'au, my taste for local fare was mostly focused on musubi and plate lunch. After high school I graduated into gardening and agroforestry, enthralled with radical self-reliance as a means to change the world. Teaching permaculture took me across the islands and the tropics. Working with homesteads and farms at some point gave way to assessing zoning code and building market systems. Over a decade in, somehow my hands are now are soft—soil supplanted by systems, planting by policy. The certainty of that young gardener has been replaced by the questioning of this PhD student. My doctoral research now focuses on the development of Hawai'i's agrofood system and food crises we faced during the twentieth century. That historical lens informs my current work on our food system responses to the pandemic.

The pandemic disruption to Hawai'i's food system is significant, but not as disordering as some previous crises. Eighteenth-century famines in the islands were driven by weather and warfare. Drought and battle decimated local production, causing starvation. In the early nineteenth century, economic factors shifted labor from agriculture to sandalwood, as the draw of a global market overwhelmed efforts at local production, producing famine (Rice). Over the next century, the global market grip grew tighter, as export agriculture and food imports both expanded. By the start of the twentieth century, most agricultural parcels, excepting plantation lands, were only five acres in size. Then in the century's first half, our food crises were again mostly driven by warfare.

During World War I and World War II, the narrowing supply coming into the islands created food system disruptions. For both wars a local governing body was formed to oversee pricing, allocate imports, and bolster local production. In the year prior to the start of WWI in April 1917, Hawai'i imported $10,000,000 of mostly staple foods (Kuykendall and Gill). By May 1917, Hawai'i's Legislature had created the Territorial Food Commission to govern production and conservation, and make the islands as "independent as possible of the mainland for subsistence." This broad ambit made it the "most powerful board ever created in the Islands" ("Territorial Food"). The commission addressed increasing the taro supply, supported a robust Women's Committee that performed statewide outreach, and funded county agents to work with small farmers, a service that then became part of UH Extension. Wheat flour shortages led to incorporating local starches into "war bread." The Banana Consuming Propaganda Committee redirected the oversupply of once exported fruit into local bakeries and homes, developing Hawai'i's taste for banana bread that persists today.

By the late 1930s, sixty percent of fresh vegetables were being imported (Magistad and Frazier). Over the course of WWII, Hawai'i food administration changed hands from the Office of Civilian Defense's Food Control Board to the military Governor's Office of Food Control. The Food Control Board developed a plan to bolster rapidly declining taro production exacerbated by labor shortages. But in its efforts to address food conservation and price issues, the board was chided for not including women, who were responsible for "90 per cent of the food purchased and prepared" ("Consumer Group"). As the conflict wore on, planning work became dominated by plantation interests, which wrongly assumed their industrial agriculture operations could easily transition to local food production. The grounding of offshore fishing fleets over fears of naval surveillance created a protein gap in local diets that Spam filled. Poke eventually returned, but Spam musubi has endured. After the war, only five percent of agricultural lands, in small parcels, were producing vegetable and fruit crops (Scheffer), and by the end of the decade, just over half of Hawai'i's food was being imported (Yamaguchi). These wartime events reveal the complexity of food crisis management, and how our responses have shaped "local" food.

Spared so far from drought and war, today's food crisis is economic. Supply chains have remained intact, although mass unemployment has drastically diminished the purchasing power of most households. Initial pandemic disruptions of restaurants, hotels, and farmers markets have carved into the bottom line of farms across the state. New relationships between farms and food banks have become lifelines for farmers and families. New funding mechanisms—federal, state, county, and philanthropic—have supported these efforts. Food hubs connecting farms and buyers have seen surges in membership, routing unprecedented amounts of local fare onto family tables.

The open questions are about how durable these changes are. Will we, as in past crises, fill our plates with so much local produce that we will no longer dine without it? When funding wanes and we trudge back to work, will our palates have been transformed? More pointedly, how do we ensure that addressing hunger and supporting local agriculture aren't just crisis responses, but new realities?

As all food crises have shown, planning in food systems is crucial. Such efforts need to be comprehensive, inclusive, and both short and long term. Akin to previous food crisis committees, but without the broad powers of government, an Agricultural Response and Recovery Working Group formed in late March. We've worked to direct resources to keep farmers and ranchers afloat, connect local production to community feeding needs, and compile opportunities for growing the agricultural sector. Yet, for all of our work, Hawai'i's food system still must deal with systemic vulnerabilities and inequalities due to our geography and global market relations. For food system resilience and equity to transition from an appetizing idea to our main course of action, we must center both sustainability and justice in our economic planning. Two good places to start are cooperative development and living wages. We need cooperative mechanisms that enable farms to overcome the mismatch between their small parcel size and the global marketplace on our shelves. We also need a living wage for all workers. Otherwise, local food will remain out of reach for too many.

Global discord and markets will continue to interweave with island lands, labors, and flavors to produce and reproduce place, people, and palates. The response decisions we make now, and the plans we set forth, will set the table for years to come. I have yet to see kalo arranged by variety in the grocery store, but in recent weeks two new poi pickups around my neighborhood have popped up.

Sure tastes like progress to me. So, when can, eat up Hawai'i. The poi is sweet.

Works Cited

"Consumer Group Agent is Urged." *Honolulu Star-Bulletin*, 21 Jan. 1942, p. 4.
"Food Commission Has Great Powers." *The Maui News*, 11 May 1917.
Kuykendall, Ralph S., and Lorin Tarr Gill. *Hawaii in the World War*. The Historical Commission, 1928.
Magistad, O. C., and T. O. Frazier. "Production and Marketing of Truck Crops in the Territory of Hawaii." *Hawaii Agricultural Experiment Station*, no. 78, April 1938.
Rice, Stian A. "Food System Reorganization and Vulnerability to Crisis: A Structural Analysis of Famine Genesis." 2018. Kent State University, PhD dissertation.
Scheffer, W. J. "Large Scale Farming in the Hawaiian Islands." *Journal of ASFMRA*, vol. 12, no. 1, 1948, pp. 70–79.

"The Territorial Food Commission." *The Maui News*, 11 May 1917, p. 4.

Yamaguchi, R. "Honolulu unloads fruits, vegetables, meats, dairy and poultry products, 1959." Agricultural Extension Service, College of Agriculture, University of Hawaii, *Agricultural Economics Report*, no. 45, May 1960.

Hunter Heaivilin is a PhD student in the Department of Geography and Environment at the University of Hawai'i at Mānoa, and works as a food system planner at his firm Supersistence.

Reopening the Hawaiʻi Tourism Economy in the Age of COVID-19

Sumner La Croix

What is revealed in the COVID-19 pandemic about Hawaiʻi's economy? It is well known that tourism is Hawaiʻi's largest private sector industry, so its sharp decline during the global pandemic comes as no surprise. What I take away from Hawaiʻi's experience over the epidemic's first few months (March through July 2020) is that no economy can function well unless its resident population is healthy. For this to happen as Hawaiʻi's visitor economy reopens means that strong measures must be taken to control community transmission. Here I lay out how this might happen, supported by Hawaiʻi's island borders

Governor Ige's proclamation in March 2020 of a mandatory 14-day quarantine of all incoming passengers was the key policy for restoring the health of Hawaiʻi's resident population, as it stopped the inflow of tourists and returning residents from the US continent who were potentially infected with COVID-19. Hawaiʻi's geographic isolation allowed this policy to be effectively implemented, as monitoring of arrivals at the state's airports allowed borders to be more effectively sealed relative to other states. But the 14-day quarantine also had the radical effect of reducing tourism arrivals by 99 percent. With tourist spending accounting for roughly 25 percent of Hawaiʻi's output, or about $2 billion per month, the state slid into depression during spring 2020, with unemployment exceeding 22 percent of the workforce. The state and county stay-at-home orders and closure of non-essential businesses and schools during March, April, and May also depressed resident spending, yet were instrumental in restoring the health and safety of the resident population. In the short run, the health of Hawaiʻi's resident population was restored by closing down much of the internal economy and virtually all of the visitor economy. As the number of interactions between Hawaiʻi residents drastically fell, the opportunities for viral transmission plunged, and diagnosed cases plummeted.

Once community transmission became very low (zero to six cases per day from mid-May to early June), stay-at-home orders were eased and non-essential businesses were allowed to gradually reopen. Though Hawaiʻi residents should have responded to more personal interactions by becoming *more vigilant* in their precautions against becoming infected, such as wearing masks in public places and maintaining physical distancing, unfortunately, many instead relaxed adherence to these requirements. In Hawai'i and across the United States, public messaging campaigns about the need to maintain safe practices were few, and generally ineffective in reaching younger people, who perceived themselves as relatively safe from serious illness after infection. As a result of this, the number of cases surged, with the 7-day moving average of cases in Hawai'i ranging from 20 to 31 between July 1 and 15.

Along with the obvious health concerns, the surge in Hawai'i cases is incredibly problematic for Hawai'i's economy and all that it means for the livelihoods of its people. Limiting the number of people without adequate food or facing eviction depends on reopening Hawai'i to visitors and their spending. Tourism, however, can only resume safely and robustly if potential tourists perceive Hawai'i to be a safe place to visit, and Hawai'i residents can be assured tourists are relatively free of COVID-19. To signal that Hawai'i is a safe place to visit depends entirely on the level of COVID-19 infection in Hawai'i. Low levels can be achieved whenever Hawai'i residents decide they must wear high-quality masks in public places, physically distance, and wash hands. But what will it take to convince more residents to behave well? Most likely, reinforcement by businesses, customers, and employees of safe practices, and public relations campaigns that positively nudge resident behavior in the right direction. Overall, there needs to be much better communication from state authorities about safe practices and their impact.

How can Hawai'i residents be assured that tourists are relatively free of COVID-19? A good first step involves the screening measures announced in Governor Ige's plan to reopen Hawai'i's tourism economy. These measures are similar to proposals by Tim Brown, DeWolfe Miller, and Sumner La Croix, and consist of pre-departure and arrival screening of visitors for COVID-19, including temperature screening, symptoms and travel questions, and a negative result for a RT-PCR test taken within 72 hours of flight departure. Any person arriving in Hawai'i without required clearance documentation would be quarantined for 14 days.

For the governor's plan to work, Hawai'i state and county governments need to strengthen quarantine enforcement beyond June 2020 levels. Otherwise, large numbers of passengers will avoid taking a COVID-19 test prior to departure and then attempt to break quarantine (Halliday). Pre-departure testing and health screenings for those flying to the islands are critical, as they also lead to safer airports and flights. Passengers who receive a positive test in their home city can recover at home, consult with their physician, and better utilize their health insurance.

Is Governor Ige's testing plan likely to work? Brown, La Croix, and Miller found that screening for high temperatures and COVID-19 symptoms in the departure city would remove about one-third of infectious passengers from flights to Hawai'i. Adding a second screen—testing air passengers for COVID-19 infection with an RT-PCR test in their departure city—would remove 80–90 percent of infectious passengers from flights to Hawai'i. This means that 10 to 20 percent of airline passengers with COVID-19 would escape detection, vacation in Hawai'i, and potentially transmit COVID-19 to other tourists and Hawai'i residents. Brown, La Croix, and Miller estimate that if tourism rebounds to half of its daily pre-COVID-19 levels, then roughly 375 visitors with COVID-19 infections will come to Hawai'i each month. These numbers could be much higher if states that send millions of tourists to Hawai'i—California, Arizona, and Texas—fail to take strong action to control their spiraling levels of COVID-19 infection. Actions taken by other US states to control their epidemic are important for Hawai'i, as a healthier visitor population reinforces the health of Hawai'i residents.

Can we handle 375+ additional cases per month? It depends on two factors. First, Hawai'i authorities must have the capacity to rapidly identify infections and respond immediately through testing and surveillance. A sound surveillance system that monitors high-risk settings in the tourism industry is important for anticipating and stemming transmission. Relevant populations for surveillance include workers with frequent contact with visitors, such as restaurant servers, front desk staff, housekeepers, and any other high-contact occupations. Any of these workers who develop potentially COVID-19 related symptoms should be offered testing, followed by aggressive contact tracing and workplace testing. Surveillance must be accompanied by rapid testing of possible cases and identification of close contacts. Contact tracing by Hawai'i State Department of Health (DOH) enables close contacts to be quickly identified, tested, and isolated. Sufficient capacity must be in place to monitor symptoms and compliance with isolation orders. DOH also must have the capacity to analyze cluster data and regularly communicate information about the cluster of cases to the public.

Does the DOH have this capacity? In August we learned that the very limited information released by DOH about cases, contact clusters, tracing times, and isolation of close contacts was due to the chaos and incompetence in DOH administration of these programs. Despite a need for several hundred more contact tracers, DOH failed to hire recent graduates of UH contact tracing programs. DOH could benefit from a rapid external review of DOH to ensure best practices are in place and short-run resource needs are met. When New Zealand found its contact tracing slow and ineffective, an external review identified ways to streamline it, and these recommendations were quickly implemented.

Second, tourists visiting Hawai'i need to be given clear guidance on measures they can take to reduce COVID-19 transmission. They should become aware that wearing a mask in a business or public space is required, that physical distancing and masking are expected at tourist attractions. The counties should put signage in public places indicating that mask-wearing is absolutely required. Educational videos should be shown on the plane and at Hawai'i's airports. It is important for tourists to understand why they need to wear masks, to understand how this protects tourism industry workers, other tourists they encounter, and Hawai'i's vulnerable populations. Tourists need to know that they can have a great vacation while wearing a mask in public.

If residents, tourists, and Hawai'i governments all take basic measures to prevent community transmission, there is a good chance that Hawai'i will emerge as a more attractive vacation destination this fall and winter. Many tourists value safe, smart destinations, and will pay a premium to visit those destinations. If Hawai'i builds a "new" reputation as a safe, smart destination, then the tourists will come, and we could experience a strong and safe revival of Hawai'i's economy.

Works Cited

Halliday, Timothy. "The Hotel Tax Should Be Raised — A Lot." *Civil Beat*, 17 May 2020, https://www.civilbeat.org/2020/05/the-hotel-tax-should-be-raised-a-lot/.

La Croix, Sumner, Tim Brown, and F. DeWolfe Miller. "Prevention of Travel-related Reintroduction of COVID-19 Infection in the State of Hawaii." UHERO, 9 June 2020, https://uhero.hawaii.edu/prevention-of-travel-related-reintroduction-of-covid-19-infection-in-the-state-of-hawaii/.

Sumner La Croix is Professor Emeritus in the University of Hawai'i at Mānoa Department of Economics and a research fellow with the University of Hawai'i Economic Research Organization. He is the author of *Hawai'i: Eight Hundred Years of Political and Economic Change* (2019).

Of Pandemics and Financial Emergencies

Will We Restructure or Transform the University?

Laura E. Lyons

I write in the midst of planning for a new academic year rendered unrecognizable from any we have previously known by a global pandemic that forced the University of Hawai'i, like many other schools, to deliver "remote instruction" for the final months of the spring semester. While trying to safeguard health and safety, faculty and administrators, including me, struggle to find the mix of face-to-face, hybrid, and online courses that will allow our advanced students to graduate, and encourage our incoming students to remain enrolled, and then stay for the spring semester.

Every day I hear from students and parents unsure of what to do. Will students be able to afford tuition, given their family's changed circumstances? If they don't attend, will rising unemployment prevent them from finding a job? Will they get housing? How can we help the student whose home lacks connectivity, or whose large household gives them little privacy to focus on their online courses? International students—who often pay tuition at higher rates than in-state students, and who, until the past couple of years, most universities viewed as an important market—grapple with changing and confusing guidelines from the Department of Homeland Security. In making their decisions to enter or stay in the US to study, these students must balance their personal health risks with potential deportation.

Overshadowing all of the unknowns for faculty, staff, and students has been an earnest, urgent, but mostly vague discussion of the inevitable budget crisis the pandemic has created. I write also having read the recently posted Agenda and Supporting Materials for the July 16 meeting of the UH Board of Regents, and it appears that the reality of budget cuts is about to get specific. On the Agenda are two approval requests from the BOR Chair, Ben Kudo. One is for a letter asking Governor David Ige to negotiate with public employee unions to defer salary increases and adjustments. The second is Board Resolution 20-3, "Proclaiming an Emergency and Directing Action by the University of Hawai'i Administration in response to the COVID-19 Pandemic."

This resolution authorizes the administration "to utilize whatever means it has" to reduce operating costs, "including but not limited to, reduction-in-force, furloughs, retrenchment, freeze or reduction in remuneration, etc." The University must present a short-term plan for this fiscal year at the BOR's August meeting, and develop a long-term plan, which may include temporary or permanent closures, reorganizations, and/or mergers of any unit, from a program to a campus. Conveying its urgency to create structural savings, the Board encourages the Administration "to utilize highly expedited processes for developing proposals for change and consulting on them." Urgent responses and consultation, however, are not easily reconciled.

Calls for restructuring have become a commonplace feature of recent budget cycles. Administrators and faculty often suggest that UH has too many four-year campuses and community colleges for our population. Some researchers ask why UH Mānoa needs to teach general education, while instructional faculty often question why researchers paid through general funds are not uniformly required to teach. Implicit in these questions are competing propositions about what the flagship research university in a state-supported system of higher education should be, and for whom. With a student population of just under 18,000, approximately 13,000 of whom are undergraduates, can UH Mānoa afford to see the excellence of our educational and research missions compete, particularly when both depend on state funding, and the Organized Research Units, while generating millions in externally funded grants, nonetheless also depend upon tuition dollars?

I have two related propositions about what the University should prioritize: students and faculty. I write this as someone with administrative experience, but not in an official capacity for the University. But first, can we agree that administrators must cut their own salaries at rates higher than those expected for other public employees? And can we also agree that an across-the-board cut will affect public employees differently, leaving some to face food and housing insecurity?

Proposition One: Any restructuring of the University must not erode undergraduate education, but should, in fact, improve it.

The BOR resolution asks that the long-term plan demonstrate how the University can "help the state recover and serve Hawai'i" while achieving "its diverse statewide mission." It's understandable that the health sciences, engineering, and technology are viewed as essential to that recovery. We are confronting a public health crisis. Producing more healthcare professionals is key to workforce development, and so is the training of data analysts, cybersecurity experts, and teachers. Even before COVID-19, concerns about climate change were fueling our students' sense that they will inherit a planet that might not recover from centuries of extractive industrial practices, driving an uptick in STEM majors as students sought degrees that would allow them to make a difference.

A college education involves the investment of time and money on the part of many. Given the funding that the state puts into the University, we have an obligation to think about our role in diversifying the economy and educating students to contribute to it. At the same time, we must not lose sight of the importance of educating students broadly to use knowledge creatively and collaboratively, not just to make their own lives better but also to imagine alternative models of success and sustainability for the communities they come from and will enter.

If we think too narrowly in terms of immediate employment, especially for undergraduates, we abdicate our other responsibilities. Public universities do not simply supply labor pools, but ensure that our economic and political structures serve the interests of the public as a whole. The domain-specific expertise employers increasingly expect from college-educated, entry-level employees encroaches upon electives and General Education requirements, which orient students toward a greater good, including what is good for Hawai'i. But few people remain in their first job, and their education should prepare them for all the occupations that follow as well as the changes in life circumstances, both individual and social, they will experience.

The challenges we face require people who can navigate the complex political and social dynamics that accompany public crises, and whose artistic interventions can shift public perceptions. Anthony Fauci's frustration with the Trump administration's failure to heed the warnings and recommendations of public health experts shows us that technical expertise, while essential, is not enough. We need people educated to higher levels of literacy and with critical thinking skills to counter the anti-science, anti-humanistic thinking of climate change deniers and social media campaigns by foreign governments interfering with elections. We also need health officials who understand the ethical dimensions of safeguarding public health. What is the metric by which we measure the return on investment of such an education?

Our island communities need the people our students will become, the skills they will have to solve difficult problems we have yet to foresee, and the knowledge and care they will have for Hawai'i.

Proposition Two: The University is better positioned to work with Hawai'i communities when more of its faculty come from them.

What continues to prevent Hawai'i's people from entering the University, as students or faculty? Education is supposed to allow individuals to transcend their personal circumstances, and it does. But this orientation frequently perpetuates brain drain, explicitly or implicitly making students choose between their communities and their own success. Many students are told their opportunities will be greater if they leave Hawai'i. But what if we imagined an education system that from the outset sought to ensure that each student's personal accomplishments will invigorate their connections and eventual contributions to the people and places they care most about?

Many of our programs—American Studies, Education, English, Ethnic Studies, Law, Music, and Political Science, and more obviously Hawai'inuiākea School of Hawaiian Knowledge—now have faculty who grew up in Hawai'i. But by their own admission, STEM disciplines have been less successful at diversifying their ranks. Even with the mandate to curtail hiring, diversifying the faculty—and the administration!—must still be prioritized. For the University to succeed, we need more faculty from Hawai'i in every program, more curricula and research focused on our natural, social, and cultural dynamics, and more administrators whose vision is grounded in aloha 'āina.

As I read Jon Osorio's piece, I was struck by how many of his listed former students are now members of the University's faculty and staff. What they and others offer is an engagement with local communities that involves teaching, research, advocacy, and activism. Though not always comfortable or lauded, their presence is transformative. While it is the BOR's mandate to ask how the University can best serve the interests of the State of Hawai'i, these faculty are asking how the University can more explicitly live up to its role as the University of *Hawai'i*? Can these different questions be reconciled to imagine both a university that is responsive and responsible to the people it is charged with serving, and a more just and sustainable future for Hawai'i?

Laura E. Lyons is the Interim Associate Vice Chancellor for Academic Affairs at the University of Hawai'i at Mānoa and a tenured professor in the Department of English.

Food Insecurity—An Institutional Response

Claudia Wilcox-Boucher

This essay is about hungry students in poverty at a community college in Hawaiʻi, and the quest for an institutionalized service to address food insecurity on campus.

I should start by admitting that I grew up in Kalihi in the 1960s and 70s, and had to run fast to hang on to my twenty-five cents lunch money. I was a master of catching the city bus, and I always knew to "squirrel" snacks. I knew all the fruit trees with easy access in a two-mile radius of my Hicks home. Fortunately, I never knew childhood hunger, as both my parents were employed (Pearl Harbor and Leahi Hospital). I was fairly popular on my street, because I could always provide after-school cookies and snacks to the neighborhood kids. I graduated from Farrington High School and received a University of Hawaiʻi Master's in Social Work in 1985, and after working two jobs (full-time Social Worker III at the Department of Human Services and part-time cruise director on a mai-tai madness catamaran), I decided that Oʻahu was too expensive for me. Despite working two jobs and feeling extremely independent, I was sneaking canned goods from my parents' pantry every chance I got.

In January 1987 I made the move to Hilo. After checking out Kauaʻi and Maui social work state jobs for a transfer, I quickly realized my money would go a lot further on Hawaiʻi island. I worked nearly fifteen years for DHS and then was an executive director for a non-profit for eight years. In 1990, I started teaching night classes at Hawaiʻi Community College (HawCC). Sociology 100 and introductory Social Sciences courses were my assignments, and I wanted students to know that despite humble beginnings they too can achieve middle class bliss if they ride the higher education train. The value of the college train? Increased earning power, improved working conditions, increased personal and professional mobility, improved health and life expectancy, improved quality of life for offspring, better consumer decision-making, increased personal status, more hobbies and leisure activities, etc., etc., etc. Want to get on board?

In 2009, I joined HawCC as a tenure-track Social Sciences instructor, and was so thrilled to be on this train. But I soon learned that despite encouraging and motivating words that students can achieve anything with education, my surroundings were not acknowledging an obvious challenge. Many students are hungry. They live with food insecurity.

Hawai'i island has the highest rate of poverty in the state, the most child deaths due to child abuse and neglect, and in a recent Feeding America survey, twenty-six percent of school-aged children shared that they were food insecure, not knowing where their next meal would come from during the weekend. According to Aloha United Way's ALICE (Asset Limited, Income Constrained, Employed) report, forty-eight percent of Hawai'i County's households are below the ALICE poverty threshold, the highest percentage of any county in the state.

The average age of a student at the Hawai'i Community College is twenty-six years old. About thirty percent identify as Native Hawaiian. Sixty percent have children and work a part-time job despite being a full-time student, or attend school part-time and work. You know the song—the high price of living in paradise. Even in Hawai'i County!

It became clear that most students are in the thick of life, and could not relate or identify to many of the sociology terms without realizing that when we discuss poverty, we are talking about the majority of the neighborhoods and large private subdivisions on Hawai'i island (catchment systems and gravel/dirt roads, marginal utilities and services). Because Hawai'i island is so large and rural, with a struggling public mass transit system, most students will spend any discretionary funds on reliable transportation. Food is a necessity you can budget. You have more discretion, or can get public assistance, especially if you have dependent children.

No matter what time of the day, in every class I teach, students are hungry. They welcome snacks, but truly fall over themselves and think you are the best if you share a pizza or crock-pot specialty. A few colleagues call me "Bananas"— mainly because I usually have apple bananas to share with students and anyone in my path. I am sure other instructors provide snacks to assist in the learning environment, but why doesn't the school take on providing a more meaningful, comprehensive service for students who are hungry?

The majority of the faculty and instructors seem to be nice well-meaning people, but where are they from and did they ever go hungry? (Diet no count!) Did they ever get free lunch or food stamps? Can they truly understand, care, or relate to the majority of students who are hungry?

Since 2010, I have coordinated and facilitated emergency food and food distributions at Hawai'i Community College. We started small, with the assistance of students who volunteered through course assignments and service learning projects. Since 2016, with the financial support of the school's student government, I have coordinated a monthly food and emergency food response.

It has been a lonely path of service. The Food Bank has always been cooperative; I worked and volunteered there for eight years. Initially using my own car, the school office, and personal funds, I managed to offer monthly food distributions and emergency boxes to students or whoever called or came to the event. Since 2017, several faculty members and instructors have helped drive the school truck to pick up the food, pass it out, and clean up. Despite volunteers serving over seventy-five students and their households per month, the school has not offered a dedicated space or position to assist, let alone provided any funding. Student volunteers from school organizations distribute the food each month.

In all the years of providing food distribution, I have received the following: twice a lecturer gave me forty dollars, which allowed me to buy cases of cup noodles to distribute, and a technician provided two cases of pork 'n' beans.

There is a campus joke that if you want a school-sponsored event to have a large turnout you need to serve food, give out bentos, or at the very least have snacks. Yet the administration and even food service programs will not make a concerted effort to feed the hungry on our campus.

How could this be? Why is it that the school does not allow food stamps at the cafeteria? Why is there such a lack of concern or care? Is liability a concern? Is it embarrassing to admit we have hungry adults on campus?

How is it that a community college in Hawai'i does not have people concerned about hunger in decision-making positions? Perhaps the UH System hires qualified people who have never experienced poverty, or who do not understand the basic challenges our students face. Is no one willing to be the food champion, and give up space or funds to support students who could use a nutritional boost—a free bag of groceries once a week, or a free sandwich or bowl of stew? Believing that a menu of cup noodles and dry ramen is a college student rite of passage is crude and insensitive.

The lack of caring is harsh in an environment that talks repeatedly about being an 'ohana and kauhale of learning, while ignoring a most basic need—food. Why does the rhetoric not reflect basic services, such as providing food for hungry students in an organized "institutionalized" manner?

How to keep students on that higher education train? Well, let's make sure they have access to food on and off campus. We can still have the status quo offerings, but because the cafeteria already takes credit cards, it can also accommodate EBT (Electronic Benefits Transfer) cards.

As one of this train's conductors, I will continue to support monthly emergency food distribution and the same day drop of commodity food from our community food bank. I will continue to respond to emergency food requests, and will offer bananas and snacks in my classes. Encouraging a more comprehensive approach to dealing with hunger on campus will probably take more politicking than I am used to, but let's start by asking colleagues and administrators, "Who do you truly care about at this community college?"

If they answer "students" then let's throw in "*hungry* students." Let's be real about the challenges they face, and how we can alleviate hunger on campus. Let's strive to offer free lunches several times a week, and allow students to buy cafeteria food with food stamps or the electronic food benefits many of them receive. Let's have the agriculture program grow greens and fruits to be given away at the distributions or at the student lounge on a regular basis. We witnessed during COVID-19 that institutions can move quickly to address student needs when forced to.

Lastly, let's hire qualified people who understand poverty, and who realize that learning happens better when someone's stomach is full, and when students know they truly matter.

Claudia Wilcox-Boucher has a Master's of Social Work and is an Associate Professor of Social Sciences at Hawaiʻi Community College.

Inu i ka Wai ʻAwaʻawa

Drink of the Bitter Waters

Mahealani Perez Wendt

It is a tough proposition: share a natural resource which is in truth a cultural resource, knowing it will be commodified, exploited solely for commercial purposes; a cultural resource that has been critical for feeding and nurturing generations of families, for growing staple food, one that is spiritual lifeblood, one from which kānaka were forcibly, involuntarily, and completely divested, and which, solely through their centuries' long struggle and sacrifice, was finally restored.

It is a bitter pill to swallow: kānaka pressured to "make nice" with "stakeholders"—many of whom were the very ones who perpetrated historic and ongoing injury—an expectation premised on kanaka magnanimity and aloha—an expectation, *as a matter of course*, that they will be only too happy to participate and dialogue about sharing, about best management practices, about *going forward*, ad nauseum. *In spite of their centuries' long deprivation. For the good of all.*

> Imua e nā pokiʻi, a inu i ka wai ʻawaʻawa.
> *Forward my young brothers and sisters, and drink of the bitter waters.*
> (Kamehameha I)

Go forward. Into another kind of existential battle, at the behest of American stake-holder democracy—aka, American capitalism most brutal.

The resource is *wai*, water—and the kuaʻāina of Maui Hikina fought long and hard for it.

They fought for wai in the 1830s and for decades thereafter, when American settlers sought to transform Central Maui, its kula lands, into sugar fields.

They fought into the 1870s, when despite their many petitions in opposition, the Kingdom of Hawaiʻi, heavily infiltrated by Westerners and in survival pacification mode, permitted wholesale diversions of water.

Kuaʻāina fought when protections within these early agreements were violated and ignored with impunity, when their loʻi, taro fields, were completely dewatered.

They fought for wai before, during, and after the 1893 coup, and after Annexation.

Their protests were renewed with the Kūʻē Petitions.

There are family stories of skirmishes, as the Koʻolau uplands were excavated for a complex ditch system to divert over one hundred perennial streams, transporting 455 million gallons per day away from the watershed—more than all of Oʻahu consumes.

The streams were completely dewatered—left desiccate and boulder-strewn where once the people gathered ʻoʻopu, hīhīwai, ʻōpae, and other traditional food.

The estuaries, muliwai, were transformed into black, foul-smelling, stagnant pools, breeding grounds for mosquitoes, wiping out limu, mollusks, and shoreline fish that grew in abundance. In the 1990s, state health officials inspected and pronounced these stream conditions "normal."

To add insult to injury, a propaganda campaign orchestrated by the corporate diverter, its operatives and supporters—including subsidiary companies, union members, politicians, and agribusiness allies—vilified the farmers through a narrative antithetical to their values, character, and motivations.

A narrative that they were *greedy*. *Greedy* for seeking return of wai. *Greedy* for attempting to grow food. *Greedy* for their ʻiʻini, desire, to carry on the legacy of their ancestors. *Greedy. Greedy. Greedy.*

East Maui families were torn apart, their loyalties severely tested as some members were forced to take company jobs to feed their families.

The farmers were maligned, treated as dangerous enemies of the state. Department of Land and Natural Resources site visits to petitioned streams were accompanied by over forty fully-armed, "locked and loaded" SWAT-team-like officers and police. As though the farmers were terrorists, a violent criminal element *in their own homeland, on the very lands they and their ancestors had always grown kalo and generously provisioned others, along the very streams and ʻauwai they had always cared for and maintained.*

Despite these formidable challenges and indignities, the kuaʻāina of Maui Hikina persevered. Against the odds, they held their heads high, courageous and persistent in their nonviolent efforts to restore the streams.

* * *

In 2020, two pandemics of equal virulence are raging across America.

At the end of August 2020 the coronavirus has claimed over 180,000 US lives—almost a fifth of the world's total, from a country with only 4.25 percent of its population.

And the malignancy of the other pandemic, systemic racism, has resurfaced with a virulence ugly as suppurating wound.

A white Minneapolis police officer knelt on a Black American's neck for nine minutes, asphyxiating him.

In many jurisdictions, and in the normal course of events, George Floyd would have been posthumously and routinely faulted for his own demise, the police given a pass. Another unremarkable day in America.

Except for a witness's video documenting Floyd crying out "I can't breathe," crying out for his mother. Documenting the white officer's callous and casual indifference, the extent of his depravity—hands in his trouser pockets, a nonchalant expression while snuffing out Floyd's life—his fellow officers' equivocation, cowardice, and complicity. But for this video, and the ensuing social media outrage, none of this would have come to light

The coronavirus pandemic's staggering and devastating toll, George Floyd's horrific suffering, and the historic maltreatment of Black Americans—all are searing to the conscience and soul. "I can't breathe" has become America's national mantra.

For many kānaka, the pain is indistinguishable from the loss of their country and just as wounding—a loss also rooted in white America's obdurate insistence on privilege and exceptionalism.

Our East Maui farmers' trauma pales perhaps in comparison, but it is poison poured from the same flagon.

America is roiling. Hundreds of thousands have taken to the streets in protest—thousands of demonstrations in four hundred American cities, with many more around the world protesting in solidarity with the profound and transcendent meaning of George Floyd's life and death.

America's Black and minority communities have suffered disproportionately and most grievously from its racist intransigence. A deeply ingrained, a stubborn, unyielding resistance to equal opportunity—equal access to education, jobs, housing, health care—has persisted for too long.

* * *

How is this relevant to kānaka, to their struggle for wai?

Simply put, their social and economic status mirrors national statistics for Black Americans and other minorities—disproportionately lower incomes, higher rates of incarceration, suicide, drug addiction, mental illness, homelessness, and high morbidity rates for chronic diseases.

Self-determination—abiding the exigencies of nature both environmental and human, a people who take responsibility for the consequences of their own mistakes and follies, reaping the rewards of right thinking and conduct—this dignifies the human condition.

Colonial oppression is its antithesis. Plenary and brute police authority imposed upon other peoples; the racist-driven force and might of America's military and state apparatus brought to bear upon kānaka, situating them in a precarious, highly disadvantageous position vis-à-vis a largely inaccessible and difficult-to-navigate legal system; forced into decades' long struggles to affirm rights which, if the state's Constitution is to be believed, are presumptively theirs to begin with; forcing and subjecting them to a tortuous political and legal system heavily weighted in favor of moneyed interests and influence—all of these elevate kānaka, including East Maui taro farmers, fishers, and gatherers, to a status implicating human rights violations.

Two hundred years of Hawaiʻi colonization have achieved no more than a veneer, a false pretext of peaceful and happy coexistence exacerbated by tourism, a grotesque contortion and charade, an appropriation that the "host culture" is forced to play along with for its very survival. Obfuscation and hypocrisy are rife, lip service paid to constitutional ideals and due process protections undermined at every turn by the state and powerful corporations. Any kanaka who believes there is justice there, think again. A most grueling path awaits the unwary kanaka who dares to so presume—who has the effrontery to provoke the status quo by naively clinging to long-discarded ideals of equality, liberty, and justice for all.

Ultimately, the East Maui farmers prevailed. Twenty-five streams were restored in 2018—the largest number in Hawaiʻi's postcolonial history. But victory came at great human cost and sacrifice—not before many farmers had passed, many generations were lost to farming, and the corrosive effects of invasive trees, plants, and animals had overwhelmed much of the ancient taro lands, streams, and ʻauwai.

America's grand experiment is failing. Kānaka never asked to be part of it; in fact, they vehemently opposed it. Our recourse is to hang on to the vestiges of what is still here for us—our ʻāina and connection to it; our families and genealogical connections to one another; our belief in balance, in a "setting things to right" cosmos which informs all human beings, including our innate goodness and generosity of spirit.

Kānaka are a pragmatic people. We are staying the course, continuing to execute a survival strategy in keeping with our proud traditions. We will continue to welcome and join with like-minded others who understand these things. We will endure, and Hawaiʻi will endure, by staying the course.

Mahealani Perez Wendt was Executive Director of the Native Hawaiian Legal Corporation for thirty-two years, receiving many awards and recognitions for her community advocacy work. She is also a poet widely published in Hawaiʻi and abroad. Originally from Kauaʻi, she and her husband Ed farm taro on his family's ancestral lands in Wailuanui, East Maui.

Political Engagement

A New Article of Lived Faith

Dawn Morais

> Where then is hope?
> not a nail hammered true,
> no joist firm without.
> Nor could roof sustain
> airborne, ceiling bone dry
> in driving rain, like spread wing
> over fledgling; grace
> beyond dumb duty. Fires fare
> in face of cold; someone invoked
> someone breathes on behalf.
>
> Daniel Berrigan, "Block Island"

COVID-19 forced all of us to hunker down in our homes. But for almost half of all the men, women, and children in Hawai'i living in or on the edge of poverty, and especially for the thousands living on the sidewalks and beaches, home is without firm joists, often without a roof, and too often without hope. Will the disease that literally takes our breath away teach us to breathe new life into our faith? Will we get beyond the beautiful hymns sung on Zoom, beyond the fervent prayers? Will faith be expressed with the same clarity and earnestness in the civic square?

It will—*IF* people in the pews—and those who have left—challenge faith leaders who have helped advance political agendas that hurt people. As the prophet Isaiah instructed, we must declare what we see with our votes, testimony, and vigilance as watchmen to ensure that public policy serves the public (Isa. 21). Some have spoken out about the need to feed the hungry, shelter the houseless, care for prisoners, tend to the sick, and more. Such advocacy can define how faith is lived here, if people of faith assert themselves as "church," and embrace engagement in political life.

The modern history of churches has too often been about shoring up those in power. Cardinal Timothy Dolan recently defended saying he admired Trump's leadership, which he "salutes," by claiming he was engaged in the "sacred enterprise of accompaniment and engagement and dialogue" (O'Loughlin). But the people in the pews feel less and less accompanied, engaged, or in dialogue with church leadership, and young people are not attracted to a corporatized church that violates their instinct for justice.

Caring for each other is the most basic expression of faith. Love God. Love your neighbor as yourself. The opulent vestments and grand cathedrals came with the institutionalization of what began as a radical call for justice and compassion.

Old habits are hard to break, but we can try. At a Zen retreat on the Hāmākua coast on Hawai'i island, host Akiko Masuda offers this prayer:

> We live in modesty and simplicity,
> palms together, head bowed in gratitude,
> giving thanks for each inhale
> and each exhale.
> We settle deeply, surrendering our bones
> and our being to the earth,
> grounded deeply in our precious Hawai'i.
> May we live fully in peace
> and service to others.

It's time to look inward and outward. Weeks into our forced COVID-19 retreat, I listened to a podcast of Rev. Jim Wallis of *Sojourners* in conversation with Rev. Eugene Cho, president-elect of Bread for the World, and a briefing by a Hawai'i legislative staffer about federal aid to address the economic fallout of COVID-19. The ministers talked about a covenantal relationship with our neighbors. About a shared humanity, something Bishop Desmond Tutu calls *ubuntu*. About the hunger of children who depend on school meals, the lack of a living wage, and racism fueled by references to the "Chinese virus." They spoke about going from the pulpit into the public square.

Running through the legislative briefing was the sense of a bureaucracy infected by its clutch on power and the purse. Advocates felt pressured not to make lawmakers look bad, despite their failure to respond to the people's dire needs. Even before the pandemic hit, nearly half were living paycheck to paycheck, with thousands on the sidewalks. But non-profits urging that priority be given to addressing hunger and shelter for families were largely drowned out by business voices.

House Speaker Scott Saiki prioritized the need to "modernize our economy," because the "future of our families and state relies upon a sound and resilient economy" ("Governor"). Our families, struggling after missing two months' paychecks, were asked to keep waiting, while legislators squabbled over who controlled the federal aid.

The faith community was missing from the team asked to map a way out of this valley of suffering. Lawmakers may have faith that people will not die waiting, but the faith leaders actually engaging with troubled families every day are not being invited to help shape the response to the crisis.

Rev. Sam Domingo, last president of the now dissolved Hawai'i Council of Churches, is not surprised. "Churches have become less relevant to our political leaders," he said to me, "They do not look to us to help guide the state through a crisis like the one we are going through now. They look to business executives."

Politicians still look to the churches for ceremony. The legislative session always begins with a Red Mass at the Cathedral. And here as elsewhere, the over-worked offering of "thoughts and prayers" professes a turning to faith in moments of despair, when the pain is visible, raw, bloody.

But much of the pain of this pandemic is hidden. It is behind the doors of homes where there is no food. Where disadvantaged children struggle without computers or broadband or parents capable of delivering effective homeschooling. Where financial stress is driving up domestic violence. The pandemic has also made visible women's heavy load as primary caregivers and as contributors to household income.

Faith should not be a prop; it should offer moral clarity publicly. Since places of worship are also places where people seek refuge, a rational approach would ensure that people of faith, and not just business leaders, plan Hawai'i's recovery. They bring the gifts and graces of faith, and an understanding of community pain beyond the abilities of most business executives.

But churches themselves must change. If "the glory of God is a living man," as the early church father Irenaeus said, churches must speak out far more forcefully against making a person work a full day, yet not earn enough to simply survive. Churches must stop giving middle-class politicians and business leaders who serve on philanthropic boards, attend church faithfully, and donate generously the comfort of thinking those actions are enough.

Churches that do not pay their workers a living wage cannot speak for the dignity of labor. Schools and churches that fire people for being openly gay cannot preach about a God who welcomes all. The oppressiveness of male clerical authority in the most intimate questions of reproduction is the last gasp of patriarchy. Clergy must accompany not just the powerful, but those the pandemic has revealed as truly *essential*: stevedores, sanitation workers, bus drivers, janitors, nurses, home care workers, postal workers, farmers, grocery store clerks, and preparers of food.

Faith should make us see, make us insist on tax fairness, on a living wage, on care of the vulnerable. It means saying "NO" publicly to the ever-widening chasm between executive pay and starvation wages. Having been, as the psalmist said, "through fire and water" we must be guided by faith to "a place of abundance for all" (Ps. 66). This concept is reflected in Hawai'i's own remembrance of 'Āina Momona, when the land did indeed provide for all.

Emerging from the hell of COVID-19, faith communities must become the living bread. We must leaven our politics—and not only with entreaty but with insistence on dignity for all. The pandemic is an invitation to rebuild. To not just sing hosannas to heaven, but also do the dirty, not always welcome work on earth of justice-seeking. Aloha. Ubuntu. A person is a person through another person because we share the breath of life.

We must accompany. We must see, and declare. Faith without engagement in our political life is a poverty we can no longer afford.

Works Cited

Berrigan, Daniel. "Block Island." *And the Risen Bread: Selected Poems, 1957–1997*, Fordham UP, 1998, pp. 245–58.

"Governor Ige Appoints Alan M. Oshima to Lead Hawaii's Economic and Community Recovery, Resilience Efforts." *Office of the Governor*, 8 April 2020.

O'Loughlin, Michael J. "Cardinal Dolan Defends Comments About Trump, Argues He Has Critics on Both Sides." *America: The Jesuit Review*, 1 May 2020, https://www.americamagazine.org/politics-society/2020/05/01/cardinal-dolan-defends-comments-about-trump-argues-he-has-critics-both.

Wallis, Jim, host. "Does Faithfulness Require Political Advocacy? A Conversation with Eugene Cho." *The Soul of the Nation with Jim Wallis, Sojourners*, 12 May 2020, https://sojo.net/media/does-faithfulness-require-political-advocacy-conversation-eugene-cho.

Dawn Morais has called Hawai'i home since 2001. Following a corporate career, she now provides communications counsel to nonprofits and teaches at the University of Hawai'i. Her writing has appeared in local media, *National Catholic Reporter*, *The Merton Seasonal*, *The Baltimore Sun*, and *Bamboo Ridge*. A dissident Catholic, she worships at St. Elizabeth's Episcopal Church in Kalihi, host to Hawai'i's first Catholic Worker House.

This Is Not a Drill

Notes on Surviving the End of the World, Again

Jamaica Heolimeleikalani Osorio

All I know:
    The ships came
    And my people started dying.
                  1778.

All I know:
    The ships came
    And my people started dying.
                  2020.

All I know:
    This anxiety and grief is new
    And ancient.

All I know:
    My Kūpuna survived too much
    for us to be taken out like this.

On January 13, 2018, Hawai'i awoke to the message: "BALLISTIC MISSILE THREAT INBOUND TO HAWAII. SEEK IMMEDIATE SHELTER. THIS IS NOT A DRILL." We shook ourselves and braced for impact for thirty-eight minutes, until notified via Twitter there was no inbound missile.

On March 11, 2020, the World Health Organization declared the vicious spread of COVID-19 a pandemic. At the end of August 2020, over 25,000,000 cases have been confirmed, resulting in over 840,000 deaths worldwide (World Health Organization). Hawai'i has endured a less staggering impact—8,339 confirmed cases and sixty-three deaths (State of Hawai'i). Over the past month I have watched many of my people struggle between their desire to return to a life that resembles normalcy and the reality of a second wave of COVID-19 spreading across our pae 'āina. When you couple this with the fact that a ballistic missile was never actually fired, one might believe that Hawai'i escaped the full trauma of these two events. I cannot help but feel, however, that considering them in relation to Hawai'i's history of mass death and displacement is already having a profound impact on how our lāhui will imagine and practice pilina into our future. Like the great dying of my kūpuna in the eighteenth and nineteenth centuries, these recent events have exposed many of the ways that colonialism has foreclosed so many of our futures and possibilities. Our population collapse, the missile crisis, and COVID-19 each represent a kind of ending. I would suggest, however, that if we are careful and intentional, they can also inspire a kind of beginning.

I begin with two simple questions. What does it means to live in the wake of these life-altering events? And how will they shape our experience as Kānaka Maoli, as we navigate what it means to live in ethical pilina to each other and our ʻāina? These questions are inspired by the work of Black futurists, who remind us that the "Apocalypse already happened: that (in Public Enemy's phrase) *Armageddon been in effect*" (Sinker), and Indigenous resurgence scholars, who reframe Indigenous "tension over membership and belonging" as a "fear of disappearing" (Simpson 176). While continuing to feel the ghost of mass death in our bones, we contemplate what it means to be terrified of our own extinction. As Kānaka Maoli, we know that our world has ended many times before, but because of the resilience of our kūpuna, it has begun "again in the morning" (Waheed). What will it take to begin again now, in ways that open futures, rather than continue to foreclose them?

My work is concerned with how aloha ʻāina articulates certain norms of Hawaiian intimacy and behavior long disrupted by forces of colonialism such as capitalism, patriarchy, and white supremacy. But so far, I've paid little attention to how mass death has also disrupted our networks of relations. So the first thing I learned from COVID-19 is that it is very hard to understand and articulate the intergenerational trauma you carry until you've been triggered. And if nothing else, these two events, the missile and the virus, are extreme examples of a cultural, communal triggering.

I am not a political strategist. I do not know how to end the mass accumulation of weapons and military strength that leaves most of the world vulnerable to displacement, disfigurement, and death. I am not an economist. I do not know how to revive our plundered economy, or to restore health and wellness to our communities in the wake of these events. But I do know enough about history and moʻolelo to be sure that returning to the status quo cannot be an option for those of us caught under the weight of the will of American and European imperialism and globalization. I know that national security has never resulted in genuine security for our people, and that the "essential" services our government has identified in the wake of this pandemic were never meant to meet the essential needs of our people. I know that when Governor David Ige instated the shelter-in-place order, I felt a kinship to my kūpuna that I had never experienced before. We have all been given a glimpse of what it means to be struck by a maʻi kaʻawale (separating sickness) that neither we or Kaluaikoʻolau can ultimately outrun. But I also know that when Koʻolau defied the orders to be taken to Kalalau alone, and fled the forces of the Provisional Government, he was not running *away* from exile but toward his ʻohana.

When our people desperately attempt to escape our death, disappearance, and extinction, we have always run *toward* something—usually each other—rather than escaping into isolation. In essence, without the survival of our ʻāina and lāhui, our individual survival is meaningless.

Few moments have displayed this as clearly as the rise of the Hui Aloha ʻĀina in the late 1890s and the rise of our mighty wave in 2019. Our kūpuna gathered the kū'ē petitions at the rock bottom of our population collapse. A once widespread and growing population of over 800,000 was then a mere 33,000 (*Act of War*). And still, aloha 'āina's magnetic force bound our people together in action.

This was also true for how our people gathered and united just a year ago to protect our Sacred Mauna a Wākea. One of the greatest lessons I learned during our time as a lāhui on the Mauna was that when we are grieving, and aspiring for something better, these feelings come with an intense, even desperate longing to be pilina with each other. We gathered in the thousands at 7,000 feet—in the bitter cold and sweltering heat, with the threat of arrest and physical harm always with us. Another lesson I am learning from all of our mo'olelo is that we passionately wish to create and live in a better future. But more than that. We desperately want to walk into that future *together*. This is why, in the absence of proper institutions of care in this time of COVID-19, our people have developed grassroots initiatives to feed our communities, to educate our keiki, and to revive our economy.[1]

In 2020, among our greatest challenges will not be just creating a new economy, or reimagining a more ethical health system, but also taking seriously how we will hold closely to each other in this time of great vulnerability. The truth is, the desire to return to "normal" ways of being in pilina with each other could be what brings about our demise. At a time when our leadership will not put the health and needs of our people before the wealth and desires of tourists and big business, we must confront our need to reimagine what it means to be in pilina. Since nearly everything we know about pilina demands showing up—to our 'āina, to each other—are we ready to reimagine our most sacred and routine ceremonies and rituals? Will we commit to new ways of practicing aloha when our survival depends on it?

I believe we are up to this challenge of creating a new world, or continuing to "live in the future," as Bryan Kuwada has written. But I also believe this will require us first to come face-to-face with our grief. We must understand how deeply the vicious and violent cycle of history has affected us. Our healing will become possible only when we acknowledge all the endings we have survived—the coming of ships, the spreading of death, the taming of industry, the carving of land, crosses, and cultures.

And I'd also suggest that the 2018 missile threat, the 2019 arrest of our Kūpuna, and the 2020 spread of COVID-19 are further traumas we must intimately engage, as we imagine who we are in the face of all these endings.

Note

1. See 'Āina Aloha Economic Futures (https://www.ainaalohafutures.com/) and *Building Bridges, Not Walking on Backs: A Feminist Economic Recovery Plan for COVID-19* (https://humanservices.hawaii.gov/wp-content/uploads/2020/04/4.13.20-Final-Cover-D2-Feminist-Economic-Recovery-D1.pdf).

Works Cited

Act of War: The Overthrow of the Hawaiian Nation. Produced by Puhipau and Joan Lander. Nā Maka o ka ʻĀina, 1993.

Kuwada, Bryan Kamaoli. "We Live in the Future. Come Join Us." *Ke Kaupu Hehi Ale*, 3 April 2015, https://hehiale.wordpress.com/2015/04/03/we-live-in-the-future-come-join-us/.

Simpson, Leanne Betasamosake. *As We Have Always Done: Indigenous Freedom through Radical Resistance.* U of Minnesota P, 2017.

Sinker, Mark. "Loving the alien in advance of the landing—Black science fiction." *The Wire*, no. 96, Feb.1992.

State of Hawaiʻi, Department of Health. "Disease Outbreak Control Division | COVID-19," https://health.hawaii.gov/coronavirusdisease2019/.

Waheed, Nayyirah. *Salt.* CreateSpace, 2013.

World Health Organization. "WHO Coronavirus Disease (COVID-19) Dashboard," https://covid19.who.int.

Dr. Jamaica Heolimeleikalani Osorio is a Kanaka Maoli wahine activist, writer, and scholar from Pālolo, Oʻahu. Currently, Heoli is an Assistant Professor of Indigenous and Native Hawaiian Politics at the University of Hawaiʻi at Mānoa. Heoli is a three-time national poetry champion, poetry mentor, and a published author. She is a proud past Kaiāpuni student, Ford Fellow, and a graduate of Kamehameha Schools, Stanford University (BA), New York University (MA), and the University of Hawaiʻi at Mānoa (PhD).

The Future Is Koa

Kyle Kajihiro and Ty P. Kāwika Tengan

We are living in a time of hulihia. As of August 2020, the COVID-19 pandemic has killed more than 800,000 people and disrupted economies and lives globally. Concurrently, the US Indo-Pacific Command has requested an additional $20 billion to enhance military bases and capabilities in the region. Many of our islands in the Pacific face military threats: a proposed operational missile launch facility and radar sites on Kauaʻi and Oʻahu, a new Marine Corps littoral regiment at Mōkapu, the destruction of native forest and CHamoru archaeological sites in Litekyan (Ritidian) in Guåhan (Guam), the expansion of US Naval bases in the Philippines, the construction of a coral reef-destroying base in Henoko, Okinawa, leaking fuel tanks in Red Hill over Oʻahu's main aquifer, and the intensification of live fire training on Oʻahu and Hawaiʻi island. Despite outbreaks of COVID-19 within the military, the Navy plans to continue with its biennial Rim of the Pacific (RIMPAC) exercise in Hawaiʻi, which poses a risk to military personnel and local communities. These conditions demand a radical reorientation towards a genuine security that prioritizes social and environmental needs.

At this time of hulihia, we argue that koa as a land/ocean-based practice of courage and warriorhood will help us to stand strong in this embattled world that our Islands and Islanders are struggling through. Koa (*Acacia koa*) is the largest native hardwood tree, used especially for canoes. Koa seeds can remain dormant in the soil for many years before a disturbance, such as the overturning of soil when invasive plants are cleared, cracks their outer layers and begins their process of germinating, sprouting, and growing into the majestic trees that provide protection and nutrients needed for a healthy forest (Kuwada; Keir). But koa also means "courage," to be "brave," and "warrior," even "soldier," and "military."

Environmental desolation caused by the military has a long history in Hawaiʻi. The military has bombed, burned, and desecrated hundreds of sites, including Kahoʻolawe, Mākua, Pōhakuloa, Līhuʻe, and Waikāne, transforming these wahi pana (storied places) into forbidden zones contaminated with unexploded munitions and toxic chemicals. By rendering the land hazardous, the military holds the future hostage—severing indigenous relations to land and foreclosing on alternative uses. Yet, like koa seeds which require scarification to germinate, military environmental impacts have also awakened koa aloha ʻāina to stand in the gap.

The many meanings of koa help to reveal possibilities of transformation in the story of our friend and veteran Uncle Joe Estores. Born in 1933, Uncle Joe spent the majority of his fifty-five years of federal service in the Army and various government agencies outside of Hawai'i, including eighteen months as a helicopter pilot in Vietnam. Before he went to war, he set up the gunnery targets at Mākua Valley. When he returned to Hawai'i in 2006, his shock at the military's environmental impacts on Pu'uloa where he grew up led him to advocate for demilitarization. He now attends cultural accesses with the Mālama Mākua organization, where he asks the valley for forgiveness for the role he played in the land's desecration, and relates stories of his personal transformation.

On one access that we both attended, Mālama Mākua leader Sparky Rodrigues, also a Vietnam Veteran, asked Uncle Joe how he overcame the conflict between his American patriotism and his Hawaiian cultural beliefs. Uncle Joe responded, "I took that American flag off my shoulder, and I put the Hawaiian flag there. I took the American heart that was inside of me, and I put the Hawaiian heart there. Different allegiance—allegiance to the land, rather than to war." As activists and scholars committed to aloha 'āina futures, we were moved by the pain and healing expressed in Uncle Joe's testimony. It helped us to see new possibilities for the future of Mākua and the Lāhui.

This notion of koa emerging from damage done to the land and our bodies in order to heal and stabilize offers an example for how to fearlessly face the current crises as koa aloha 'āina—warriors dedicated to the land/nation. On a larger scale, groups like the Protect Kaho'olawe 'Ohana (PKO) and Mālama Mākua have transformed the collective trauma of military destruction of 'āina into a space for more koa aloha 'āina to sprout. From 1976 to 1990, the PKO organized to stop the bombing of Kaho'olawe, and in the process sparked an 'Ōiwi cultural and political resurgence. The severe ecological and cultural degradation of Kaho'olawe called forward the (re)emergence of 'Ōiwi ceremonies, language, history, and ea. Many returning 'Ōiwi veterans from the Vietnam War became koa aloha 'āina with the PKO. Struggling to heal Kaho'olawe helped these koa to heal their traumas of war and find alternative life-sustaining futures. Many went on to become community leaders dedicated to restoring land, growing food for their communities, and educating future generations.

Arundhati Roy reminds us that a moment of crisis forces us "to break with the past and imagine [our] world anew. . . . It is a portal, a gateway between one world and the next." This invocation of crisis-as-portal brings to mind the 'Ōiwi concept of kīpuka—a change of form (puka, hole), and especially an oasis of forest that persists after the landscape has been devoured by Pele's hulihia and regenerates life. We see this regeneration in the global rising of Black, Brown, and Indigenous peoples to protect their lands and communities. From July 2019 to March 2020, thousands of Kānaka 'Ōiwi and supporters maintained an occupation at Pu'uhonua o Pu'uhuluhulu to protect Mauna a Wākea (Mauna Kea) from the construction of a

Thirty Meter Telescope (TMT). The Stop RIMPAC Coalition is working to end RIMPAC exercises. And Black Lives Matter protests continue to rock hundreds of cities around the world, demanding an end to racist violence, and a defunding of the police and the military.

In 1992, a ceremony was held on Kahoʻolawe to dedicate a stone platform for reinterring iwi kupuna (ancestral bones), marking the transition from military to ʻŌiwi use. Parley Kanakaʻole named the structure "Kahualele." "Kahua" can mean a foundation, seed, fruit, egg, or word. "Lele" means to leap or fly. He wanted this event of replanting to fly and take root elsewhere.

We offer some thoughts about regenerative futures for Hawaiʻi, in hopes that they too might lele to take root in fertile soil:

- Support abolitionist calls to defund the police and military, redirecting those funds to human and environmental needs. Jobs created in this way will boost economic recovery and provide crucial services for our communities and the ʻāina. This complements various local post-pandemic recovery initiatives, such as ʻĀina Aloha Futures and *Building Bridges, Not Walking on Backs: A Feminist Economic Recovery Plan for COVID-19.*
- Close and convert military bases to other productive uses, such as affordable housing and facilities for education, research, technological innovation, social services, community organizations, and especially ʻŌiwi serving programs. Building on the experiences of Kahoʻolawe and other military land restoration projects, Hawaiʻi firms and workers can become leaders in the growing field of environmental restoration of former military sites.
- Fund the tuition and living expenses of displaced workers so they may learn essential skills for the new economy. This investment in workers could be modeled on the GI Bill for returning veterans of World War II. These educational programs should develop capacities for creating socially just and ecologically sustainable futures. Veterans and formerly incarcerated persons could work on ʻāina restoration projects as part of their reentry programs.
- Make Hawaiʻi into a peace center based on understandings of *genuine security* as articulated by the International Women's Network Against Militarism. An independent, neutral, and demilitarized Hawaiʻi could be an international meeting place.

We must discard the "old normal" which led to this catastrophe, and boldly move into that kīpuka of change—mindful of the risks, and attentive to opportunities for more sustainable futures. The saying "E ola koa" (Live like a koa tree) is a wish for a long and sustaining life, one that calls us to courageously confront and overcome the multiple challenges ahead.

The future is koa.

Works Cited

Keir, Matthew. Laukahi Hawai'i Plant Conservation Network. Personal communication with Ty Tengan, 13 Dec. 2017.

Kuwada, Bryan Kamaoli. "We are not warriors. We are a grove of trees." *Ke Kaupu Hehi Ale*, 6 July 2015, https://hehiale.wordpress.com/2015/07/06/we-are-not-warriors-we-are-a-grove-of-trees/.

Roy, Arundhati. "The pandemic is a portal." *Financial Times*, 3 Apr. 2020, https://on.ft.com/2N9x6wn.

Kyle Kajihiro is a peace and social justice activist and lecturer in Geography and Environment and Ethnic Studies at the University of Hawai'i at Mānoa.

Ty P. Kāwika Tengan is an associate professor of ethnic studies and anthropology at the University of Hawai'i at Mānoa.

Waiʻaleʻale

Mehana Vaughan, Monica Montgomery, and Kristine Kilikina Luebbe

Growing up on Kauaʻi, I was taught that Mount Waiʻaleʻale was the wettest spot on earth, and we keiki memorized this as part of what made our home unique and special. Within the past decade, Waiʻaleʻale has been surpassed by places like Puʻukukui on Maui. This is one small example of how what we know and rely upon about the places we call home is changing with the weather. People on Kauaʻi know firsthand the impacts of climate change, affecting traditional practices such as salt-making in Hanapēpē, and making hurricane threats more frequent. From April 14–15, 2018, an extreme rainfall event scoured the entire island, particularly catastrophic along the northeast shore, in the moku of Haleleʻa, where I grew up. One local rain gauge logged 49.6 inches of rainfall in 24 hours, a national record.

This piece shares my own experiences of those days and the months that followed, along with lessons gleaned from over seventy interviews with Kauaʻi ʻohana, first responders, community organizers, government officials, and leaders who lived through the rising waters and responded to their aftermath. Recommendations for adapting to what interviewees called the "new normal" are interspersed with stanzas of a poem presented at the 2018 Kauaʻi Community College commencement ceremony, a month after the April floods.

* * *

1. Waiʻaleʻale (billowing or rippling waters)
At one AM on April 15, 2018,
my husband and I are awakened from sleep
by rain so hard I feel our roof will cave in.
It has been raining all day,
on and off, for a month here in Haleleʻa.
But this rain is different. This rain thunders.

Minutes later my husband's fire department radio
starts to crackle with 911 calls from Hanalei.
"A woman caller with three children says
the water is two feet from their door
and rising quickly. What should she do?"

One of the firemen radios in that they can't reach her house by truck
due to water ten feet deep on the highway. They launch a jet ski,
which sucks debris into its engine and stalls.
Ten people need to be evacuated from the emergency shelter
at the local elementary school.
It is flooding too.
We are up and texting friends in low lying areas to see if they are alright.
Texts bleep back. "We are fine. We are on the second story
and the water is a foot from the door. Thanks for checking on us."
Our cell service goes dead.

    Lesson #1 - Mahalo: Be thankful every day and remember what matters.
    Life, loved ones, living here, together.

    Lesson #2 - ʻIke ʻĀina, ʻIke Wai: Know your home's history and place names,
    the past pathways and spirit of its waters. Water always returns.

2. Kawaikini (multitudinous waters)
Overnight rivers across the island lunge from their paths.
Kīlauea River rises 35 feet within ten minutes.
Keapana Valley becomes a river.
Trickles of water along Power-Line road
swell to rip houses from their foundations
spilling avalanches of boulders down the hillside.
Waikomo Stream makes her way into Kōloa homes.

At dark four AM, my friend, a single mother, plunges through water up to her chest,
with her mother, each carrying one of her three-year-old twins.
Had they waited five minutes, all would have been swept away.
In Wainiha a landslide blocked the river
and the water coursing through another friend's home
stopped, pooled, and began to circle.
Then, she says, she really got scared.

Bays turn mud brown, ironwood trees ripped out by their roots rest on reefs.
Landslides close the highway to Hāʻena in six separate locations.
Each ahupuaʻa is cut off, isolated along the coast.
This coast our kūpuna traveled by canoe and foot trail.

In the floods, the multitudinous waters of Kauaʻi returned to their paths,
reclaimed the character of their names.

Waikomo—water that enters
Wailapa—enlivened waters
Wainiha—waters that rage.

> Lesson #1 - Kilo: Reinvigorate observation and connections to 'āina. Educate and prepare.

> Lesson #2 - Mālama: Take Care of the Land. Empower groups to plant natives to hold slopes; clean stream channels and 'auwai, maintain lo'i and green spaces, clear rubbish and invasives, so that water can safely flow to sea.

3. Ho'okahi wai o ka like (the sameness of a single shade of dye—unity)
After the flood the people of Kaua'i went into action.
Off-duty firemen went door to door
to ensure neighbors were safe,
worked for days on end though their own homes flooded.
Surfers on jet skis ferried mothers home to their kids,
kids at sleepovers home to their parents.
People stood shoulder to shoulder, loading food and water, tools and chainsaws
on to boats running down the coast to cut off areas.
Neighbors mucked out homes, dried photo albums,
took muddy bedding to wash and return folded,
lugged wet mattresses that strangers with trucks showed up to haul away.
A young mother of three created a google survey on 'ohana needs.
Moms took it door to door in their own neighborhoods across the island,
then went back and back again, till people felt comfortable asking for help.
Cooks set up kitchens to feed flooded families and volunteers.
Operators on excavators and Bobcats cleared mud as high as the power lines,
making it possible for state crews to access the highway within four days.
People saw needs and responded, applied their skills,
found ways to help, and just jumped in.

> Lesson #1 - Pilina: Know your neighbors and look out for one another.

> Lesson #2 - Mākaukau: Develop community-led disaster management and action plans; don't rely on outside or official response.

> Lesson #3 - Ho'ona'auao: Reinforce existing community capacity, offer training in needed areas.

4. Mohala i ka wai ka maka o ka pua—
(Flowers thrive where there is water, as people thrive in good living conditions)
Kaua'i is not new to natural disasters.
When asked how her family survived Hurricane 'Iniki in 1991,
Aunty Anabelle Pa Kam responded . . .
"I guess the way we grew up, because we never had money, money was nothing to us. You know, everything was hand-me-down. And I was happy to have the hand-me-downs. We didn't need anything new. We learned survival. That's how, when 'Iniki came, we could live. We didn't need anything. We could live off the land. And that's what I teach my children and my grandchildren, how to live off the land."

In Kīlauea town, after Hurricane 'Iniki,
work groups collected sheets of tin roofing blown off homes,
hammered and straightened them, then went house to house
nailing them up so everyone had dry places to live.
Groups of women made lunch for the workers, kids brought ice and soda.
Families moved in with neighbors, cooking meals together.

In a hurricane everyone is affected, homes damaged,
no water, no electricity, all together.
In a flood, some people's homes are obliterated.
In those that stand, black mold creeps up walls.
While others' lives go on as if nothing happened.

> Lesson #1 - Ea: Increase self-sufficiency through local food production and job diversification. Create jobs in mālama 'āina.

> Lesson #2 - Hana: Employ locals for post-disaster roles and funnel relief funding directly to communities. Fund positions and people, not just infrastructure.

> Lesson #3 - Lōkahi: Build partnerships between communities and all levels of government, enhance communication, and devolve decision-making.

5. Waiwai (plentiful water, riches or wealth)
'Āina, left alone to rest, will recover.
Many resources will replenish on their own.
Without tourists packing the beaches,
Turtles returned to dig nests,
schools of fish spilled into shallows
empty of snorkelers to feed
crabs burrowed into sand undisturbed by footprints.

Local families also returned,
no fighting for parking, hustling to beat the crowds,
bringing their kids to experience 'āina
the way they knew it as kids
and never thought it could be again,
renewing connections to ancestral places,
gathering to practice and restore.

How can people reside and raise families in the places they grew up?
How can they care for 'āina they can no longer access?
How can we have quality tourism without bringing ever more visitors?
How can homes wash away without contaminating the ocean,
shorelines move to accommodate the sea?
How to capture abundant water for when there is drought,
deliver emergency aid and communication by drone?
How to create jobs caring for 'āina that help 'ohana to thrive?
How can communities stay close as they grow?

In April of 2018, there was no loss of life.
No high surf to push the water back to land.
A chance to reflect, reset, and reimagine,
work to create a new system
while living in the one we have.

> Lesson #1 - A'o aku, A'o mai: It was a miracle no one died, a blessing and chance to learn.

> Lesson #2 - 'Āina: Our environment is changing. Pay attention. Cultivate natural infrastructure to catch water and cultivate resilience.

> Lesson #3 - Huliau: Don't work to return to "normal." Let places rest. Limit visitors in vulnerable areas. Rethink rebuilding and zoning. In a previously unimagined present, re-envision the future.

Ho'omoe wai kāhi ke kāo'o . . .
    Let us all travel together like water flowing in one direction . . .

Mehana Blaich Vaughan is a mother of three children from Kalihiwai and Namahana, Kaua'i. Her work focuses on enhancing community efforts to care for the places that nourish and sustain them.

Monica Montgomery is from the Pacific Northwest. She completed her MS at the University of Hawai'i at Manoāand has had the great privilege of working in Hawai'i, learning from and supporting community efforts to govern natural resources.

Kristine Kilikina Luebbe is a graduate student with the Department of Natural Resources and Environmental Management at the University of Hawai'i at Manoā.

Collaborating authors: Derek Esibill, Kammie Tavares, Elaine Vizka, Alexis Stubbs, Danielle Bartz, Cameron Ogden-Fung, Carolyn Flacker, Nelson Masang, Jr., Kai Hoshijo, Emma Brown, Roberto J. Porro, Ku'ulei Freed, J. Kahaulahilahi Vegas, 'Alohi Nackachi, and Matt Ito.

II
Resources and Values—
Turning to Our Strengths

Pehea lā ke kanaka i ʻapo ʻia ai e ka ʻāina?

How are we Kānaka perceived by the ʻāina?

We Da Waiwai

Loke Aloua

Moʻokūʻauhau
Who you? Where you from?
Who me? I one Hoapili.
Kauoha-bound kiaʻi to loko
An oath you can't let go, no.
Waiwai stirs the soul.
Mahi iʻa, wen da fish we raise is for loko, kānaka, and Kanaloa.
Hui, mai poina, no foget' those old ways!
Pāpā told me, "No can eat money"
Kapu Kanaloa.
Remember that pilina
Held on through change by kūpuna during onslaught of foreign ways
Wea da kiaʻi stay?

Menehune
Early morning, late night cloaked by darkness
Removing invasives, protecting Kanaloa, it's a constant fight choking waiwai.
Like foreign badge, ranger, laws, authority bar us from setting waiwai, us kiaʻi, our *ea*
free!
Someone yells, "ho, duck low, look da flashlight!"
End up just one lawaiʻa passing by.
Those adda' guys dey no scare me.

Lock us up, throw away da key!
We are *kiaʻi*.

Kani ka pū
Dig deep
Feet kiss kelekele feel Papa's heartbeat.
Removing decades of lepo when our people were forced to leave.
Clogging pūnāwai bugga no can breathe.
If no can breathe how you goin' eat?

No wai, no *waiwai*!
Waiwai calls on our
Courage to have foresight
Discipline for hard times
Bigger than I for we.
Reclaiming hands to 'āina touch her tenderly, mindfully, that wahi you feel
Das *us.*
We are *'āina.*
She is we.

Hūlalilali
Living kahiko
Birthing mo'olelo
Creators our story will be told.
Names unleashed beneath kou trees, salty mist coats lips, sweat drips.
Mo'o slither on blankets of yellow heart leaves while 'a'ama cling kua side.
Those stones we stack no wait for permits and permission to act.
We are *Kaiāulu.*
Taking our Hawai'i back.

Hō'ailona
I see a shimmering sea
Filled with waiwai old timers speak.
One throw, pau fish, go home, share, kaukau, 'au'au, sleep.
Nobody go hungry, life is sweet!
Take what need, set the rest free.
Nets rip from big fish, not catching pōhaku in an empty sea.
Wa'a reclaiming ocean side
Ko'a fed, regenerating.
Limu blossoming beyond da maka can see bugga form one thick sheet.
Those fisheries that sound so waiwai no can believe,
That's where we going be, but you gotta believe, have the courage to dream.
Remember the mo'olelo, those kūpuna who made we.
We are *waiwai.*
Dream.

Loke Aloua is a kama'āina from the Kona District on Hawai'i Island. Her lineage binds her to Hawai'i and Maui. She is a kia'i loko for Kaloko Loko I'a.

Ahupuaʻa Values Should Enlighten Next Generation Investing in Hawaiʻi

Neil J. Kahoʻokele Hannahs

In January 2020, representatives of pension funds, government, foundations, grass-roots organizations, private equity, and venture capital gathered on Maui for an Ahupuaʻa Investment Summit to identify key components of a blueprint for next generation investing in Hawaiʻi. The sponsors designed the program for this diverse audience to explore what investors can learn from the Hawaiian ahupuaʻa system of natural resource management and governance. I was honored to be invited to offer background on the ahupuaʻa and history of investment in Hawaiʻi.

My own introduction to this kanaka maoli practice of land management came in 1974, when I accepted a position at Kamehameha Schools. Across the hall was a talented team of graphic artists that included Marilyn Kahalewai, who painted a colorful depiction of an ahupuaʻa on a four foot by six foot canvas. Decades later, Marilyn's art is still the first image to appear in an internet search for "ahupuaʻa." The work was commissioned as a curriculum tool that traveled the state with cultural resources brought to life by brilliant and revered teachers. But a summary in the instructional guide reveals unintended evidence of a culture demeaned by colonizers and self-suppressed to facilitate survival in a society dominated by patronizing forces. The poster is described "as a visual springboard for any discussion of Hawaiian life *from the days before foreign influences forever changed the environment and lifestyle of the Hawaiian people*" (emphasis added). A review of the guide extended a backhanded compliment that also trivializes the rendering's value: "Although intended for . . . the classroom, the poster would look neat on a kid's bedroom wall or on the wall of your study."

A half-century ago, our highest hope for memorializing cultural practices was to uplift the esteem of our youth before steering them toward acquiring knowledge that would prepare them to serve as good and industrious citizens in a world that each day was evolving ever further from the lifestyle represented in the painting. Any thoughts that we might have had to regenerate abundance in native forests depleted by over-harvest and exotic species, to return water to streams, sucked dry by plantation diversions, in order to grow kalo and community in loʻi overtaken by weeds and waste, and to rebuild fishponds eyed by developers for their ocean-front-age real estate value, were dismissed as the nostalgic pipedreams of those who would impede the unstoppable march of progress.

Fortunately, these relentless pressures could not squeeze the life out of a people resolved to sustain their existence and identity.

The tides of change did not deter the Polynesian Voyaging Society from launching traditional voyaging canoes, undertaking epic voyages of discovery, and collaborating with Kamehameha Schools in planting hundreds of acres of koa trees in Keauhou, Ka'ū that will provide canoe logs for future generations.

The currents of industrial agribusiness thinking did not drown the dreams of kalo farmers along the eastern coast of Maui and in the valleys of Nā Wai Ehā, who fought to return waters to streams and revive life on land and in the sea.

The riches promised by land developers did not seduce activists, who inspired citizens to defend cultural landscapes, restack the scattered stones of our cultural sites, and reinvigorate impaired ecosystems.

"Makamalunohonaokalani" by Marilyn Kahalewai. Used with permission from Kamehameha Schools.

The gains did not come easily, and my meetings today on the State Commission on Water Resources Management bring monthly reminders of the losses along the way. It ought not to have been such a struggle—not in a State with a Constitution that includes protections for Traditional and Customary Rights, and a Preamble that states "We, the people of Hawaii . . . mindful of our Hawaiian heritage and uniqueness as an island State, dedicate our efforts to fulfill the philosophy decreed by the Hawaii State motto, 'Ua mau ke ea o ka aina i ka pono.'"

The problem is that global capital deployment strategies do not spring from our Constitutional intent, manifesting instead those "foreign influences [designed to] forever change the environment and lifestyle of the Hawaiian people." In defensive response, we establish convoluted regulatory processes to minimize or mitigate adverse impacts. But at best, it is an exhausting effort to manage unremittting decline.

So, how do we stem the surge of economic developments that ravage our natural resources, erode our cultural heritage, and compromise our future? Acknowledging that Hawaiian ancestral practices are well adapted for fostering long-term sustainable well-being is a worthy start. The *Hawai'i 2050 Sustainability Plan* takes a step in that direction with its finding that the people of Hawai'i "want a vibrant, diversified economy, a healthy quality of life that is grounded in a multi-ethnic culture and Kanaka Maoli values . . ." (v). "The values of the ahupua'a system ensure that people respect the air, land, water and other scarce natural resources that make life sustainable from the mountains to the sea" (8).

At the Ahupua'a Investment Summit, I pointed the way for prospective investors by drawing their attention away from the images in ahupua'a renderings and toward three unseen investment parameters that guided behavior—values as relevant to us today, if not more.

I began with **investment horizon**. This defines the period of time over which benefits are generated. Modern investors project the flow of capital over the defined period to calculate a net present value. Two tenets of this analysis are that more is better than less and sooner is better than later. Therefore, the process includes a discount rate to reduce the value of future returns, and to reward performance that produces as much as possible, as fast as you can.

This stands in stark relief against the sustainable principles of ahupua'a management motivated by intergenerational equity and lāhui preservation, as captured in a chiefly directive of Kamehameha I: "When cutting the wood for the ali'i, be thinking of the young trees for the young ali'i. After we have gone, they will not be poor because we did not understand that this source of wealth will benefit the young ali'i in the future."

I also discussed the importance of **investment scope**. The notion of unbridled liberty held by some raises expectations that they have a right to do whatever they want on their land, in their business, with their money, for their industry. They bristle at requirements to assess impacts of their actions upon ecological systems, cultural assets and practices, or societal relationships and equity.

Such a perspective is misaligned with the understanding of interconnected systems foundational to ahupua'a management. What happens upstream will always affect what happens downstream. Our economic development strategies should recognize these impacts, and foster symbiotic relationships.

Finally, I addressed **investment benefit**. There is no credible defense for today's economic systems that distribute wealth so disproportionately. There is no responsible rationale for ignoring the alarming growth in the number of productive workers who are imperiled as wages fail to keep pace with the escalating costs of survival. There is no motivation for industrious effort when the fruits of the harvest are reserved for a privileged few.

Our ancestors understood that people thrive where living conditions are good. Mōhala i ka wai ka maka o ka pua (Pukui 237). Rather than passively *take* the capital market's foreign ideas of investment and development, it is time to actively *make* the capital market that honors and perpetuates our values. The 'Āina Aloha Economic Futures (AAEF) movement has developed a balanced scorecard that can serve as the blueprint for next generation investing in Hawai'i that Ahupua'a Investment Summit attendees agreed is needed. The AAEF tool includes criteria that:

- Foster a vibrant natural environment;
- Enhance community well-being, resilience, engagement, and empowerment;
- Support Hawaiian cultural vitality;
- Contribute to a circular, regenerative, and equitable economy;
- Promote community-supported energy sustainability; and
- Build food security and self-reliant community food systems. ("AAEF Assessment")

With such investment and policy guidance, the ahupua'a will be more than a cherished memory upon a child's wall. Instead, the values reflected in that image will again produce the abundance that will nurture the flowers to unfurl and our people to thrive.

Works Cited

"AAEF Assessment Tool for Policies, Projects, and Programs." 'Āina Aloha Economic Futures, http://bit.ly/ainaaloha-tool.
Hawai'i 2050 Sustainability Plan. Hawai'i 2050 Sustainability Task Force, State of Hawai'i, Jan. 2008, http://files.hawaii.gov/dbedt/op/sustainability/hawaii_2050_plan_final.pdf.
Natural Resources Management Plan. Kamehameha Schools, 2011, https://www.ksbe.edu/assets/site/special_section/land/pdf/NRMP_Flier.pdf.
Pukui, Mary Kawena. *'Ōlelo No'eau: Hawaiian Proverbs & Poetical Sayings.* Bishop Museum Press, 1983.

Neil J. Kaho'okele Hannahs is founder and CEO of Ho'okele Strategies LLC, former director of the Land Assets Division of Kamehameha Schools, and co-founder and director of the First Nations Futures and Hawai'i Investment Ready programs. He has served on the State of Hawai'i Commission on Water Resources Management since 2016.

An Aloha ʻĀina Economy—
Give, Take, Regenerate

Kamanamaikalani Beamer

We were sitting at a stunningly beautiful round table, made out of what looked to be a six-inch thick slab of koa. The wood grain was so spectacular that I inched my dinner plate over a bit so I could admire the pattern.

Usually held at the second or third home of a one-percenter, such gatherings have never been entirely comfortable for me. I start feeling uneasy when security for the gated community grants me entrance. The food is usually good, and the conversations can be engaging enough to keep my interest. The problem is that I just can't get past this lingering disquiet—one difficult to describe, but what I will call a feeling of inequity.

That night there was so much to look at. Stunning ocean views. A picturesque sunset. An infinity pool. And a front door that probably cost as much as the down payment on my house. Yet this was supposed to be a chance to gather insight and perspective from a person with national networks and powerful government contacts who might assist us in reaching our last fundraising goal for a project.

When I mentioned "ecological peace and social justice," and said that "we want to advance aloha ʻāina as a way of being for the world,"[1] the expression on the face of our hoped-for comrade abruptly changed. So as not to incriminate anyone involved, let me just say that our proposal was not embraced—although we eventually did find the needed support. But inching toward transparency, I will report that I was suddenly defending myself against allegations that I was trying to take society back into a past where we lived in "grass huts" and survived "off of only the fish we caught."

Perhaps the most important lesson for me was how angrily some intelligent and decent Americans react to the idea that aloha ʻāina could shape our future. At that moment, I did not know that I would spend much of the next decade explaining how aloha ʻāina could inform how we can envision and how we will operate our future economy. I had not even heard the term "circular economy" then, though the next few years of my professional career would take me on a voyage to where I can now clearly "see the island."[2] But a colleague from the University of Augsburg, Germany saw it after my first presentation there. "This aloha ʻāina can help to save our world," he said.[3]

This essay will discuss how aloha 'āina and a circular economy will be essential and instrumental for the future of Hawai'i. I've recently stopped using the term "subsistence" to describe the ho'okele waiwai of our ancestors. It is true that the innovative agricultural and aquacultural systems of our Kūpuna took only what we needed from nature to subsist as a society with little to no waste, thereby preserving precious resources for future use and future generations. But I have come to recognize the veiled Anglo-European economic assumptions lying behind labeling a society's primary mode of production as one designed simply to "subsist." For two thousand years, our ancestors did much more than this. We created regenerative agricultural and aquaculture systems that were aligned with and took advantage of ecosystem niches to produce food in abundance for generations. We innovated lo'i systems, developed new varieties of ancestral plants to push the limits of production, and utilizing the power of the tides, we farmed algae to feed herbivorous fish. Dr. Peter Vitousek has called Hawaiians the world's best agriculturalists. We also established institutions such as kālai'āina, which ensured a substantial redistribution of wealth with each new Mō'ī, preventing that vast acquisition and retention of wealth seen among the one percent today.

When our ancestral economy is classified as "subsistence," much if not all of this rich history of innovation disappears. Even more destructively, this branding has carried within it the justification for replacing the existing economy, often violently, as part of the workings of imperialism and linear "progress." The replacement economic systems seek to maximize the extraction of natural resources in their drive to get products to markets. Among the results are surplus and excess, significant waste, and environmental damage on a scale that has plunged our planet into a climate crisis. In the pursuit of endless growth, through colonialism and imperialism, these linear economic systems have exploited, then destroyed ancestral economies around the world.

International efforts today are trying to reassess the benefits and the consequences of such economic systems on the natural resources and human communities of our planet. We are currently extracting and consuming resources at a rate that would require 1.75 earths to be sustainable. By 2050 we will need the equivalent of two earths (Brears). As part of their efforts to mitigate the damage or develop resilience within the global climate crisis, significant swaths of nations have embraced the concept of a "circular economy," and are setting goals for achieving it.

A circular economy (CE) seeks to decouple economic growth from environmental degradation. The European Union has an action plan to shift toward a CE as part of its 750 billion Euro COVID-19 recovery plan. Individual cities such as Amsterdam have developed CE policies and strategic plans for making their economies circular. Unlike linear economies, where goods and services are produced through a process often described as *take, make, use, waste,* a CE operates on a model devoted to reducing resource consumption, recapturing resource materials from products, and then repurposing those formerly "wasted" materials into new products. CE proponents seek to eliminate waste as much as possible from production, reuse resource materials, and power manufacturing though renewable energy. They are also dedicated to creating a more equitable and just economic system. Inspired by the closed loop systems that have made life possible on mother earth for billions of years, the concept of a CE offers some hope.

* * *

Establishing an aloha 'āina based CE in Hawai'i would be one of the most revolutionary, productive, and beneficial things our generation could do. An aloha 'āina economy, one also devoted to a living wage and health care for all, could not only replace our current antiquated and destructive economy established primarily in plantation era Hawai'i, but also lead us into a more humane and productive future. GDP cannot register the value of the fulfillment and love that results from living and being provided for by aloha 'āina.

Like the hana of the skilled mahi 'ai and lawai'a of old, an aloha 'āina circular economy should be based on a *give, take, regenerate* model. Examples are already underway—the Waipā Foundation on Kaua'i; He'eia and West O'ahu; Hāna, Maui; Moloka'i; and in pockets on Hawai'i island. With the right leadership and policies, imagine what large scale efforts we could initiate to address the impacts of tourism by mandating the use of products whose waste can be turned into resources for regenerative agriculture? Imagine if instead of the existing policy, we required power companies to purchase power from any community or household that can install systems—as is the case in much of Europe. Isn't it peculiar that even as they are creating their own solar farms, these companies will not allow families to be compensated for supplying the grid?

There is so much we can learn from global best practices regarding circular economies. But we also have never lost aloha 'āina, and we now have international allies—as did the aloha 'āina diplomats of our past. We cannot let our progress be slowed by those still supporting the cruel and obsolete economic systems of the past centuries. We need to move forward.

I mua.

Notes

1. I have been educated and inspired by fearless aloha 'āina such as Kekuaokalani, Manono, Liholiho, James Kauli'a, Anakalā Eddie Ka'anā'anā, Uncle Calvin Hoe, Carlos Andrade, Kaleikoa Ka'eo, Ka'eo Duarte, Kawika Winter, Hi'ilei Kawelo, Ka'iulani Murphy, Keli'i Kotubete, Kanekoa Schultz, Kalā Hoe, Kapua and Stacy Sproat, Malia Akuatagawa, Mehana Vaughn, and many others. Also, see my essay "Tūtū's aloha 'āina grace" in *Value of Hawai'i 2*.

2.   Often referred to by Pwo Navigator Nainoa Thompson, this phrase has been recaptured by Neil Hannahs as a metaphor for vision in leadership and seeing our way to a new future. As Nainoa has said, if you as the navigator lose sight of the island in your mind and spirit in the midst of the voyage, you and the collective effort are lost.
3.   I have been greatly informed on circular economies through a collaboration with Dr. Axel Tuma and Dr. Andrea Thorenz and the students of the Resource Lab, Institute of Materials Resource Management, University of Augsburg.

Work Cited

Brears, Robert C. *Natural Resource Management and the Circular Economy*. Palgrave Macmillan, 2018.

Dr. Kamanamaikalani Beamer is a professor at the University of Hawai‘i at Mānoa, with a joint appointment in the Richardson School of Law and the Hawai‘inuiākea School of Hawaiian Knowledge. He is a father, farmer, and aloha ‘āinaist.

Hawai'i and Tourism Reimagined

John De Fries

At a gala banquet in 2018 at the Hyatt Regency Waikīkī, Nainoa Thompson was being honored by the Aloha Chapter of the prestigious tourism organization, Meeting Professionals International (MPI), for his contributions and achievements in the category of Hawaiian Culture. Nainoa was humbled as an honoree, yet perplexed about why an ocean voyaging navigator was receiving a tourism award.

Being with Nainoa caused me to recall that in just over three years at sea, the crew of Hōkūle'a had visited 150 ports, engaged more than 100,000 people in eighteen nations, voyaged through eight Marine World Heritage Sites, and was received at the United Nations on World Oceans Day 2016 by Secretary General Ban Ki-Moon—a protocol usually reserved for heads of state and leaders of global stature.

Known as Mālama Honua, this worldwide voyage was an epic achievement for all of Hawai'i, sharing our message of caring for our planet in all that we do. That evening in Waikīkī, Hawai'i's visitor industry was honoring Nainoa as president of the Polynesian Voyaging Society and as a global ambassador from Hawai'i.

Prior to the presentation, Nainoa shared a thought with me. What if we thought of tourists as students and Hawai'i as a school? What if we taught them how we mālama Hawai'i, so when they go home, they can mālama their own families and places?

This thought was profound and prescient, as less than two years later a global pandemic would bring the visitor industry as we knew it to a grinding halt.

Waikīkī as Home and a Place of Learning

Nainoa's message affected me viscerally, because we were in the heart of Waikīkī—just four blocks from where I was born and raised. Millions of people from around the world come to know Waikīkī as the mecca of Hawai'i's visitor industry, I came to know Waikīkī as the piko of my family life.

Nainoa's concept of Hawai'i as a school took me back to those childhood memories. The highlight of weekends was going fishing with my Uncle John, whose 'ohana lived next door. Our fishing grounds at Waikīkī Beach were five to eight feet deep, starting at the "Deep Holes" seawall promenade (in alignment with Kapahulu Avenue) and extending west to the Halekūlani Hotel. It was during those times—the early 1960s—as a ten-year-old with Uncle John that I learned three essential qualities about Waikīkī Beach. It was a source of food, a source of medicine, and a place of recreation for our families—in that order.

Although he didn't talk about it much, I knew that Uncle John was bothered that the oceanfront row of hotels was being built too close to the shoreline. Besides the aesthetic impact of high-rises on the Waikīkī shore, my uncle knew about the ocean's tidal patterns and the contraflow of subsurface waters from the hillsides of Mānoa, Makiki, and Pālolo.

In my late teens, Uncle John and my father's sister, Aunty Emma, told me about my great-grandfather's concerns about shoreline hotel construction and fluctuations in the subsurface water table. He predicted that "one day, Waikīkī will choke on its own sewage."

Fast forward to March 24, 2006, when 48 million gallons of raw sewage was dumped into the Ala Wai Canal due to a ruptured line. A government official issued the following statement: "Pumping sewage into the Ala Wai Canal prevented the waste from backing up into homes, hotels, and businesses located in Waikīkī and nearby areas." Upon reading this, my thoughts immediately drifted back to my great-grandfather's prophetic words.

He Lani Ko Luna, He Honua Ko Lalo—Connections Between Heaven and Earth

My paternal great-grandfather had a deep understanding of water and its flows in the ocean and beneath the land. My maternal grandmother was in tune with the celestial knowledge of our ancestors, those who looked to the heavens to understand natural patterns and human behaviors. My first few years of life, when she raised me, and the summers I later spent with her in Hōlualoa, Kona, on Hawai'i Island, shaped my lifelong fascination with the heavens.

In October of 2017, observatories on Haleakalā and Maunakea detected the first known interstellar asteroid passing through our solar system. It was given the Hawaiian name 'Oumuamua by the distinguished Hawaiian language expert Dr. Larry Kimura, an associate professor of Hawaiian Language and Studies at the University of Hawai'i at Hilo.

His translation of the name is the "advanced scout-messenger from the distant past," from that place our ancestors referred to as Pō. This name led me to ask: "What message is 'Oumuamua bringing to us?"

About six months later, on May 3, 2018, the volcanic eruptions of lower Puna on the east side of Hawai'i Island began and continued in unprecedented fashion for five months, with lava fountains of up to 300 feet.

This awesome display and the magnitude of these eruptions caused me to ponder even more deeply the possible connections between this volcanic activity and the discovery of 'Oumuamua.

Talking with friends and colleagues during the summer of 2018, I began to describe this new sensation I was feeling—that we in Hawaiʻi were experiencing the beginning of a transformation that our ancestors referred to as huliau—the turning point in a time of change.

My feeling was reaffirmed in July 2019, when Maunakea Access Road was blocked by the kiaʻi, a well-organized coalition of Native Hawaiians and kamaʻāina joining those who had dedicated decades to protecting Maunakea. The blockade and the puʻuhonua that grew around it were unified in opposing the building of the Thirty Meter Telescope. After three months of this standoff, in an op-ed for the local media, I said in part:

> The law and order upon which our civil society is reliant has been supplanted, for now, by a socio-cultural phenomenon and vision of Hawaiʻi's future—a future where we as Native Hawaiians assert the inherent right to self-determination. This political force is resounding on Maunakea and throughout the State, thus producing the current quandary that must be resolved for the well-being of Native Hawaiians and for Hawaiʻi as a whole.

From Huliau to Hulihia—A World Turned Upside Down for the Better

As many tensions in Hawaiʻi were coming to a head, the COVID-19 pandemic wrapped around the world. With leisure travel essentially shut down globally due to public health restrictions and concerns for personal well-being, Hawaiʻi's visitor-reliant economy came to a standstill.

"Professor Pandemic" has walked into the global classroom with a life-threatening reminder that for too long, humans have encroached into the natural habitats of wildlife, increasing the number of animal diseases transmitted to humans. During the course of study for this pandemic, the worldwide lesson plan and the local homework assignment is to restore a better balance in how we live in relation to all life forms and living systems.

For me, the lessons of my grandparents and family, of growing up in Waikīkī, of ʻOumuamua, the Puna eruption, the movement to protect Maunakea, and now this pandemic crystallize into a collective mandate for all of us to mālama, to care for and nurture, all life.

Perhaps ʻOumuamua is delivering this message celestially. Perhaps mālama was the lesson learned by those who cared for neighbors throughout the Puna eruption. Mālama is certainly the refrain sung by the fearless kiaʻi on Maunakea. It is also the wisdom Nainoa and the crew shared on their worldwide voyage. And mālama must be the guiding principle as we reimagine Hawaiʻi not as a destination for passive recreation, but for active and serious contemplation of how interconnected we are with the heavens, oceans, land, and to one another.

As protective restrictions in Hawaiʻi and around the world are lifted, tourism's recovery will be slow and long, causing financial pain and suffering for thousands of Hawaiʻi families. But we must not squander this opportunity by reopening too hastily, before we have carefully considered our future, and reimagined Hawaiʻi's tourism-based economy.

Adopted policies such as the Aloha+ Challenge and the Hawaiʻi Tourism Authority's new strategic plan give me hope, and efforts such as the ʻĀina Aloha Economic Futures initiative give our community the opportunity to shape that future.

This global condition of hulihia calls on us to emerge with new ways to innovate, survive, and thrive. Our children and generations to come are counting on it. Mālama pono.

Work Cited

De Fries, John. "My Turn: Maunakea can be beacon for us, other countries." *West Hawaii Today*, 12 Aug. 2019, https://www.westhawaiitoday.com/2019/08/12/opinion/my-turn-maunakea-can-be-beacon-for-us-other-countries/.

John De Fries was raised in Waikīkī at the advent of tourism's ascent to the center of Hawaiʻi's economy. He has worked as a tour director, resort and real estate developer, director of economic development for the County of Hawaiʻi, and executive director of the Native Hawaiian Hospitality Association. He currently serves as President and Principal Advisor of Native Sun Business Group, and on the boards of Kualoa Ranch, Bishop Museum, the Keāhole Center for Sustainability, and the Julie Ann Wrigley Global Institute of Sustainability at Arizona State University. He and his wife and business partner, Ginny, reside in Kona.

Ka ʻĀina Moana

Noelani Puniwai and Kaʻehukai Goin

Noelani

I have spent the last few months sharing a tide pool along the shores of Makuʻu with my children and haumāna. Coming here to cool off after a humid Puna day immerses us in this ʻāina. Taking the short hike out to the tidepool, we pass hala, naupaka, and coconut trees. Along the coast, we breathe in the limu kohu, pālahalaha, and ʻakiʻaki growing among the lava cliffs covered in ʻopihi, hāʻukeʻuke, and ʻaʻama crabs. We see many families casting lines and reading books. The shores of Makuʻu have once again become a place of welcome and the building of community.

The coastline is where I call home, where I come to reconnect and kilo, where I practice my love of Kanaloa. Being blessed with so much extra time to experience this ʻāina has me reflecting on the relationship that our people today have to ʻāina and moana. Are we swimming in the same spaces as our kūpuna? Are we harvesting from places of abundance or scarcity? Are we witnessing the demise or resurrection of our ocean resources?

Kaʻehukai

From the beginning of time, our kūpuna were pono and paʻa with everything that encompasses ʻāina. The Kumulipo, one of many cosmogonic genealogy chants tying us as kānaka o Hawaiʻi to our ancestors, shows us our relation to koʻa, hāloa, nā akua, and the pae ʻāina itself. For our kūpuna, being related to everything that is ʻāina was not a far-fetched idea. What they did in the past is what we, the younger generation, are aspiring to do in this modern day. Yet for some reason many of us are still insecure—one of the many reasons, perhaps, we are having a hard time finding our own identity as young kānaka within the lāhui. What can we bring to the table to raise and hoʻoulu lāhui?

When I was growing up, the term "Hawaiian" carried a different weight and value for me. Confused and uneducated, I was adding to our people's problems instead of contributing solutions for how our nation could once again be a thriving proud people. It took me a long time to get over my poʻo pakikī ways. My education pathway is what saved me, reintroducing me to my kūpuna, and not just my koko

Hawai'i, but all my ancestors, and helping me to recognize what they have contributed to who I am. Knowing that I carry on their names, I must make sure that I will be a positive light for the next generation.

Coming from O'ahu, when we would holoholo, or harvest resources, I had a "me before them" mentality and not enough of a "kākou thing." Blinded by ignorance and Western ideals, I can now see how depleted O'ahu resources are when compared to the rest of the pae 'āina. Spots where we used to ku'i 'opihi at Ka'ena Point not five years ago have been ravaged. Where I whipped for papio as a kid on the south side of O'ahu, I can either no longer go, due to foreign development, or the area is so polluted with trash that fish no longer reside there.

Now that the world is under quarantine, this is accelerating. People are going fishing to keep from going stir crazy, but they do not fully understand and respect that this is our "kākou" resource, or that there is a proper way to take care of and sustainably harvest these marine resources. From mauka to makai, all the resources that sustain us are gifts from nā akua, and are an extension of ourselves.

As Noe and I sit, reflect, and share our journeys traveling these islands we call home, I realize how blessed I am to have the opportunity during this crazy pandemic to be a contributor of solutions for the nation. Studying and learning how Hawai'i Island's fishing communities protect, manage, and sustain their marine resources is truly essential for the future of all keiki o Hawai'i. What I have regained on Hawai'i island is hope. I see that there is a way kānaka can practice the ways of our kūpuna in this modern era. Pele is still listening. Wākea is still here. Kāne is still flowing. And Kanaloa will flourish all around us.

Noelani

I was raised on the Island of Hawai'i, in the districts of Puna and Hilo. I spent my childhood diving in the tidepools of Kapoho, hiking the forests of Ola'a, paddling in the bays of Hilo One, and especially, swimming in the rivers of Pi'ihonua. All connected by water, these are places of abundance, even as they shift and change with time. I share these spaces and experiences with my keiki and haumāna; telling them the mo'olelo, feeding them of these places, and spending time he alo a he alo.

In school, I was trained to see the decline of our environment—overpopulation, global change, ozone hole, etc.—and the loss of our resources—losing our rainforest, coral reefs, extinction of species. I became a scientist to learn how to save my home, my ocean, but I soon learned that to save these places, I also needed to become a Hawaiian. I needed to aloha 'āina, to mālama 'āina, and to share these wahi pana with others. I needed to reach people through their love of the 'āina and their hope for the future, not through their pain and fear for what they will lose.

Now as a scientist and a professor, I look to my kūpuna for inspiration on how to restore the health of our reefs and shorelines, our forests and gardens. As a teacher, I look to my haumāna for inspiration from their passion and commitment, and for kuleana to our places into the future. As a mother, I look to my keiki for inspiration from their love and pilina, and hope that they will take their love for the ʻāina into all that they do. As a daughter of the Hawaiian and sustainability movements, I have been blessed to "be immersed" in communities across this pae ʻāina, inspired by those working hard to restore abundance, creating ʻāina momona. I no longer see what we have lost in our environment. Instead I see the potential, the momona that can once again be found, as our people reconnect to each other and to the ʻāina.

Hoʻoʻiʻini

I've spent time this spring and summer hearing from communities that kilo their resources, visiting different kai with Kaʻehukai, and witnessing families fishing and gathering. Being part of nā hui gathering across our pae ʻāina that are connecting to and taking kuleana for their fisheries shows me that our ocean will be productive again. As a kumu, I must be supporting and training the next generation to know their resources, to foster pilina with these places, and to have a harvesting strategy for each resource that ensures its continued abundance. To kilo is not just to monitor our environment and record change, but to act responsibly from what we witness. To eat and harvest from her sustainably.

I believe that the building of pilina—to places, to seascapes, to Kanaloa—is our only pathway to a future abundant ocean where we can continue to gather and feed our lāhui. Many kānaka love to swim, surf, fish, paddle, kilo, and be immersed in the depths of Kanaloa. This time at home has allowed families to reconnect and return to harvesting the bounty of Kanaloa. It is now our kuleana to awaken our pilina with these spaces, and to raise kiaʻi that may once again aloha Kanaloa. Our ocean warriors are the best observers of our ʻāina. They witness the changing tidal levels, the direction of currents, the decline and abundance of resources. Recognizing their knowledge, we challenge them to share it with the lāhui, so that Kanaloa's energies, inhabitants, and abundance will survive.

As we hike the cliffs of Makuʻu as teacher and student, Kaʻehukai and are dedicating ourselves to ensuring that the ocean and our people will survive and flourish. We know in our naʻau that Kanaloa is alive and thriving. Our life journeys have carried us into these spaces. We must now bring others with us, so that they too awaken their kuleana to this ʻāina moana.

Noelani Puniwai was raised among the forests and coastlines of Puna, Hawai'i Island, and currently lives near Maku'u with her three children. She brings her love of the ocean to her students at the University of Hawai'i at Mānoa, Kamakakūokalani Center for Hawaiian Studies, where she teaches courses in mālama 'āina and aloha Kanaloa.

Raised in the concrete jungle of Makiki, O'ahu, **Ka'ehukai Goin** hiked the trails of 'Ualaka'a, and fished, dove, and surfed the south shores of town. He comes to break boundaries and misguided cycles of kānaka like himself, and to help the lāhui prosper for coming generations by showing them that he has traveled a similar path, and that our akua, oceans, and people will always be here.

From Wai to Waiwai

D. Kapua'ala Sproat

In 2010, my essay in the first *Value of Hawai'i* pondered "Aia i hea ka wai a Kāne? Where are the waters of Kāne, the waters of life?" This traditional mele from the Island of Kaua'i celebrates fresh water's invaluable role as a kinolau (physical embodiment) of akua Kāne (one of the four akua of the Maoli pantheon) and the very lifeblood of Hawai'i's land, culture, and Indigenous People. Starting with this mele framed wai as waiwai (wealth), so that our community would respect fresh water as the life-giving resource that it is, rather than simply as a commodity. I also traced the decline in Hawai'i's wai, due largely to centuries of "extraction" management by plantation agriculture, which is exacerbated by global warming.[1] Despite decreasing supplies and lax commitment to monitoring and proactive management, demand had continued to climb, as a privileged few appeared content to take from our common heritage without ensuring that resources could sustain such withdrawals. I lamented the entitlement and gamesmanship of Hawai'i's post-plantation economy, and resource managers' lack of resolve to make the decisions necessary to restore balance for Native Hawaiian communities in particular. Given sugar's decline, revisiting the siphoning of streams and groundwater to subsidize industrial agriculture was just common sense. But powerful corporations and political interests had other priorities. It was as simple and as complex as that.

Despite the challenges of this quest for pono, in 2010, I had hope for the future. I noted how years of private appropriation inspired the 1978 constitutional amendments and 1987 Water Code—Hawai'i Revised Statutes chapter 174C. Despite the lack of financial and human resources at the Commission on Water Resource Management (the "Water Commission"), the entity charged with bringing the law to life on the ground and in our communities, I emphasized the law's *potential*. The Commission's own lack of political will had provoked litigation, and I highlighted struggles in Waiāhole, O'ahu and Nā Wai 'Ehā, Maui, where communities rose up and deployed the law's power successfully to secure some measure of justice for fresh water resources, and the communities and cultures depending on them. Though decisionmakers clung to the vestiges of plantation agriculture despite widespread closures and a slide towards urban development, communities legally forced decisionmakers' hands. After over a century of diversions, protracted litigation in Waiāhole, Nā Wai 'Ehā, and elsewhere restored water to streams, confirming that the public trust doctrine was Hawai'i's law of the land. Under the constitution, the Water Commission holds fresh water resources in trust—not for any individual or company, but for present and future generations.

Then battles raged on O'ahu and Maui. Today, attention has shifted to Kaua'i, Moloka'i, and Hawai'i island in particular, and expanded to include groundwater. The Water Commission has embraced some change. Better educated and culturally grounded commissioners and staff, including Native Hawaiians, have been more proactive. For example, for the first time the Commission initiated minimum flow standards for streams on Maui, Kaua'i, and Hawai'i island *without* the threat of litigation. In Waimea, Kaua'i, proceedings over minimum flow standards were resolved *without* an extended trial. These are small but positive steps in the right direction. But other issues remain, with both the Water Commission and its sister agency, the Land Board, including litigation over East Maui's water.

In 2010, I called for investment in Hawai'i's wai, and urged readers to look beyond the law to ensure that resources are protected into the future. Community members cannot rely on government agencies alone for action, and individuals and decisionmakers must dig deep to find the political will to move beyond the plantation past. Some redistribution of resources is necessary. Streams must be restored, uses made more efficient, and alternative sources—such as brackish or reclaimed water—developed and utilized. A decade ago, we had the technological capacity and social responsibility to do more with less, so that Hawai'i's natural systems and cultural practices dependent upon them—Indigenous and local—could endure. That capacity and responsibility has only increased.

* * *

Although it dominates this era, COVID-19 is only the latest malady to visit Hawai'i's shores. Kānaka 'Ōiwi endured devastation by western-introduced diseases since the late 1700s, so Native Hawaiians and others already familiar with genocide know to take pandemics seriously. In 2020, as COVID-19 ravages the world with no signs of slowing, we in Hawai'i must forge our own path forward. Life as we knew it in December 2019 will not return for a long time—or at least not until a vaccine is available to all. COVID-19 has laid bare Hawai'i's vulnerabilities, and especially our dependence upon things beyond our shores—tourists, airlines, multinational corporations, governments, the military, and more. But during a global pandemic, Hawai'i's isolation can and should be our strength. We must fix what's broken, and give Hawai'i the best chance of ensuring that management decisions and implementation funding are determined by needs, culture, science, and policy, instead of mere politics.

Just as the Black Lives Matter movement drew attention to the structural and institutional racism undergirding American society, COVID-19 should inspire Hawai'i to take its own sobering look at how colonization's legacy still controls our land and water resources. By definition, colonization involves appropriating then controlling a place and its resources for one's own use. Never OK, this happened quite often, and its influence continues. Perhaps one silver lining of COVID-19 is that it can embolden resource managers to finally manage wai proactively as waiwai, for the benefit of all of Hawai'i's present and future residents. The Water Code and Commission have had the necessary legal and adaptive management frameworks in place for decades. What has been missing is leadership and funding.

* * *

In 2020, our natural and cultural treasures, and wai and waiwai in particular, remain largely in the hands of plantation descendants or their beneficiaries. Two centuries after the missionaries' arrival, and the subsequent explosion of sugar plantations and industrial agriculture, it is past time to rewrite Hawai'i's social contract. Plantations once used public trust resources for private gain, in exchange for community "benefits." That contract overlooked harm to natural resources, workers' rights, and Indigenous communities and culture. That era has ended; or, should have.

Hawai'i's last sugar plantation shuttered operations on Maui in 2016. Yet from Hawai'i island to Kaua'i, the ditch systems that transported water across ahupua'a (watersheds) and entire islands remain in place. In some areas, such as on Kaua'i, plantation descendants still control vast tracts of land and the water infrastructure that feeds them. On Moloka'i and Maui, companies bought former sugar, pineapple, or ranch lands and their irrigation systems, including wells. Farms are planned in some areas; developments in others. Both could perpetuate colonization's legacy. With respect to natural and cultural resources and Indigenous rights, Hawai'i's laws are grounded in restorative justice, but they must be brought to life in our communities. Decisionmakers must harness the courage to do what justice and our resources require. These are not mutually exclusive. Business cannot continue as usual.

In this era of the virus, decisionmakers must invest in Hawai'i's waiwai by redistributing fresh water, and managing and protecting resources in response to a warming planet. Streams must be restored to recharge related ground water supplies, especially those overlying aquifers that supply drinking water. As Hawai'i's trustee of wai, the Water Commission has the legal and moral authority to initiate such actions by mandating the abandonment of relic plantation systems no longer being used, rather than allowing them to be banked for future development. If systems do remain in place, they must be maintained and meet safety standards. Reservoirs, for instance, must be lined and optimally placed, with automated systems installed so that intake levels and releases can be adjusted remotely. If wai is really going to be stewarded mutually as waiwai, then as a community, we must determine the best mechanisms—a cooperative, public utility, or something else—to manage (or co-manage) larger systems such as the one that takes water from East

Maui streams. And, wells must be optimally (not conveniently) spaced. As decisionmakers and beneficiaries, we must interrogate colonialism's legacy in Hawai'i's water resources, and then redress it.

Eia ka wai a Kāne. Here is the water of Kāne, the water of life.

Note

1.   For over a century, water resources were "developed" and then managed for plantation agriculture, principally sugarcane. Massive irrigation systems took water from wet, windward, predominantly Native Hawaiian communities to the drier leeward and central plains of most islands. This significantly damaged the resources themselves, and the natural and human communities relying upon them.

Work Cited

Sproat, D. Kapua'ala. "Water." *The Value of Hawai'i: Knowing the Past, Shaping the Future*, edited by Craig Howes and Jon Osorio, U of Hawai'i P, 2010, pp. 187–194.

D. Kapua'ala Sproat is Professor of Law at the University of Hawai'i at Mānoa and Director of Ka Huli Ao, an academic center that promotes education, scholarship, community outreach, and collaboration on issues of law, culture, and justice for Native Hawaiians and other Pacific and Indigenous Peoples. She is also Counsel at Earthjustice.

Renewable Energy—Stop Burning Stuff

Henry Curtis

I am sitting on my lanai, listening to the wind rustling in the swaying branches, hearing the birds, observing nature.

How did we get here? Where are we going? Age-old questions made more relevant by the COVID-19 pandemic that stripped away the veneer, exposing the social weaknesses of our overdependence on tourism and imports. The pandemic propelled the planting of residential food gardens. I am digging in the dirt, pulling weeds, respecting nature about what to grow where.

We must talk about bias. We all have biases. Self-examination is critical. The future needs to focus on sustainable lifestyles with far less inequality. Racial tensions are less than many other places, but only haoles think racism doesn't exist on the islands. The future needs to be based on aloha, laulima (working together), mālama ʻāina (caring for the land), pono (right, just), and kūlike (equity).

I grew up in the 60s. It was a time for questioning, for challenging authority, for looking beyond inaccurate governmental pronouncements. I traveled throughout California, door-to-door, talking to people about pesticides, pollution, and other environmental issues. For the past quarter-century, I have represented Life of the Land in more than fifty administrative, regulatory, and contested case proceedings before the Hawaiʻi Public Utilities Commission, where we have been admitted into far more electric and gas proceedings than all other environmental and community groups combined. We encourage others to intervene.

Energy is what enables change. In a general sense, we eat food to provide us with energy. We see light energy. We hear noise energy. We smell aromatic energy. The funny thing about energy is it can't be created or destroyed. It exists forever, although it often changes form.

The other funny thing is since energy can't be created or destroyed, there is no such thing as renewable energy. We give names to several types of energy to make it easier to grasp. We have clean energy, dirty energy, blue energy, green energy, and renewable energy, with no clear definitions of what is meant by any of them.

When we talk about energy, we often mean something useful that we can move from one place to another, like gasoline, kerosene, propane, jet fuel, and electricity. We also sometimes mean the infrastructure, such as transmission lines, wind turbines, and power plants.

In a very general sense, renewable energy can be thought of as something we can get directly from nature, while fossil fuel is vegetation that died eons ago and over time has become coal, gas, or petroleum. This analysis is from the 30,000-foot level. If we dive into the weeds, then we would find that every government has a unique political definition of what is and isn't renewable energy. Hawai'i legislators have produced at least five fundamentally different definitions of renewable energy in the past twenty years. Currently, the Hawai'i definition of renewable energy includes chopping down the Amazon rainforest, flying the trees to Hawai'i, and burning the wood. State law says this is carbon neutral. Obviously, it's not!

Burning anything creates air pollution that impacts the health of all living things and releases greenhouse gases. Burning biomass and garbage often generates more greenhouse gases per unit of electricity produced than burning coal. We must stop burning stuff.

Life of the Land supports community-friendly, non-combustion energy sources. We strongly believe that any solution needs to be real and not pit communities against each other. Energy facilities should be part of the community they are placed in. Together, we must find ways that allow all people to have access to clean water, local food, reliable energy, and equity.

I have sought to bring the community perspective and values into energy proceedings. Life of the Land advanced the Public Utilities Commission's understanding of electronic filings, equity, justice, climate change, cultural impacts, geographic impacts, and competing land uses.

Our path forward must be influenced by recent events.

Hurricane Maria hit Puerto Rico in September 2017. The cyclone cut diagonally across the island from the southeast to the northwest, separating the major population areas from the major power plants. Resilience requires the generation of energy to be located near where it is needed.

Hurricane Lane barreled towards O'ahu in August 2018. The Hawai'i Emergency Management Agency determined that if the storm had maintained its strength for another twenty-four to forty-eight hours, the economic damage would have exceeded $10 billion, more than 10 percent of the state population would have required short-term shelter, and over eight million tons of debris would have needed to be cleared from roads.

Currently, Hawai'i has a three-day supply of medicine, a five-day supply of food (excluding prepackaged military meals), and a thirty-day supply of fuel. Only Moloka'i has more than a one-day supply of freshwater. The other islands depend upon electricity for water pumping.

The COVID-19 pandemic is changing how energy is used. Meetings and conferences are being held via videoconferencing. Working at home is on the rise. Our economic future must be diversified rather than dominated and controlled by tourism. Building a social safety net so that everyone has enough food, water, and internet access is critically important.

The cyclones and pandemic have created the opportunity to rethink our future. We can design and build local sustainable communities that power themselves with local power and local microgrids. By working together and learning from each other, we can grow our own food, produce our own energy, rebuild the social safety net, and create a more just and equitable society.

Community is important. Together, each community must address where food and electricity are generated. We must work together to find community solutions for many issues: health, food, education, affordable housing, climate change. Too often in the past, site selection was based on mainland capitalists seeking profit maximization, and rural communities were run over.

The phenomenal growth in rooftop solar has enticed dreamers to realize that a new future is possible. Life of the Land believes that the electricity scenario must be based on low-cost, low-impact, local energy sources: solar, wind, hydro, ocean. Each moku and ahupuaʻa can generate its own electricity and handle its own waste. Ground and marine transportation must be powered by electricity. The amount of energy needed to power a car using gasoline is nearly three times greater than the amount of energy needed to power a car by electricity. Cars should be powered by electricity made without burning things.

In the last fifteen years, Hawaiian Electric has signed contracts for imported rainforest palm oil biodiesel, for clear-cutting Hawaiʻi forests to generate electricity, for microwaving Kaʻū crops into biofuel, and for creating intrusive Kahuku wind-based electricity. In each case, Life of the Land fought the proposal. We won some; others are ongoing disputes. Life of the Land also filed the first two climate change cases before the Hawaiʻi Supreme Court. We won both, forcing the Public Utilities Commission to analyze greenhouse gas emissions for all proposed gas and electric facilities.

The state should examine renewable energy projects holistically to see how they interface with job training, local employment, and climate change. We must subsidize construction and job opportunities in economically-challenged areas— for example, building solar-powered affordable housing and community centers with community gardens.

The technology exists for buildings, electric grids, and vehicles to share electricity, with any one of them providing power to the other two. Rooftops are an excellent place for solar panels and microturbines. Propellers on the floor of gravity-fed storm drains and canals can provide power during rain events, when not as much solar is available.

Tax breaks should be provided for people who do not own a fossil fuel-powered vehicle, regardless of whether the person owns an electric vehicle or has no vehicle at all. The government should also offer free electric-powered bus service, with expanded routes on all islands.

I am a firm believer in the rights of nature as well. Plants and animals do not exist on this planet merely to meet our needs, or so we can observe them. They have their own right to exist. Sustainability requires reimagining and rethinking the entire ecosystem—the plants, animals, water, rocks, agriculture, energy, and educational systems.

We need to expand interdisciplinary thinking, cutting across silos to see and develop the big picture. This will require an engaged community. All voices must be at the table, including seniors and young people. Competing ideas make us stronger. Superficial sound bites should be replaced with deep analyses of viable alternatives.

The fires of change require friction. I am an optimist.

We can make the change. We must make the change. We will make the change. We are the change!

Henry Curtis is a justice advocate, community organizer and facilitator, researcher, peer reviewer, moot court judge, and energy expert, associated with Life of the Land, Community Alliance on Prisons, Hui Aloha 'Āina o Ka Lei Maile Ali'i, and journalist/publisher of Ililani Media (2,000 articles on Hawai'i technology and politics).

E Pū Paʻakai Kākou

Charlie Reppun

My dad, a family doctor, was always involved in community and world politics. In the early 70s, my brother Paul and I, a few years out of college, didn't want to do that. We wanted to be part of the back-to-the-land movement. One of Dad's patients found us land in Kaʻalaea, where we started growing taro. With more luck and connections, we ended up in Waiheʻe, and finally Waiāhole. That was forty-five years ago.

From day one, we learned that farming was no escape from politics—land use issues, water issues, community issues. Although food is connected to everything, the capitalist economic system has disconnected most of us from knowing that who grows food and how we get our food are integral to world history and current events—slavery, Hawaiian sovereignty, women's rights, health disparities, climate change.

Driven by a mindset of perpetual growth for private profit, our capitalist agricultural system relies on "cheap" labor largely performed by people of color, devalues gendered household labor, trades farmland for urban use when the price is right, and avoids paying for environmental costs. Although we in Hawaiʻi are isolated, the food and values that we import connect us to this system.

Labor and race. Seventy percent of the 2.5 million US farmworkers are undocumented, with seasonal work, low pay, and few rights. Our local farms struggle to compete with continental farms that save money through cheap labor practices. Half of Hawaiʻi's own hired farm laborers work 150 days or fewer per year. And while demographic data on Hawaiʻi's farmworkers are scarce, we know that more than half of our farm "principal producers"—those making the most decisions— are white, despite making up only one fifth of the state's total population.

Gender. In Hawaiʻi we have almost as many unpaid as hired workers. While we have no statistics on how many of these unpaid workers are women, we know that nearly two-thirds of farm "principal producers" are male.

Urbanization. On Oʻahu, approximately 9000 acres of agricultural land were rezoned to urban in the last thirty to forty years—and this is an underestimate, because it does not count conversions of less than fifteen acres.

Climate change. The agricultural sector produces ten percent of US greenhouse gas emissions. The impacts of climate change on agriculture in Hawaiʻi have not been well studied, but so far the outlook is negative. Indigenous farming practices could play a role in increasing agricultural resilience.

Hawai'i must tackle these food issues with an understanding of their linkages to capitalism. Since the first *Value of Hawai'i* ten years ago, communities, individual farmers, and farm organizations have addressed food self-sufficiency through innovations in growing and distribution—but not on a large enough scale, or with a systemic scope. The State and County agricultural self-sufficiency goals and policies now in place will be difficult to implement as long as the capitalist economy continues to define growth and wealth in narrow and destructive ways.

In Hawai'i, economic growth is tied to population growth. In 1997, I wrote an article called "Population Growth Economics." Our community was trying to restore water to Waiāhole stream. The argument against this was that the diverted water would be needed for "inevitable population growth." During that struggle, we learned about population policies established by the Hawai'i State Temporary Commission on Population Stabilization in 1971. For instance, it was official City policy to "control the growth of Oʻahu's resident and visitor populations in order to avoid social, economic and environmental disruptions," and to "seek a balance between the rate of in-migration and out-migration by reducing in-migration." The City was also required to "participate in State and Federal programs which seek to develop social, economic, legal, and environmental controls over population growth" and to "publicize the desire of the City and County to limit population growth." Observers at the time acclaimed these actions of Governor John A. Burns as historic.

But no political analysis or practical steps have ever been taken to implement these policies. Development advocates and government planners have concluded that we cannot control population growth—that in fact, our economy depends upon it. In the four decades we've been farming, battles over the agricultural land rezoning and stream diversion for urbanization have been constant. Enter **steady state economics**, a system that defines sustainability as balancing population and economy with the capacity of Earth's ecosystems and our social systems (Center for the Advancement of a Steady State Economy). As the current pandemic reveals the injustices and vulnerability of our current economy, lots of ideas are being shared for what a Hawai'i steady state economy would look like. Whether they use the term "steady state" or not, the "ʻĀina Aloha Economic Futures Declaration" and *Building Bridges, Not Walking on Backs: A Feminist Economic Recovery Plan for COVID-19* both place ecology and people's health above short-sighted definitions of economic growth.

This takes us back to who grows our food. Can "we, the people," grow food in more just and sustainable ways, in keeping with a steady state vision? To do so will require many hands and a unified movement.

Protein. In a steady state economy, instead of being diverted, our streams would flow to the ocean, restoring all of the estuaries that support healthy fisheries. Reclaiming the 400+ fishponds that Hawai'i once had will be a critical step toward protein self-sufficiency and community-level organizing and resource management.

Vegetables. They can be grown in every backyard and in open spaces, public and private. Detroit offers an inspiring example. More than 23,000 residents maintain 1,500 individual gardens (Urban Land Movement). The Detroit Black Community Food Security Network is in the vanguard of the urban garden movement, working in the city and nationally toward racial and economic justice.

During WWI and WWII the victory gardening movement ignited twenty million gardeners, producing forty percent of the country's fresh fruits and vegetables. To address the issue of climate change, people today are adopting the same strategy. Climate Victory Gardeners know how to grow food, and the ecological and human costs of how it gets to our table. This movement means more people are organized and lobbying for changes to our food system. Global networks—Slow Food is another example—will have an increasingly significant impact here in Hawaiʻi.

Protein in the ocean, vegetables in the garden. What about **starch**? We have ʻuala, sweet potato, and ʻulu, breadfruit, but from a cultural and health perspective, the most important is kalo, Hāloa, the elder brother of people. It is currently grown on many scales—from large farms to backyards to pots in high rises—but we need more places where people can grow more kalo. In the last ten years, many Hawaiʻi nonprofits have gotten into kalo farming, recreating extended family and community-based food production. In the ahupuaʻa of Heʻeia, Oʻahu, two nonprofits, Kākoʻo ʻŌiwi and Papahana Kuaola, are restoring wetlands, planting kalo, and providing farming space for families and individuals.

Hāloa has been feeding my family and teaching us how to take care of him physically and politically. Little did we know when we went "back to the land" that our farm would become a community gathering place and a "school" where we would teach and learn. Little did we know that our lives would be enriched not only through the physical act of growing food, but by getting to know people from around the world on their own food journeys.

Our farm was historically a home for Hāloa, and to restore that home and start our food journey, we were generously given huli. In turn, we give huli to others. Huli also means to turn, flip, transition to another form. And it is the most powerful metaphor for understanding the politics of food in Hawaiʻi. We need to turn our food world around, flip the social power dynamics, propagate new ideas, and transition into a lifestyle and steady-state mindset that allows us to live sustainably.

In the past four years, I have witnessed four of the largest local demonstrations I can recall: the women's march, the youth-led rally for climate action, the march for Mauna Kea, and the march for Black Lives. Climate activist Greta Thunberg tells us that "we have passed a social tipping point. We can no longer look away from what our society has been ignoring for so long, whether it is equality, justice, or sustainability. There is an 'awakening' in which people are starting to find their voice."

Growing food awakens you to these huli movements. By building connections between these movements, we have a chance to make systemic change. Food brings us together. E pū pa'akai kākou.

Works Cited

"'Āina Aloha Economic Futures Declaration." 'Āina Aloha Economic Futures, 19 May 2020, https://www.ainaalohafutures.com/declaration.

Building Bridges, Not Walking on Backs: A Feminist Economic Recovery Plan for COVID-19. Hawai'i State Commission on the Status of Women and the Department of Human Services, State of Hawai'i, 14 Apr. 2020, https://humanservices.hawaii.gov/wp-content/uploads/2020/04/4.13.20-Final-Cover-D2-Feminist-Economic-Recovery-D1.pdf.

Kurashima, Natalie, et al. "The potential of indigenous agricultural food production under climate change in Hawai'i." *Nature Sustainability*, vol. 2, 2009, pp. 191–99.

United State Department of Agriculture. "2017 Census of Agriculture." AC-17-A-51. USDA, National Agricultural Statistics Service, Apr. 2019.

Charlie Reppun and his extended family live on their taro farm in Waiāhole, O'ahu. His wife Vivien, son Fred, and niece Ke'alohi contributed significantly to this essay.

The State of Our Starch

Noa Kekuewa Lincoln

Rice. So much about Hawai'i's contemporary food system can be summarized in just this one crop. Hawai'i consumes more rice per capita than any other state, importing over 140 million pounds annually. Although Hawai'i can grow rice, and grew substantial amounts of it in the past, only a handful of token acres remains under cultivation today. White rice, by far the preferred form in Hawai'i, is milled and polished to remove the bran and germ, stripping much of the fiber, minerals, antioxidants, vitamins, amino acids, and lignans. The result is an "empty carb" that is rapidly digested, causing spikes in blood sugar levels and potentially increasing the risk of Type 2 diabetes.

Most people know that Hawai'i imports about 85–90 percent of our food. But while half of our daily calories come from carbohydrates—mainly grains and starchy tubers—Hawai'i produces less than 0.5 percent of those carbohydrates locally. If we want to talk about food security, we must reckon with the fact that to feed people, we need starches. While local production of baby cucumbers, mushrooms, and tomatoes may be quite good—60 percent of our fresh fruits and 30 percent of our vegetables are produced in-state—our self-sufficiency in the critical staple food category is virtually nonexistent. Even production of kalo and 'uala, the staples of our ancestors, no longer contributes signficantly to feeding Hawai'i. The 'uala we do grow is largely exported, while we import kalo from elsewhere in the Pacific because we do not grow enough here to satisfy the small local demand.

Crisis and Carbohydrates

Consideration of carbohydrates is important because we can never just talk about food production, but must address the whole system of activities and services that comprise a *food system*. A food system can be very simple, but becomes complex rapidly when we take into account that crops may need to be harvested, washed, packed, refrigerated or processed, stored, transported, marketed, wholesaled, retailed, and finally prepared and consumed.

Even in the best of times, concerns have been raised over the industrialization of agriculture, the environmental impacts of our food supply, and our extremely low food security. The economic crisis accompanying the COVID-19 pandemic has exacerbated these issues, showing us that our food system priorities may be all wrong—a subset, unfortunately, of much broader issues of our national and global economic system.

This is exemplified by the huge hits to local farmers resulting from the tourism shutdown. Although there are still 1.4 million people in Hawai'i who need to eat, many farmers have suffered tremendous losses because their markets were, by and large, based on supplying restaurants and hotels. That we take care of tourists before our own communities, that the cost of local food is out of reach for many local families but tourists have no problem paying for it, that in many cases we do not have even the basic infrastructure needed to support a robust local supply chain, are all indicative of long-term misplaced priorities and resources that fly in the face of our cultural values, the essential needs of our communities, and even the stated priorities of our state's constitution.

Growing Indigenous Roots

Two years ago, my graduate seminar asked the simple question "What is Indigenous agriculture?" We had surveys and discussions with a range of farmers, practitioners, academics, and even politicians to gather perspectives and opinions on the topic. While there were no conclusive answers, there were clearly several major themes, as illustrated in a word cloud generated from the students' reports.

First and foremost, more important than food or crops or land or practices was the central concept of people. This took the form of family, community, and to a lesser extent, the lāhui.

A word cloud created from the written transcripts of the speakers and subsequent discussions exploring the topic of "What is Indigenous agriculture?" in contemporary settings. Created by author.

This is important. More often than not when we talk about Indigenous agriculture, we emphasize things such as the methods, the crops, or the farmer's ethnicity. But our ancestors operated within a society both supporting and supported by the values, norms, and behaviors of the collective. Everything from decision-making and resource laws to peer pressure was situated within a cultural framework. But because of the new socioeconomic system that was imposed on Hawai'i, we are severely lacking this aspect of Indigenous agriculture today.

I think there are two major areas where we can make substantial changes and advances in this realm. The first is more practical and relates to the social structures that we use to conduct agricultural, and indeed all, business. In the modern world the corporate structure dominates, which prioritizes short-term individual gain with no personal responsibility. This flies in the face of core Hawaiian values, such as kuleana (the reciprocity of rights and responsibilities), laulima (cooperation), and ho'omau (to perpetuate and preserve).

Indigenous Business

Creativity is essential to building organizations that embody the social structure and values of indigenous agriculture in the contemporary system of business dealings. Cooperatives offer some solutions. Our farm, Māla Kalu'ulu Cooperative, is piloting a *workers' cooperative* farm for restoring traditional breadfruit cultivation. Unlike a nonprofit, those who come and work on the farm to experience and learn are not just volunteers, but partners with an ownership stake, contributing their time and patronage to a common effort. Through the investment of mostly sweat equity, they work together to become legal owners of a farm business model that offers a proportionate share of productive income and equal input into decision-making. Participants earn a stake in the game, rights to the land, a voice at the table, and a fair share of the bounty.

Kuleana.

On a larger scale, this effort has spawned the Hawai'i 'Ulu Producers Cooperative, a *producers' cooperative* that collectively processes, markets, and distributes traditional staples. By pooling and leveraging resources, multiple farms band together to accomplish what no one farm could on its own. Just as 'auwai were built, maintained, and owned by communities, the infrastructure of the 'Ulu Co-op (certified kitchen, machinery, storage, etc.) is collectively owned and used by the farmers. Just as no 'auwai could be built alone, no one farm could afford and manage the infrastructure the 'Ulu Co-op has assembled. Coming together to benefit all.

Laulima.

Other organizations, such as MA'O Organic Farms, are utilizing hybrid for-profit and nonprofit business structures to fold together multiple goals. This has allowed stronger embedding of culture and values into the overall model. Farming can be conducted in ways that have longer-term outcomes and impacts, rather than being driven solely by an economic bottom line (but not ignoring it either).

Recognizing that our actions affect our communities and environment—possibly long beyond our own lives—those impacts need to be considered in our decision-making.

Ho'omau.

While each of these structures has its own advantages, challenges, and short-comings, they are being created within the opportunities and confines of our current business environment while incorporating methodologies and practices that better encompass our traditional values.

The Nature of Value

The second area is more esoteric, and concerns the value of food. Is growing food just another form of resource production? Or is there more that is derived?

In the past, agriculture was paramount not only to the prosperity of the people, but to all aspects of society. Agriculture was therefore wrapped in worldview and spirituality. Kalo is an ancestor and provides a familial connection to the land. Kalo was a mentor, teaching family roles and responsibility, relationships, and values. Kalo was an indicator of our environmental health and management. Food was not only something that sustained us physically, but used to reinforce community relationships through the giving and sharing of food, used to connect to our ancestors and provide self-identity, and used to celebrate and appreciate. Agricultural landscapes were not simply extractive areas for food production, but landscapes that were appreciated, utilized, and enjoyed. Farming was not just hard labor, but practiced with song and enjoyed with family. There was a quality of life associated with productive agriculture that elevated it beyond an economic resource, and leveraged it to recognize that this is the life we have. Every moment and every action should sustain the health of ourselves, our communities, and our land. It is only when we truly value what is important that we can change our priorities. Recognizing the value of our food and agriculture is a critical first step to changing and supporting local agricultural production.

Imua

While it is easy to point out what is wrong in our current system, building new pathways is the real challenge. We must find ways to create the food system, and indeed the world, that we want.

Dr. Noa Kekuewa Lincoln is a professor of Indigenous Crops and Cropping Systems at University of Hawai'i at Mānoa, co-founder and president of Māla Kalu'ulu Cooperative, and a member of many boards and advisory councils for a range of agricultural and land management organizations.

Food of Our Future Grows from Seeds of Our Past

Staff at Kuaʻāina Ulu ʻAuamo

"Food sovereignty" is an increasingly used term in Hawaiʻi, but many may not know its origin, meaning, or application to our community. First developed in 1996 by La Via Campesina—an international movement of rural people—the *Declaration of Nyéléni* at the first global forum on food sovereignty in Mali, Africa in 2007 defines it this way:

> Food sovereignty is the right of peoples to healthy and culturally appropriate food produced through ecologically sound and sustainable methods, and their right to define their own food and agriculture systems. It puts the aspirations and needs of those who produce, distribute and consume food at the heart of food systems and policies rather than the demands of markets and corporations.

Food security concerns itself with food access in the conventional transnational context. Undergirded by ecological and human rights for all, food sovereignty recognizes a local right to determine and transform one's own food systems. Over 2,500 miles from anywhere, Hawaiʻi has many unique reasons to see food sovereignty as a response to the precarious dependency of our current food system. Eighty-five to ninety percent of our food is imported. Much of it is processed and of low nutritional value. The COVID-19 pandemic makes our food system challenges glaringly obvious. As we rebuild, concern grows over whether the government and current food systems can address these challenges. As with care for our greater environment, it might be better if a vision and cultural shift in our food systems starts from the ground up, with Hawaiʻi's people.

Indigenous and local culture and history can guide us. Prior to Western contact, Hawaiʻi was food self-sufficient, supporting a population estimated to be close to one million people, almost as many as the 2010 US Census estimation of 1.365 million. Today, a traditional Hawaiian diet, made up of seafood and traditional crops such as taro and sweet potato, is a recognized contributor to improved health, especially for Native Hawaiians who experience health disparities per capita. We see pathways in the rigorous epistemology of pre-Western Hawaiʻi, which many in our communities work to carry forward today. It offers a very different relationship to our food, places, communities, politics, and each other.

Hawaiian Food Sovereignty of the Past: 'Āina Momona

Native Hawaiians developed food, environmental stewardship, customs, and traditions and expertise based on intimate knowledge and long-term multigenerational ecological observations. Traditional food systems produced a resource surplus that exceeded population needs. True on the land and in the sea, this state is referred to as 'āina momona, an abundant productive ecological system that supports community well-being. Food sovereignty is part and parcel of seeking 'āina momona. Hawai'i's people and biocultural resources—storied landscapes, sacred forests, agroforests, streams and rivers, agricultural fields, fisheries, fishponds, and reefs—are deeply damaged by over 200 years of political, economic, and social upheaval and change. Rarely do people, even residents, understand Hawai'i's historic and ongoing role in the US campaign of influence in the Pacific and Asia, or the consequences of colonization on Native Hawaiians. Few know of the historical erosion of Native Hawaiian governance, the overthrow of the internationally recognized Hawaiian Kingdom, the post-overthrow policies to wipe out Native Hawaiian language, culture, and identity, or the historical and ongoing severance of relationships and familial connections to ancestral lands and the natural world.

But not all is lost, nor were Native Hawaiians idle in the last two centuries. In the lessons learned from the past lies a path toward a better future. Prior to the overthrow, Native Hawaiians developed an evolving governance system that integrated community and resource management practices for 'āina (referred to then as the ahupua'a or moku system), and 'āina-based leadership embodied in leaders called konohiki. Leadership with a konohiki mindset connected better with and involved communities to care and govern their place. Hawaiians also became one of the world's most literate populations, entered into treaties with other nation-states, and published books on history, tradition, and culture still used today. In preserving a sense of cultural and national identity, they planted seeds for future generations to reconnect with each other, their culture, their places, and even the world. Those seeds germinate today.

The ongoing Native Hawaiian movement emerging from the 1960–79 renaissance based its attendant values, customs, and practices on the foundations left by previous generations. This traditional ecological knowledge (TEK) includes cultural legacies retained by 'ohana and individual kūpuna (elders), kumu (knowledge sources), kahu (guardians), kāhuna (priests), and loea (experts and professionals) who preserved traditions through practice or oral history.

Hawaiian Food Sovereignty of the Future

Because of such threats as the current COVID-19 pandemic, climate change, sea-level rise, natural disasters, and labor issues such as shipping or airline strikes, Hawai'i must move away from dependency on imported goods which make up ninety percent of our food. To achieve food sovereignty, we must draw upon our community spirit and Hawai'i's TEK.

Three community movements in Hawaiʻi ground their actions and advocacy in the idea that "I ka wā ma mua, ka wā ma hope," the future continues from the path laid behind us. Each effort bridges people to place through a community-based biocultural resource management strategy to restore nearshore fisheries, loko iʻa (fishponds), a traditional aquaculture practice and the celebration, stewardship, and restoration of native limu (seaweed).

Community-based Subsistence Fishing Areas (CBSFA)

In 1994, Hawaiʻi policymakers passed the CBSFA law (HRS 188-22.6) inspired by the konohiki practices of Moʻomomi, Molokaʻi, and Governor Waiheʻeʻs Molokaʻi Subsistence Task Force to reaffirm and protect fishing practices customarily and traditionally exercised for purposes of Native Hawaiian subsistence, culture, and religion. Government leadership took almost twenty years to pass the first CBSFA rules in Hāʻena, Kauaʻi. Today three other communities are in the queue for rulemaking: Moʻomomi, Molokaʻi; Kīpahulu, Maui; and Miloliʻi, Hawaiʻi island. These communities work together in the spirit of lawaiʻa pono to fish virtuously, to fish Hawaiian, and to care for their fisheries.

Loko Iʻa

Found nowhere else in the world, ancient Hawaiian loko iʻa were a technologically advanced, efficient, and extensive form of aquaculture. Indicators of ʻāina momona, they provided much of the protein in the traditional Native Hawaiian diet, and retain the potential to contribute to healthy and robust food systems and fisheries. Over recent decades, Hawaiian communities and kiaʻi loko (fishpond guardians and caretakers) worked to restore loko iʻa and reclaim the knowledge and practice of loko iʻa culture. Recognizing shared challenges to increase collaboration and accelerate restoration and food production, kiaʻi loko from six Hawaiian Islands formed the Hui Mālama Loko Iʻa, a network of loko iʻa and kiaʻi loko. Since 2004, Hui Mālama Loko Iʻa has met annually to strengthen relationships and share experience and expertise.

Limu

Limu had a significant role in many aspects of Hawaiian culture and ʻāina momona. Nowhere else in the world was limu used as extensively. Hawaiian people gathered it for food, medicine, and spiritual purposes. Along with fish and poi, limu was the third major component of a healthy traditional diet by providing flavor and key vitamins and minerals.

Revival and perpetuation of TEK and connections to limu will also develop the biocultural systems that limu depends upon, and that depend upon limu. To carry out this crucial pathway to ʻāina momona, a new, burgeoning, and multigenerational movement formed the Limu Hui.

Building Movement Networks for Community Resilience

Kua'āina Ulu 'Auamo (KUA) means "grassroots growing through shared responsibility." KUA—or "backbone"—gathers, organizes, mobilizes, and supports community-based natural resource management networks—communities, practitioners, families, individuals, and organizations—who work to perpetuate TEK and build a stronger sense of local governance and empowered management of place. KUA reinvigorates sentiments and traditions of laulima, aloha 'āina, and mālama 'āina as embodied in TEK and its attendant values, ethics, and regional place-based practices. KUA's community-driven approach supports E Alu Pū, a network of thirty-six mālama 'āina (natural and cultural resource stewardship) groups, Hui Mālama Loko I'a, a consortium of over forty fishponds and fishpond complexes, and the Limu Hui, a network of native seaweed gatherers, growers, and stewards.

The waiwai (value) of Hawai'i lies in its people and brings them together to work towards 'āina momona. E Alu Pū, Hui Mālama Loki I'a, and Limu Hui efforts have sprouted the seeds left by our kūpuna. They can teach, guide, and spearhead this work; however, the true revival of our loko i'a, limu, fisheries, wahi pana, and ahupua'a depends on the development of a whole community. Food sovereignty is an ecosystem of which we are all a part. Every Hawai'i resident and visitor has a function. How will you activate your role? What seeds will you plant today? It will take a whole community to move us away from our current corporate and foreign food overdependency and toward more sustainable livelihoods and food systems.

Work Cited

Declaration of Nyéléni. Declaration of the Forum for Food Sovereignty, Nyéléni, Mali, 27 Feb. 2007.

This essay is the collective mana'o of **Kua'āina Ulu 'Auamo** staff derived from numerous conversations on this subject.

Kevin Chang and Miwa Tamanaha, Co-Directors, Kua'āina Ulu 'Auamo
Brenda Asuncion, Hui Malama Loko I'a Coordinator
Alex Connelly, E Alu Pū Coordinator and Program Assistant
Ginger Gohier, Community Outreach and Engagement Coordinator
Wally Ito, Limu Hui Coordinator
Kim Moa, Communications Coordinator
Lauren Muneoka, Program Associate and Technical Specialist
Niegel Rozet, Planner

Toward a Smaller, Smarter Correctional System for Hawai'i

Meda Chesney-Lind and Robert Merce

One of the most troubling developments in Hawai'i over the past forty years has been the dramatic increase in the state's jail and prison population. The trend began in the early 1970s when Hawai'i, like most other jurisdictions, enacted "tough on crime" laws that put more people behind bars for longer periods of time, particularly for drug offenses. In just four decades Hawai'i's combined jail and prison population increased 670 percent, and the incarceration rate increased 400 percent (*Creating*). Hawai'i didn't just follow mainland mass incarceration trends, it led them. In the 1980s the average annual increase in Hawai'i's prison population was the second highest in the nation (Langan et al. 2).

As Hawai'i's prisons became dangerously overcrowded in the mid-1990s, we sent hundreds of inmates to private prisons on the mainland, but we didn't change the policies driving the prison population, and so the number of people behind bars continued to grow unabated. Hawai'i currently has more than 27,000 people under some form of correctional supervision, and although the incarceration rate has declined slightly in the past few years, it is still so high that if Hawai'i was a country rather than a state, it would rank among the top twenty incarcerators in the world (*Creating*).

The problems with Hawai'i's correctional system go far beyond the number of people we incarcerate. Native Hawaiians are overrepresented at every stage of Hawai'i's criminal justice system, making up 21 percent of Hawai'i's general population, but 37 percent of the prison population (*Creating*).

Does our correctional system work to prevent future crimes? The average recidivism rate in Hawai'i for those who spend more than one year in prison is 59 percent, which means that our system fails more often than it succeeds (Wong).

And of course, the cost of our correctional system is unsustainable. It costs $198 a day, or $72,000 a year, to incarcerate a person in Hawai'i (*Annual Report* 16). The Department of Public Safety's budget is more than $226 million a year, and the State is planning to build a new jail to replace the O'ahu Community Correctional Center (OCCC) at a cost of $525 million, or $380,000 per bed (*Final Environmental* 49). The State also plans to spend $45 million to expand the Women's Community Correctional Facility (WCCC), and it is planning to build new medium security housing units at the prisons on Maui, Kaua'i, and Hawai'i island (*Creating* xiii).

Fortunately, there are evidence-based solutions to many of the issues facing our correctional system. Hawai'i should immediately transition to a more effective correctional model that focuses on rehabilitation instead of punishment. The new model should incorporate best pracitices from countries like Norway that follow the "normality principle" in which prisoners live in comfortable private rooms, wear normal clothing, and follow a normal daily routine of working, shopping for food, cooking, cleaning, and socializing.

One of the biggest obstacles to reforming Hawai'i's correctional system is the State's plan to build a 1,380-bed jail on O'ahu to replace OCCC. There is no question that OCCC needs to be replaced—it is old, dilapidated, and overcrowded—but the jail that the State is planning to build is based on outmoded ideas and a failed planning process. If it is built, it will produce poor outcomes for decades and significantly undermine other reform efforts.

The first question a community should ask when planning a new jail is not "How big should it be?" but "How small can we make it?" Hawai'i officials never asked that critical question, and the State has no plans to address the policies that are driving the OCCC population. This is a huge mistake. Just a few days in jail can "increase the likelihood of a sentence of incarceration and the harshness of that sentence, reduce economic viability, promote future criminal behavior, and worsen the health of those who enter—making jail a gateway to deeper and more lasting involvement in the criminal justice system" (Subramanian et al. 5).

Planning for the new jail should wait until we have policies in place to significantly reduce the jail population by: (1) expanding the use of pre-arrest diversion programs that refer clients to social services and case management instead of putting them in jail; (2) expanding the discretion of police officers to issue citations in lieu of arrest for offenses up to and including most non-violent class C felonies; and (3) expanding residential treatment programs for crimes related to addiction or mental illness (*Hawai'i Criminal*).

We should also end the money bail system because, as the Hawai'i Criminal Pretrail Reform Task Force said, "there is virtually no correlation between the setting of a particular bail amount and whether the defendant will commit further crime or engage in violent behavior when released from custody" (*Hawai'i Criminal* 68).

In addition, we should stop using the jail to sanction probation violators who have not committed a new crime. They do not pose a danger to the public, and it costs close to $60,000 a day to house them in the jail.[1] If we address the foregoing issues we can build a smaller and smarter jail at a fraction of the cost of the jail the State is now planning to build.

Finally, many of the people in OCCC are poor, mentally ill, and charged with homeless-related offenses such as sitting or lying on a public sidewalk. These people repeatedly cycle through our jails and emergency rooms, receiving fragmented and costly care that fails to address their underlying needs. One of the primary functions of the new jail should be to assess the medical, social, and financial needs of these people, treat them while in jail, and provide them with a discharge plan that will ensure access to services and continuity of care when they are released.

The dramatic increase in Hawai'i's jail and prison population over the past four decades can be reversed without compromising public safety. Indeed, in 2017 Hawai'i's violent crime rate was eight percent below the crime rate reported in 2008, and the property crime rate decreased twenty percent during the same period, suggesting that Hawai'i's incarceration rate is largely unconnected to declining crime levels in the community ("Crime in Hawaii").

Hawai'i's reliance on mass incarceration is a corrosive trend that wastes lives and money, but it can be reversed. Opportunities for real and lasting change in our correctional system abound. What we need is the political will to reduce our jail and prison populations, and revitalize our communities with the savings that accrue from smarter criminal justice policies.

Note

1. As previously noted, it costs $198 a day to incarcerate a person in Hawai'i. At any given time there are about 300 probation violators at OCCC (*Department of Public*). With 300 inmates at $198/day, the cost is $59,400/day.

Works Cited

Annual Report FY 2019. State of Hawaii Department of Public Safety, 2019, https://dps.hawaii.gov/wp-content/uploads/2019/11/PSD-ANNUAL-REPORT-2019.pdf.

Creating Better Outcomes, Safer Communities: Final Report of the House Concurrent Resolution 85 Task Force on Prison Reform to the Hawai'i Legislature, 2019 Regular Session. HCR 85 Task Force, Hawai'i Judiciary, Dec. 2018, https://www.courts.state.hi.us/wp-content/uploads/2018/12/HCR-85_task_force_final_report.pdf.

"Crime in Hawaii 2017." State of Hawaii Crime Prevention and Justice Assistance Division, 11 Jan. 2019, https://ag.hawaii.gov/cpja/crime-in-hawaii-2017/.

Department of Public Safety End of Month Population Report. State of Hawaii Department of Public Safety, 31 Jan. 2020, https://dps.hawaii.gov/wp-content/uploads/2020/02/Pop-Reports-EOM-2020-01-31.pdf.

Final Environmental Impact Statement (EIS) for the Replacement of the Oahu Community Correctional Center, Expansion of Women's Community Correctional Center, and New Department of Agriculture Animal Quarantine Station. State of Hawaii Department of Accounting and General Services (DAGS), 26 June 2018, http://oeqc2.doh.hawaii.gov/EA_EIS_Library/2018-07-08-OA-FEIS-Replacement-of-Oahu-Community-Correctional-Center.pdf.

Hawai'i Criminal Pretrial Reform: Recommendations of the Criminal Pretrial Task Force to the Thirtieth Legislature of the State of Hawai'i. Criminal Pretrial Task Force, Hawai'i State Judiciary, Dec. 2018, https://www.courts.state.hi.us/wp-content/uploads/2018/12/POST_12-14-18_HCR134TF_REPORT.pdf.

Langan, Patrick, et al. *Historical Statistics on Prisoners in State and Federal Institutions Yearend 1925–86.* Bureau of Justice Statistics, U.S. Department of Justice, May 1988, https://www.ncjrs.gov/pdffiles1/digitization/111098ncjrs.pdf.

Subramanian, Ram, et al. *Incarceration's Front Door: The Misuse of Jails in America.* Vera Institute of Justice, Feb. 2015, http://www.safetyandjusticechallenge.org/wp-content/uploads/2015/01/incarcerations-front-door-report.pdf.

Wong, Timothy. *2017 Recidivism Update.* State of Hawaii Interagency Council on Intermediate Sanctions (ICIS), July 2018, https://icis.hawaii.gov/wp-content/uploads/2018/08/Hawaii-Revidivism-2017.pdf.

Meda Chesney-Lind is a professor of Women's Studies at the University of Hawai'i and past president of the American Society of Criminology.

Robert Merce is a retired lawyer. He recently served as vice-chair of the House Concurrent Resolution 85 Task Force on Prison Reform.

Labor and Social Justice against the Colonial University

A Union for Radical Solidarity

Executive Committee of Academic Labor United

This violence is being perpetrated by our boss, David Lassner. Together, we have the power, knowledge, and solidarity to find another way forward. We must be a union that will always stand up for our fellow workers, and never stand with a boss that routinely disregards our dignity, futures, and now physical safety. An injury to one is an injury to all.

Benton Rodden, former ALU Chair

Aloha kākou. We are members of Academic Labor United (ALU), a graduate student committee organizing for graduate assistant (GA) unionization at the University of Hawai'i. We invite you to envision with us a coalitional labor and social justice movement that reaches across Hawai'i Pae 'Āina and the boundaries that imperialism has forced between our bodies, and that strives towards transformational labor power and radical solidarity.

ALU formed in 2017 in response to the university administration's continued and active exploitation of vulnerable student workers. As the discrepancy between our wages and cost of living continues to grow, the UH administration is increasing its reliance on our cheap labor for teaching, research, and administrative work. For years, they have not intervened in cases of exploitive supervisors abusing graduate workers. Trying to wait survivors out, bureaucratic inefficiencies stall grievances for months. And even though public sector workers won the rights to strike and bargain collectively in the 1970s, the State of Hawai'i and UH are denying GAs these same rights.

Efforts at GA unionization in Hawai'i have been years in the making. In fact, our cause has a genealogy stretching back nearly two centuries. While many believe the earliest Hawai'i labor action was a Kanaka Maoli worker walkout at the Kōloa sugar plantation in 1841, Kanaka Maoli students working the printing press at Lahainaluna school struck for higher wages in January of 1839. That school's post-secondary program anticipated the University of Hawai'i.

True to its foundations as a missionary school, UH is deeply rooted in histories of settler colonialism, militarism, and capitalism. The flagship campus sits on "ceded lands," the term the US State of Hawai'i uses for those lands seized from the Kingdom of Hawai'i after the illegal overthrow by American businessmen and military in 1893. At the summit of Mauna a Wākea, the UH-managed Mauna Kea Observatories, slated for a massive thirteenth telescope complex despite decades of opposition from the Kanaka Maoli community, also rest on "ceded lands." Written by our then-chair on the day that the kūpuna protecting Maunakea were arrested, this essay's epigraph provoked vocal opposition and silent resentment from parts of our own membership. While many of our leaders and organizers, past, present, and future, Kānaka Maoli and settlers alike, put their bodies between the mauna and a heavily militarized police force, some of our membership benefit academically and professionally from summit telescope development. Like many Hawai'i labor unions, composed of workers in tourism, development, education, and so on, we wrestle with our need for economic security as exploited workers, and our complicity with our workplace's settler colonial violence. At Pu'uhuluhulu, however, the UH administration unmistakably participated in capitalist class traditions of employing the police as a private security force against its own workers, and the colonial higher education tradition of inflicting violence on Native bodies to advance research objectives. Also tools of the brutal US imperialism regime, these actions are inseparable.

As a unionization organizing committee, we believe that labor struggle is essential to our collective liberation, and that social justice movements must address labor to win the radical change they seek. The move away from considering labor as essential to social justice work over the past few decades is understandable. Business model unionism, where representatives act as third-party negotiators between bosses and workers, is not advocacy for workers' rights, but a concession of workers' agency. This model has neutered workers' power and bred working class mistrust.

ALU is organizing a union run by workers, fighting for and uplifting our comrades—solidarity, whose central message, coined by the earlier labor movement, is that "an injury to one is an injury to all." Although critical theorists have armed us with the tools to see our individual oppressions as intersecting, the basic principle has not changed. ALU and all unions are workers collectives, including every worker. In violent struggles such as protecting Maunakea, as an organization ALU is therefore not an ally. That would imply that ALU's struggle is not a direct struggle against settler colonialism. Such a stance would however erase our Kanaka Maoli members. Because we cannot be free until they are free, we stand in *solidarity* with kia'i mauna, as we do with Black Lives Matter, because our members are Black as well. Or as ALU comrade Joy Enomoto says, "Black lives matter in the Hawaiian Kingdom."

As labor organizers, we must return to the movement's radical roots. As social justice organizers, we must include labor once more as a central piece of our collective movement. If imperialism exploits labor to extract resources from stolen Indigenous lands and convert it into capital, fighting this system demands that you either take control of the land, as was done on Kahoʻolawe or Maunakea, or withhold your labor. If ALU had been organized enough to strike in solidarity with our Kanaka Maoli comrades during the 2019 standoff on the Ala Hulu Kūpuna, we could have shut down UH operations completely, crippling the institution forcing TMT construction. Simply put, we have to hit wherever it hurts.

In reality, this is extremely complex. Many ALU organizers and members are settlers—including those writing this essay—and the university is a colonial legacy project. The anti-colonial struggle within UH is a fight we want to advance, but also a source of great internal tension. The ALU Executive Committee believes that dismantling Hawaiʻi settler colonialism when perpetrated by the university is part of our duties. But we represent graduate workers who participate and profit from the university's settler colonialism. We are striving to unite a diverse graduate student population, without watering down our stand on intersectional struggles. While we cannot, and do not want to remain silent on social justice issues affecting our members, expressing radical politics or claiming ideological purity serves nearly no one if we can no longer turn out a large portion of our members. A union's power lies in its workers standing together.

Because a union always has to come back to the table, though some members disagreed with our then-chair's statement on Maunakea, they will return to join us in fighting for sick leave, higher wages, and collective bargaining. Our work is political education rooted in solidarity, in identifying our intersecting struggles and collective oppressors. To this end, in the fall of 2019, we held "Maunakea Talk Story" events every few weeks, providing forums for difficult conversations about settler colonial violence and science. These were productive, but the vast majority of the work still needs to be done. When we contact members or hold events, some folks still renounce their ALU membership because of our chair's statement. But new members have sometimes been referred by folks who previously renounced their membership. We have hope.

Labor organizations working towards radical intersectional solidarity must avoid focusing on immediate material gains to engage membership, and commit to personal and societal transformation on a deeper level. The COVID-19 pandemic has revealed the deep structural oppressions most apparent during times of crisis, as well as our deep need for loving communities. We have the chance to hulihia in Hawaiʻi Pae ʻĀina—to build a movement so strong it alters our landscape. No single event is the hulihia. Our sick leave petition was not, and even though it drew nearly 20,000 people together, the Black Lives Matter protest on June 6, 2020 was not either. The hulihia is that we witnessed that a community of labor, Indigenous, and social justice organizers can pull together one of the largest mass protests in

Hawai'i history in about one week. ALU is not a hulihia, but we hope to be part of one. As organizers, our task is to dismantle one imperialist institution among many in this archipelago, becoming in the process part of one great and mighty wave. One movement.

Graduate workers are often seen as "in transit"—from elsewhere, going somewhere else soon. But a PhD at UH frequently takes seven to ten years, and over sixty percent of graduate students qualify for in-state tuition. They did not move here simply to attend school. Many are parents or caretakers. We are responsible for much of the teaching and mentorship of undergraduate students, and through these connections and our research work, we profoundly affect this place.

We vow not to be moved by the forces of our intersecting oppressions as we join in solidarity to become a movement itself, emerging from the earth to carve out our own landscapes.

Works Cited

Enomoto, Joy. "Where will you be? Black Lives Matter in the Hawaiian Kingdom." *Ke Kaupu Hehi Ale*, 1 Feb. 2017, https://hehiale.wordpress.com/2017/02/01/where-will-you-be-why-black-lives-matter-in-the-hawaiian-kingdom/.
Rodden, Benton. "Message on Events at Mauna Kea." Email message, 17 July 2019.

This essay was written by Lucie Knor and Alex Miller on behalf of the executive committee of Academic Labor United, and does not reflect the opinions of the entire organization.

Lucie Knor is an activist and PhD student in oceanography from Bremen, Germany, currently living in Mānoa, and vice chair of Academic Labor United.

Alex Miller grew up in the Susquehanna River valley, now studies dance at the University of Hawai'i at Mānoa, and is communications chair of Academic Labor United.

The Sustaining Force of Sports

Michael Tsai

The vitality of a community's sporting life reliably indicates its greater social, economic, and even political well being. The degree to which residents can engage in non-purposeful recreational play or participate in organized sport programs, and can consume as spectators amateur and professional sports, either live or via a myriad of electronic media, reflects and contributes to the quality of daily life in Hawai'i. It is worth reflecting on what we value as a sports culture, and on what we can do to preserve the sustaining force of sports in our community.

Participation

With year-round temperate weather, a broad network of parks and recreational facilities, and ready proximity to hundreds of miles of public trails and the surrounding ocean, Hawai'i is a player's paradise. Residents and visitors keep busy some seventy-five golf courses across the state. More than sixty active canoe clubs offer recreational and competitive opportunities for thousands of paddlers in multiple age divisions. In Honolulu alone there are ninety-one public tennis courts, nearly all regularly trafficked. On any given weekend, hundreds, sometimes thousands, of recreational athletes participate in road races, triathlons, time trials, open-ocean swimming competitions, and other events.

But access to recreational and organized sport is not equal across race, regional, and socioeconomic lines. While two-thirds of Hawai'i residents technically live within a half-mile of a park, the concentration of parks and population in Honolulu heavily distorts this measure. Of course, enjoying recreational sports depends not just on access but also on the quality of experience. Maintenance of parks, trails, and beaches can therefore significantly impact their accessability and the health and safety of visitors. For many residents, particularly on O'ahu, however, such recreational experiences can be compromised by the encroachment of homeless encampments and by the crush of ten million visitors per year.

Ala Moana Beach Park is a hub of local recreational activity. By day, runners, cyclists, swimmers, surfers, stand-up paddleboarders, canoe paddlers, volleyball players, and other everyday athletes share the hundred-acre space. Local park users are also accustomed to the steady stream of Japanese wedding photographers and their clients traipsing through recreational areas, and to the throngs of visitors who, spurred by guidebook recommendations, line the shore to take smartphone photos of the sunset. But a hard line was drawn in 2019, when the city approved a private developer plan to build a $3 million playground, complete with zip lines, within the park. While promoted as a gift to the city, the project seemed more of a gift to residents of the pricey condominiums nearby. The resulting public outcry effectively scuttled the project, a victory of sorts for residents weary of seeing public spaces usurped for private interests, and perhaps a message to lawmakers that recreational spaces must be preserved and enhanced in ways meaningful to their host communities.

Native Hawaiians and Youth Sports

The significance of youth sports in Hawai'i is compounded by their relation to educational opportunity. Children with potential at an early age are encouraged to specialize in a sport, and guided to private sports clubs and off-season camps to supplement the training and playing opportunities offered by their school athletic programs. Talent can help to secure entry into one of the elite private schools, a common goal for families seeking to escape the perceived inadequacies of the state's chronically underfunded and underperforming public school system.

But private clubs can cost thousands of dollars per season, and young athletes with working parents may not have transportation to practices and games, perpetuating differentials in opportunity that stretch beyond the field. An Aspen Institute report specified that Native Hawaiian youth, particularly those living in rural communities, are disproportionately impacted by a lack of transportation to recreational centers and the inability to pay for private sports programs.

There are no easy solutions here, but a starting point could be for the state and counties to fund low-cost, well-staffed, park-based athletic programs as an alternative to costly private programs that take youth athletes out of their neighborhoods.

UH Sports

Despite lukewarm student support and continual budget shortfalls requiring regular loans from the university to the athletic department, the University of Hawai'i remains the state's top spectator draw. In 2019, the athletic department ran a deficit of $2.94 million, necessitating a $13.6 million loan to defray $51.3 million in expenses.

Only a handful of sports—football, men's basketball, men's and women's volleyball, and baseball—break even or generate a profit. The heaviest investment is in football, which supports the largest number of scholarship athletes and incurs the largest operational expenses. But the investment return, relied upon to help fund the non-revenue-generating sports, is negatively affected by high travel costs, travel subsidies paid to visiting conference opponents (a unique requirement of

Mountain West Conference affiliation), low student fee support, and a zero share of parking and concession fees from Aloha Stadium, where it plays its home games.

To avoid contraction of non-revenue-generating sports—a scenario that would endanger compliance with Title IX, which requires equal access to participation opportunities for men and women—and to establish a sustainable financial model for the athletic department, UH will need greater annual appropriations from the state, and find new ways to maximize its operating revenue. If local sports fans will not accept eliminating football or dropping it to the Division III level, as some have suggested, it may be time for UH to seek separate support for programs that ensure Title IX compliance, through dedicated state funding and private booster support.

Sports Marketing

Each year, the Hawai'i Tourism Authority spends roughly one-tenth of its nearly $80 million budget on sports marketing. The investment is meant to maintain and build a sports tourism sector, which HTA values at $150 million.

Prior to the game's relocation in 2015, the National Football League received an annual subsidy of about $5 million to hold the Pro Bowl in Hawai'i. The HTA claimed that this subsidy secured an event that annually drew as many as 47,000 visitors, and promoted Hawai'i to millions of TV viewers. But a 2015 analysis by the North American Association of Sports Economists estimated that the actual number of additional visitors during the period was between 5,596 and 6,726. This analysis supports research indicating that subsidized sporting events have minimal economic benefit for the host community.

The Professional Golfers' Association is now HTA's most prominent sports affiliation. The state signed a four-year, $2.1 million extension with the PGA to continue hosting championship events on O'ahu, Maui, and Hawai'i island. The arrangement provides promotional opportunities for Hawai'i's $1 billion golf industry, and for the state as a whole. HTA sponsors dozens of other events, many tied to local sporting traditions such as the Nā Wahine O Ke Kai Canoe Race. In addition, HTA supports events packaged with outreach programs, such as a Los Angeles Rams youth football camp held in advance of an exhibition game against the Dallas Cowboys in 2019.

The state does not provide direct financial support for Hawai'i's largest and most economically impactful sporting event—the Honolulu Marathon. Staged each year on the second Sunday of December, traditionally a slow tourism period, the race draws tens of thousands of participants from Japan via aggressive in-country marketing by sponsor JAL and its subsidiary travel business JALPAK. While the Honolulu Marathon Association no longer commissions an annual economic-impact study, it previously reported over $100 million in economic activity related to the event each year. But that figure only accounts for total spending, and not for the amount that actually stays in Hawaiʻi. More telling is the $4 million to $6 million in direct tax revenue, which benefits the local economy. The other major state-hosted international endurance event, the Kona Ironman Championship, claims $30 million in economic impact, with an outsize sphere of benefit to the many private, locally owned businesses in the area.

In recent years, HTA has increased its involvement with UH athletics, a positive refocusing that bears watching. For a 2019 UH-Washington road game in Seattle, HTA paid $50,000 for an alumni reception, tī leaves for Hawaiʻi fans, and flights for the UH cheer team, who joined UW cheerleaders in a visit to a local children's hospital. By investing in the top local sports attraction, HTA can continue to promote Hawaiʻi tourism in meaningful ways while also helping to preserve revenue-generating UH sports and the non-revenue-generating sports they support.

Works Cited

Aspen Institute. *State of Play Hawaii.* Washington, D.C., 2019.

Associated Press. "Title IX a Major Factor as Colleges Begin Cutting Sports to Meet Budget." *Portland Press Herald*, 27 May 2020.

Civil Beat Editorial Board. "Children's Playground a Bad Fit for Ala Moana Park." *Civil Beat*, 20 Nov. 2019.

Hawaii State Golf Association. *Course Listing*, 2019.

Hawaiʻi Tourism Authority. *2019 Annual Report to the Hawaiʻi State Legislature*, https://www.hawaiitourismauthority.org/media/4052/2019-annual-report-to-the-hawaii-state-legislature.pdf.

Hiraishi, Kuʻuwehi. "Sports Tourism in Hawaiʻi in 2019." *Hawaiʻi Public Radio*, 4 Feb. 2019, https://www.hawaiipublicradio.org/post/sports-tourism-hawai-i-2019.

Lewis, Ferd. "UH Athletics Operated at Nearly $3 Million Deficit in 2019." *Honolulu Star-Advertiser*, 6 Dec. 2019.

Michael Tsai is an assistant professor of English at Kapiʻolani Community College and a former reporter and columnist for the *Honolulu Star-Advertiser*. He is the author of *The People's Race Inc.: Behind the Scenes at the Honolulu Marathon* (2016).

The Value of Mele

Kainani Kahaunaele

How much is mele or music a part of your daily life? Has your attention to mele increased to get you through your day, especially in uncertain COVID times? Have you been watching local and worldwide live stream concerts or social media posts of friends and family making music? It's ironic how musicians, who seemed to be the first profession to go under, are now playing an essential role in nurturing our communities' wellbeing through mele, as we navigate our new normal.

Like most colleagues in Hawai'i's music industry, we went from full calendars of gigs for this year to zero in about two weeks. Because I was recording my newest album on another island, the travel ban also stopped my production dead in its tracks. As a kumu of mele research and Hawaiian music performance at Ka Haka 'Ula O Ke'elikōlani College of Hawaiian Language and Literature at UH Hilo, I had to deal with drastically altered class meetings and participation by moving to online learning, losing much of the social connecting force that making music provides. As the boss of mele in my household, however, we have never played so much music together.

Mele—Hawaiian songs and chants—are our primary sources, literature, and vehicles to celebrate, revere, grieve, recount, love, and request. The carefully woven lyrics are primary, holding Hawaiian language knowledge and worldview, pearls of wisdom from our ancestors, and experiences of the haku mele, or composer. An understanding of mele language, a working knowledge of a variety of mele, 'ōlelo Hawai'i proficiency, continuous practice, and collaborating with experts bring the mele to life. In our schools, community life, and families, mele is more than background music. It is the soundtrack of our lives, and an integral link to our past, merging with current events and our visions of the futures.

No Ka Haku Mele

For the first time, we're witnessing Hawai'i with no visitor industry, our main economic engine. This is mind-blowing for all—and a wish come true for some. Musicians, hula dancers, sound techs, and others serving tourists and locals are having to get creative. Many musicians are still playing as a matter of practice and healing. But no paycheck. The crisis has however given us time to refine, rejuvenate, talk shop with colleagues, share music, and refine again. And haku mele is an option many are exploring.

Haku mele is the careful selection, weaving, and crafting of words and ideas through the Hawaiian worldview, based on a foundation of older mele. It requires Hawaiian language proficiency and delivering mele through chant or singing. As in many cultures, mele composition is highly regarded for its poetry, power of language, and appeal to our emotions, spirituality, environment, and fellow man.

Two stars guide my haku mele practice. "I ka 'ōlelo nō ke ola, i ka 'ōlelo nō ka make," there is life and death in words, and "'O 'oe ka luaahi o kāu mele," you, the composer, are the victim of your mele. These 'ōlelo no'eau show us how important it is to watch your words, lest you suffer the consequence. They also affirm the powerful benefit of mele that are "pili," or put together well. The lyrics are primary; the music helps lift the message, intention, and vibe. The vocal delivery—pronunciation and phrasing—can make or break your mele, which is primarily about the 'ōlelo. Luckily, you can make every delivery better—but only if you are aware.

This excerpt from "Waipunalei," my recently composed mele, reminds me of the healing power of our natural environment, and particularly our forests, in these COVID times.

Ua ano ka nahele	*The forest is silent*
'A'ohe lele manu o kula	*For no birds dwell in the plains as preparation*
Ia uka wehiwehi	*In this verdant forest*
'Elua kāua i ke kilikili ua	*Here we are in the fine rain*
I kolu i ke 'ala anuhea	*Where the cool fragrance of the forest joins us*
Līhau mai nei ke oho palai	*The palai ferns are fresh and moist*
Ua la'i i ka lau lā'au	*Contentment is found*

When our forest thrives, the kai thrives, and kānaka thrive too. Experiencing our 'āina, paying attention to the nuances, and seeing the world through mele language is exhilarating. Whether in the forest, at the beach, or at home, mele can be the vessel to transport you between space and time.

The Life of Mele in Our Community

The Hawaiian entertainment industry deserves lots of credit for our unbroken tradition of Hawaiian music, carrying mele and cultural knowledge that could have been lost and forgotten. Beaten out of many of our kūpuna, our language was on the brink of extinction, but music and mele provided safe spaces for it to continue and thrive, even if it meant singing mostly to visitors. Through mele, 'ōlelo Hawai'i was still relatable and practical, and mele was also maintained in the Hawaiian churches, hālau hula, and 'ohana.

As our education system evolves in these COVID times, this is an opportune moment to imagine how we can amplify the role of mele in our schools. In Hawaiian education-based schools, mele are important throughout the daily school curriculum—from chanting genealogies, ceremonies, and formal speech making, to collecting and analyzing scientific data. The chosen mele are functional, enjoyable, and nurturing for the student's identity and skill sets. With more training and grounding in mele language and Hawaiian language arts, I hope to see even more use of mele as empowering tools, and avenues for expressing and connecting student ideas. More online learning platforms may grant schools more access to mele, musical, and hula experts of Hawaiʻi to plant seeds of inspiration, and to nurture the spirit and creativity of students. Hiring mele practitioners as more than guest speakers, and especially working musicians now unemployed due to the pandemic, would benefit all.

I was recently part of a Zoom gathering of wāhine from across Hawaiʻi sponsored by Ka Waiwai Collective. We discussed how we are doing, what we were noticing as we kilo our natural environment, and how we are dealing with it all. One of my roles was to wrap the gathering up with mele. I decided to sing an island medley, and to get the ladies to sing along and hula when their island song was sung—to make themselves known. The mele totally lifted up the scene. Seeing all the ladies having fun in a collective setting and connecting to mele and place wrapped us in rejuvenation and gratitude. Even during social distancing, when our communities claim their spaces and storied areas with mele wahi pana, we all holomua. When we sing these songs *together* and feel the connecting force of mele, the lifting is lighter. This is not only for good singers. When we sing together with intention, aloha, and pride, we fortify the community and spirit. Valuing the mele of all your areas—in residence, in ahupuaʻa, in district, or on the highest peak—sets these select mele or pōhaku into the foundation, the house structure, that lives within.

I envision more time for our keiki and ʻohana to work in mālama ʻāina and connect with the mana of the land, equipped with mele to reinforce their foundation. I envision more appreciation for Hawaiian music in the home, with multigenerational gatherings, with storytelling and kanikapila. I envision Hawaiian education laden with functional, practical, and well-made mele to stir the hearts and minds of our kānaka, elevating the value of mele, of our world, and of ourselves.

Start at Home

As we get used to quarantining, or staying in our ʻohana bubble, making music is one of the most heartwarming activities we can do. Start with the mele that take you back to your favorite places or people. Perhaps your children have never heard of your connection to a particular mele. Go over the words and get those stories going. Record the storytelling. If you don't have instruments to play, pull up the song on your playlist and sing along. Create an ʻohana playlist of favorite mele. A little ʻohana competition can go a long way to foster mastery and confidence.

The kuleana and practice of mele in my household is essential. It's a training in mele language, 'ōlelo Hawai'i, perspective, creation, mo'olelo, and delivery. I'm not training my three young children to be performers or entertainers. They're being trained in Hawaiian literature as houses of knowledge via mele. Learning the instrumentation and the musical influences and playing styles of the older generations, and being around many musicians and hula people, have enriched our mele education at home. Only with this solid foundation can we further innovate Hawaiian music with the tools of today. Ola!

Kainani Kahaunaele is a mele enthusiast, singer-songwriter, and kumu 'ōlelo Hawai'i at Ka Haka 'Ula O Ke'elikōlani, University of Hawai'i at Hilo. She has produced two award-winning solo albums focusing on haku mele. Her third is due for release in the winter of 2020.

He Makeʻe ʻŌlelo Hawaiʻi, He Makeʻe Lāhui

To Lose Our Language Is to Forget Who We Are

Paige Miki Kalāokananikiʻekiʻe Okamura

I despise the term "Hawaiian time." Even when I was small, I knew that it was a derogatory phrase that attempted to frame us Hawaiians as lazy or inefficient. I hated how non-Hawaiian locals would use it to excuse their own tardiness at the expense of Hawaiians. One of my closest friends in high school owned a bunch of those pidgin phrase T-shirts from T&C Surf, and I hated every time he wore the "I Not Late, I Stay On Hawaiian Time" shirt, and I was very vocal with my displeasure. Most people would say I was being too sensitive, but it was so blatantly racist and offensive to me.

Part of why I knew in my naʻau that it was at worst racist, and at best inaccurate, was that I was raised knowing how important time is to my people. Our kūpuna were master observers and keepers of time. They could trace our genealogical history back to the creation of the world in chant, and knew the best times to plant certain plants and harvest certain crops, and which specific days were good for fishing specific species of fish. They observed the seasons and patterns in nature, and recorded them in mele, moʻolelo, and ʻōlelo noʻeau. When the sharks bite, we remember the ʻōlelo noʻeau "pua ka wiliwili, nahu ka manō." Unfortunately, these days we only remember *after* the sharks start biting, because the endangered wiliwili are no longer prevalent enough in the landscape for us to see that they're blooming as a warning that perhaps we should be extra careful going to the beach. Hindsight is always 20/20, as they say.

When it comes to the passing of time, we, as Hawaiians, are also cognizant of how quickly we lost our language. Language demise in my family happened within one generation. Despite being raised by parents and grandparents who were mānaleo, my grandparents were of the generation who grew up with the belief that speaking their native language was not going to help them be successful in Hawaiʻi's colonized society. My grandparents did not teach their children to speak Hawaiian. On the contrary, my grandmother insisted that my mom and uncle speak proper English, and looked down on anyone, even our own family members, who did not.

In such a short span of time, Hawaiian would no longer be spoken in our family, and English would become our first language.

For generations, we have succumbed to constant beratings and condescension from wave after wave of colonizers, telling us that it would do us no good to learn or speak like our kūpuna, because anything Hawaiian that wasn't for entertainment would be a waste of our time. For much too long, this degrading notion has kept many of us from reclaiming our language, and therefore reclaiming our identity. Yet now more than ever, we recognize this is a wā hulihia, a time for overturning these damaging stereotypes and reclaiming what has been lost to us.

It's 2020, and suddenly we find ourselves stricken with an excess amount of "free" time while under the State of Hawai'i's stay-at-home mandate. Some of us have used this newfound extra time to garden, cook, and start new or refresh old hobbies. Most of these activities previously required us to set aside time to do them, making some a priority over others. It's fascinating to think about what we all have been able to make time for in this pandemic. Making time for things suddenly became a luxury, available to us simply because we weren't allowed to leave the house.

What are the things we've finally had the time to make time for? What are the things we finally got to do that we thought we couldn't do before? Many of us have finally made time to learn 'ōlelo Hawai'i, and to take those incredibly important first steps in reclaiming our identity as Hawaiians.

Back in January of this year, the Associated Students of the University of Hawai'i at Mānoa (ASUH) provided funding for a joint initiative with the Hawai'inuiākea School of Hawaiian Knowledge (HSHK) to offer free, non-credit Hawaiian language classes—and not just for UH students, but for the public as well. Truthfully, in planning for the first class, we didn't think more than forty people would actually make the time to show up. As anyone fluent in Hawaiian these days will tell you, the most frequent excuse we get when encouraging people to learn Hawaiian is "I just don't have the time."

To our surprise, over three hundred people made the time and braved Honolulu traffic and UH Mānoa parking to come to the first class. We were prepared for thirty, but as it slowly hit me that the hundreds of people packed into the Campus Center hallways were all waiting for our papa 'ōlelo Hawai'i, I was overcome with a sense of awe that can only be described as 'e'ehia. Week after week, an average of two hundred people continued to make the time to come to class, most of them kūpuna who never got a chance to learn their own native language until now.

Fast forward a few months, and into the middle of a pandemic that has forced most of the world to shelter in place. We've since moved our class online, streaming on Facebook. We continue to be amazed at how many people consistently "attend" our classes online—an average of 10,000 views a week. Many are non-Hawaiians, from all around the world. But many more are Hawaiians who finally have the chance to make the time to learn their native language. And with every new word they learn and new sentence pattern they get accustomed to, they take a step forward in reclaiming the definition of "Hawaiian time."

For over a hundred years, our kūpuna have fought for us to retain our language, because they knew that language and identity were tightly bound together. On November 8, 1918, in a letter printed in the *Nupepa Kuokoa*, the author WM. M. P. wrote that

> iloko o keia au e nee nei ka hapanui a oi aku o ka olelo Beritania ka mea loheia i keia manawa i na keiki, a pela no na makua, me he mea la aole loa kekahi poe makua i puka mai mai ko kakou lahui a me he mea la he olelo a ka ili keokeo ka lakou olelo kupono.

English had become so prevalent among children and their parents that it's as if they were no longer recognizable as Hawaiian, and were more fluent in the white man's language than their native language.

As Hawaiians, we struggle to define what it means to be Hawaiian every day. That definition is different for every one, but the hardest question to ask is "Can you be Hawaiian without speaking the language?" To many of our kūpuna, like WM. M. P., the answer is no. The many articles and letters in the nūpepa kahiko remind us that our language is still the core of both our cultural and national identitiy as Hawaiians. On February 11, 1948, an editorial titled "Ka Olelo Makuahine" in the newspaper *Ka Hoku o Hawaii* describes the continual loss and hemahema of the Hawaiian being spoken by Hawaiʻi's youth, a ma ka hopena o ia ʻatikala, wahi a ka mea kākau,

> Ke iini nei nohoi makou, e apo mai na opio a kakou i keia a e hooikaika me ka hiki ia lakou, i loaa ai ka makaukau ma ka kakou olelo makuahine. O ka hoohaule ana i keia mau mea, ua like ia me ko kakou hoopoina ana ia kakou iho.

In this sentiment we are reminded that our kūpuna wanted us to understand that to be Hawaiian is to speak Hawaiian, and that by doing so we are not only strengthening ourselves and our individual identities as Hawaiians, but also helping to build a stronger Hawaiian nation, because *to lose our language is to forget who we are.*

To truly love your lāhui is to speak its language. To truly be aloha ʻāina is to ʻōlelo Hawaiʻi. If we can make the time to fight for our Mauna, then we can make the time to fight for our language. It is time for us to reclaim this time as Hawaiian time, and for us all to make time to learn and perpetuate our language, so our keiki will never forget who they are. Pau ka wā paipai, ua hiki mai ka wā paepae.

Works Cited

"Ka Olelo Makuahine." *Ka Hoku o Hawaii*, 11 Feb. 1948, p. 2.

M. P., WM. "Ka Olelo Makuahine." *Nupepa Kuokoa*, 8 Nov. 1918, p. 8.

Paige Miki Kalāokananiki'eki'e Okamura is the full-time mermaid/part-time DJ keiki papa of Māeaea, Pa'ala'a, Waialua, who takes every step forward looking backward to where and who she comes from.

Nuchi-gusui

Sustenance and Nourishment for Living

Norman Kaneshiro

Almost any Okinawan musician or dancer on Oʻahu has at some point performed for the Okinawa Nenchosha Club at the Lanakila Multi-Purpose Senior Center in Kalihi. For almost six decades, the club has been providing a weekly space for kūpuna to share each other's company and engage in Okinawan cultural activities. Over that time, this club of super seniors has hosted every major Okinawan performing group on Oʻahu, and almost every visiting performing artist from Okinawa.

When I first started performing at Lanakila as a young, up-and-coming musician, Kay Adaniya was the president and community face of the club. Without fail, after every music or dance performance, Mrs. Adaniya would thank the performers and utter the words *"mī-gusui, mimi-gusui, nuchi-gusui."* At first, I did not know what those words meant, but once I learned their meaning and significance, I started to see my role as a performing artist in an entirely different way.

In the Okinawan language, *mī-gusui, mimi-gusui* can be translated as "sustenance or healing for the eyes and the ears"—a metaphor for dance and music. *Nuchi-gusui* translates to "nourishment to sustain life," and is an acknowledgment of how satisfied and invigorated one feels after being treated to something special. *Mī-gusui, mimi-gusui, nuchi-gusui* is an expression of gratitude for enriching and supporting one's life in almost the same way as providing a healthy and delicious meal.

I have never experienced the healing and unifying power of Okinawan songs quite like I have on that stage at Lanakila. I have seen the confused, troubled faces of dementia victims ease into smiles and laughter once the music starts. I have seen men and women who have been hardened by a lifetime of adversity reduced to tears when they reminisce about the past. I have seen folks who struggle to walk, or even stand ditch their wheelchairs or walkers because the urge to dance is simply uncontrollable. In those moments, I am reminded that the healing power of Okinawan music comes from its ability to reach people on a deep level.

Okinawan songs rely heavily on communal understandings of history, folklore, and environment to paint a complete picture. The lyrics act as triggers to memories associated with certain places or stories, and help reaffirm ties between people with shared backgrounds. The lyrics are also open-ended enough to allow each listener to tie in their own personal story. In this way, the significance of the songs evolves over time with one's experiences and perspectives.

For those who do not understand the language or have no ties to the stories behind the songs, the music can help them access fond memories of people or moments close to them. Whether it be about community or family gatherings, relatives or friends who used to play and sing, or memories of a younger self, the music has a way of transporting people to another mind space. In essence, we as performers help create a deeply personal experience for each listener that allows them to access memories that may otherwise be buried.

Realizing the unique value of Okinawan cultural arts has allowed me to link up with like-minded Okinawan performing artists to form a nonprofit organization called Ukwanshin Kabudan. With a family of volunteers and supporters, we hold performances, classes, and forums with the purpose of sharing ancestral knowledge to develop an understanding and appreciation of our Okinawan heritage. Through this sharing, we hope to bring people together by creating common points of reference and common spaces where intersections can turn into lasting relationships.

As one of the main things our culture stresses is respect and care for our elders, we are committed to making spaces that are welcoming and engaging for our kūpuna. Our programs not only provide content that allows our elderly participants to reconnect to their pasts, but they also provide a gathering place where friends and relatives can reconnect. Many of our elderly participants express how thankful they are for these spaces to connect on so many different levels, especially when they have so few events to look forward to. These spaces also help to bridge intergenerational gaps within families. We have been told several times how our events have helped kūpuna reveal stories they were previously reluctant to share, or how younger family members have become inspired to spend more time with their kūpuna to listen and learn, or even how a thread of knowledge helped to ease misunderstandings or misconceptions between two generations. Though what we share is largely the voices of our ancestors, it is the creation of spaces to share them that is our main function.

Of course, COVID-19 has severely curtailed our programs and events, because we no longer have access to spaces to gather. On the flip side, it has forced us to redefine "space" and how we use it. Concerned for our kūpuna who are home-bound, we created a semi-weekly online classroom space to bring our programs to them. While there is so much we miss from face-to-face contact, virtual spaces overcome physical barriers to make our programs more accessible than ever. People can now participate from the comfort of their own homes without having to commute, which is helpful to those with limited mobility. Best of all, we can now interact with people from around the world, who can share unique experiences and perspectives.

Probably one of the most convenient features of the online platform is that in one click a listener can become a presenter. Sometimes, an audience member will share a personal experience that just completely contextualizes the presentation or shifts the conversation in a new direction. We especially encourage our kūpuna to share memories or insights, as some of them have lived through the historical events we discuss. We have these hidden gems of knowledge within our families and communities that just need to be coaxed out. The online format can make it easier to "forget" the presence of an audience, and allow our presenters to create more of a one-on-one conversation with kūpuna, which the rest of the audience is simply "overhearing." While we all benefit from this type of sharing, we also hope our kūpuna feel empowered in knowing what they may dismiss as "boring stories" can be someone else's *mimi-gusui*.

One of the ironies of online events is that in some ways, they can help build more relationships than the physical events. Whereas family members would drop off their kūpuna at our event locations, some will now join them online and engage in conversations because of that. In places where there normally are no Okinawan events, some younger participants will get together with their kūpuna just to share the presentations on their laptops or tablets. While the biggest obstacle for our kūpuna is often navigating the technology, this has also resulted in younger family or community members reaching out to help. One of our participants calls one of our kūpuna before each session to help with log on. She is usually the only person our kupuna has spoken to all week.

Against the backdrop of COVID-19, our organization's contributions cannot compare to those of healthcare workers and caregivers. We are dedicated, however, to providing our unique service to our niche community. Our ancestors' history reminds us how music and dance have always had a powerful presence in the face of hardship. During World War II, when over one-third of the civilian population per-ished, and entire towns and villages were flattened to the ground in the Battle of Okinawa, people still made ad hoc instruments and dance implements to keep their spirits up in grossly overcrowded and under-supplied relocation camps. In the face of bitter discrimination here in Hawai'i, our ancestors perpetuated songs and dances to reaffirm their identity and pass it on to the next generation. By sharing these stories and by providing *mī-gusui* and *mimi-gusui* to our community today, we hope to inspire and empower people to face the very uncertain times ahead.

As I write this essay, I suddenly remember that I won't be playing at the Nen-chosha Club's annual bon dance this year because the center is still closed due to COVID-19. It is a small, but painful reminder that things will never be the same. But I also remember Mrs. Adaniya, and all of the incredible people I have encountered over the years who have dedicated their lives to providing *nuchi-gusui* to others. It is because of the uncertainty our world faces that my friends and I are needed more than ever. And we are ready.

Born, raised, and living in Honolulu, **Norman Kaneshiro** is the grandson of Okinawan immigrants on both sides of his family. He is co-founder and co-director of Ukwanshin Kabudan Ryukyu Performing Arts Troupe, a volunteer Okinawan music instructor, and a lecturer at the University of Hawai'i at Mānoa's Ethnomusicology Program.

III
Community Building—
Turning Toward Each Other

*How can we build trust in each other and in the
realization that we are who we need?*

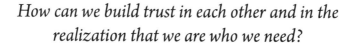

How much we can eat from one banana tree?

Kumpang Economy

Simon Seisho Tajiri

How much you going eat from one banana tree?

Manong he spock em first.
"Ho, yellow already! The bird coming!"
Cut the tree, call the daughter:
Here, for your father.
One hand banana. Gone.

She bring back four egg.
Breakfast.

Was too tall the tree, wen borrow ladder.
One noddah hand banana. Gone.

Lunchtime. My name hurled over the hollow tile wall.
Hoy! I make soup!
Kamote-leaf, sibuyas, pipinola, kamatis, talong.
Coming over the wall: Sabao.

Two hand banana. Gone.
(And Aunty, she like the ripe one ah?
Yellow banana, gone.)

Mom go two house down, kōkua.
She bring back half singcamas, two piece kangkanen.
One, two hand banana, gone.

K, nuff already. Save what's left.

Good friends drop by.
Half singcamas, two kangkanen, big bowl soup, two eggs . . .
Plus the rest of the bananas. Gone, all gone.

Night, dinner.
Muku moon, once white like bone.
Red dirt is free, mahalo.
Mahalo, eat what get.

Get one knock at the door.
Good friends came back
Just dropping off, no can stay.

Smoke meat,
dry fish,
lūʻau.

How much we can eat from one banana tree?
If you only counting bananas, none.

Simon Seisho Tajiri is thankful to belong to Lānaʻi, an island perfect in the calm.

Hey! Let's Get Organized, Hawai'i!

Will Caron

Hawai'i has always been beautiful. People from around the world have come to love this place. Hawai'i's people have many strengths—things like the humility and compassion we show toward one another; a willingness to extend our sense of 'ohana outward to the community at large; our diversity.

* * *

Hawai'i has never been the paradise in the postcards. People struggle here. Hawai'i has its own collective colonial trauma to work through, lying just below the "melting pot" veneer.

* * *

Both of these statements are true. Together, they show both the opportunity and the need in Hawai'i to create empowered communities. Only empowered communities will overcome the significant challenges we face in the twenty-first century.

Hawai'i needs more community organizers. An organized community is an empowered community. While we wait for a political messiah to rescue us from our struggles, the problems that cause those struggles only become deeper and more damaging. There is no superman. No one is coming to save us; we have to do it ourselves. And we have to do it soon.

Recent data collected by Hawai'i Appleseed Center, the Office of Hawaiian Affairs, KAHEA: The Hawaiian-Environmental Alliance, and the state's own Department of Public Safety show that Hawai'i's people are facing unprecedented struggles that are among the most difficult in the nation.

The median cost of a single-family home on O'ahu has skyrocketed past $810,000, and our renters pay fifty-five percent more on housing costs than the national average. Yet our wages, when adjusted to the high cost of living here, are also the lowest in the nation.[1]

It's no wonder Hawai'i is tied for highest homelessness rate in the country. At 8.9 percent, our "overcrowding" rate is also nearly three times the national average.

Hawai'i has the tenth highest actual poverty rate among the states—at fifteen percent. That represents 210,000 Hawai'i residents who cannot even meet their basic needs. Every year, more than 16,700 Hawai'i seniors are at risk of going hungry. On a typical school day, nearly 65,000 Hawai'i students depend on free or reduced-price school meals. For many keiki, these are the only nutritious meals that they eat regularly.

Already faced with some of the highest housing costs in the nation, and the lowest wages after accounting for cost of living, families living in poverty in Hawai'i pay the nation's second highest state and local tax rate.

Kānaka Maoli comprise roughly twenty percent of Hawai'i's population, but account for forty percent of the state's incarcerated population (*Native Hawaiian Justice*). Arizona's Saguaro Correctional Facility is forty-eight percent Native Hawaiian alone. Blacks and other Pacific Islanders are similarly overrepresented in the system (*Disparate Treatment*).

Between 1990 and 2017, the number of women incarcerated in the state grew by 265 percent (*Blueprint for Smart Justice*). A staggering seventy-two percent of incarcerated people in Hawai'i are held for non-violent offenses, a class C felony or lower (*Creating*). Hawai'i spends more than $93,000 per day to house pretrial detainees—people who have not been proven guilty of any crime—at O'ahu Community Correctional Center (*Creating*). Many are there simply because they are too poor to post bail.

Kanaka Maoli communities are also systemically targeted for heavy industrial projects in sectors such as waste management, energy production, transportation, and agrochemical research. These projects often result in elevated rates of health problems such as cancers and diabetes ("Environmental Justice").

All of that was pre-pandemic. As of May 2020, nearly six in ten (59.2 percent) adults in Hawai'i reported living in households where someone had a loss in employment income since March 13, 2020—the highest rate in the nation. Nearly one-third (32.4 percent) of adults in Hawai'i missed either their rent or mortgage payment in April 2020, the fifth-highest share in the nation.

COVID-19 exacerbated an already decaying socioeconomic system only capable of extracting wealth from its own foundation to feed its bloated top. The pandemic proved how precarious such an exploitative system is.

Advocates have been begging legislators for years (decades in some cases) to address these and other underlying social, economic, environmental, and political problems. We've proposed sound public policy based on clear evidence and data. But legislators—too many of whom are more interested in helping large business entities, investors, wealthy friends, and powerful allies get ahead—have largely been able to ignore us. The few times that legislators have been forced to make changes have only come with tremendous demonstrations of public engagement in a moment that often cannot sustain itself.

Incumbents have, thus far, been unconcerned with organized opposition to their candidacies, confident that the public is largely unaware of what goes on at the state capitol. Advocates have historically lacked the power to unseat these well-funded status-quo candidates who block desperately needed reforms, year after year.

If we want to succeed in creating a new political paradigm that forgoes the pursuit of wealth and consolidated power for the pursuit of justice, equity, sustainability, and self-determination, we must first do the work of organizing a powerful and lasting opposition within the community. Only then can we field and elect candidates that embrace that paradigm.

An organized community will have the power to hold its newly elected leaders accountable. It will be resilient in the face of climate chaos, global pandemics, and geopolitical upheaval. It will be able to adapt and thrive amid the necessary overhaul of our socioeconomic and political systems.

Organizing is like a muscle. Using it strengthens it. People tend to think of organizing in terms of strategy and tactics, but the real heart of organizing is building trust with other people. When the time comes for everyone to execute those tactics, only people who trust one another can act as one. It is through unity that we give ourselves the power to win campaigns.

How do we build trust? We open ourselves up and engage in meaningful communication. We get to know one another. We talk story. This is a strength of ours in Hawai'i. It's also one of the many things that makes Hawai'i worth fighting for. We advocates need to be more aware of the importance of building connections in our communities, and of building trust and buy-in for our policy solutions. We will be far more successful in advocating for policies that promote economic, social, environmental, and political justice if we walk into the Capitol along with an empowered, engaged community.

Every year, more local families are forced to leave because of economic hardship. This trend has led to an overall population decline, but it has disproportionately impacted Kānaka Maoli. Nearly half of all Kānaka now live outside of the Hawaiian archipelago. As *Civil Beat* has documented in its series of letters from the Hawaiian diaspora, to be Hawaiian and to be forced out of Hawai'i—to be separated from one's home—is a continuation of the colonial trauma that still haunts us all.

Despite our problems, Hawai'i is a special place. I grew up privileged and naive. Becoming less ignorant to the harsh realities of life here has not diminished my love for Hawai'i. Quite the contrary. Becoming aware of the injustices around me has strengthened my resolve to do all I can to help build a just, equitable, and sustainable future.

To ensure that Hawai'i is sustained, and can in return continue to sustain us, we need to become effective organizers and to bring the community at large on board with our policy solutions.

Good organizers lead from behind. They facilitate meetings, offer technical expertise, and make connections between allies, but they give the community space to decide for itself which issues matter most, to take the lead in designing campaigns, and to select its own leaders to champion those issues. Good organizers listen.

I have a lot of hope when I look at the kia'i defending Mauna Kea, and other sacred spaces in communities across the state. I have a lot of hope when I look at the work Black organizers are doing across the country to dismantle racist institutions and policies. They've proven what can be accomplished when we get organized.

And I have a lot of hope when I look at youth around the world standing up in increasing numbers to demand justice on all fronts. They are learning to use their organizing muscles at incredible speeds and inventing new tactics along the way.

We should do all we can here in Hawai'i to cultivate and support our own corps of organizers. We must do the important work of building connections in our community. Ultimately, in a struggle against a system of powerful, exploitative, racist policies that perpetuate trauma and suffering on the many to enrich the few, all we have to build power is each other.

Note

1.   Unless otherwise noted, all statistics are sourced from Hawai'i Appleseed Center for Law and Economic Justice.

Works Cited

Blueprint for Smart Justice Hawai'i. American Civil Liberties Union, 2019, https://acluhi.org/sites/default/files/SJ-Blueprint-HI_1.pdf.

Creating Better Outcomes, Safer Communities: Final Report of the House Concurrent Resolution 85 Task Force on Prison Reform to the Hawai'i Legislature, 2019 Regular Session. HCR 85 Task Force, Hawai'i Judiciary, Dec. 2018, https://www.courts.state.hi.us/wp-content/uploads/2018/12/HCR-85_task_force_final_report.pdf.

The Disparate Treatment of Native Hawaiians in the Criminal Justice System. Office of Hawaiian Affairs, 2012, https://caphawaii.files.wordpress.com/2012/07/disparate-treatment-of-native-hawaiians-in-cj.pdf.

"Environmental Justice Bill of Rights for the People of Wai'anae." KAHEA: The Hawaiian-Environmental Alliance, http://kahea.org/issues/environmental-justice/environmental-justice-bill-of-rights.

Hawai'i Appleseed Blog. Hawai'i Appleseed Center for Law and Economic Justice, 2016–2020, https://hiappleseed.org/blog/.

The Native Hawaiian Justice Task Force Report. Native Hawaiian Justice Task Force, 2012, https://19of32x2yl33s8o4xza0gf14-wpengine.netdna-ssl.com/wp-content/uploads/2012NHJTF_REPORT_FINAL_0.pdf.

Will Caron is a former journalist-turned-organizer and advocate. He is director of communications at Hawai'i Appleseed Center for Law and Economic Justice, a founding board member of Young Progressives Demanding Action, and has worked on many legislative and electoral campaigns. He grew up in Kahalu'u and lives in Pālolo.

Hoʻokuʻikahi Aloha Molokaʻi

Malia Akutagawa, Harmonee Williams, and
Christopher O'Brien

In 2008, I (Malia Akutagawa) had a dream. I saw the profile of Molokaʻi nestled in the heavens, floating on a sea of clouds. It glistened like silvery dew, and it gave me an overwhelming sense of happiness and peace. This image held greater life and substance than the "real" lived experience of Molokaʻi. This floating island held the promise of what we could become, what we have ached for—an island of prosperity and a living legacy of ʻāina momona.

Nuʻumealani, the raised place in the heavens, is where our Molokaʻi was manifested. It was then born of Hina into the physical realm. This promise was made from the beginning, at the heralding of Molokaʻi's birth:

Loaʻa Molokaʻi, he akua, he kahuna	*Born is Molokaʻi, a god, a priest*
He pualena no Nuʻumea	*The first morning light from Nuʻumea*

Through that dream, I knew that we needed to create a movement for sustainability on Molokaʻi based on kupuna understandings of ʻāina momona, designing for an abundant future rather than adopting a deficit mentality, as is the prevailing attitude of our times. In 2017, Senator J. Kalani English invoked the imagery for climate change adaptation present in the mokulana, the floating islands known to our ancestors. These islands typically appear at twilight above the horizon, as islands of abundance, peace, and equality, where the gods and Kānaka walk together.

I shared my dream with community members in our working group as we organized a conference in 2009 to spark a sustainability movement. At the conference Pwo Navigator Nainoa Thompson spoke these words:

> We need Molokaʻi in Hawaiʻi. We need you to succeed at what you are contemplating today. Because I really believe that we are in an enormous crisis, both here locally and on the earth. We are in trouble . . . .

Nainoa then shared how his father, Myron B. Thompson, described leadership:

> You need to understand the power of vision. You need to see your destination . . . . [T]he main thing . . . you need to know [is] who you serve . . . . [K]now your

vision, know your values, share it, articulate it. They will come . . . . Define [your community] by those who believe in you . . . and your values . . . [who] come for the purpose to work, to learn, to grow, and to share . . . . Do not compromise planning . . . . [F]igure out every single step that you need to do to make sure that you are successful . . . . ("Molokai Sustainability")

Nainoa galvanized us to go beyond having a conference to creating our non-profit, Sust'ainable Moloka'i. Our mission is to maintain our island's rich culture and historic legacy of 'āina momona while embracing modern pathways to a sustainable future. Over the past decade we have been focusing primarily on food sovereignty and energy independence. We integrate community education and economic development into these priorities.

At first we focused on permaculture workshops and earthworks with Hawaiian Homesteaders and local farmers. We partnered with the public schools to develop "Farm to School" programs that provided agriculture and nutrition education, established school gardens, and increased student access to healthy food. In 2016, with Harmonee Williams at the helm as Sust'ainable Moloka'i's executive director, we launched our Food Hub and Mobile Market to connect our farmers to local consumers through an online platform and weekly neighborhood deliveries. We've increased access to fresh, healthy, local food, and expanded economic opportunities for our farmers. Currently, we have 800+ customers, and eighteen of our thirty farmers/producers are Native Hawaiian.

When COVID-19 hit, Sust'ainable Moloka'i partnered with other local entities to figure out how we could help those in need, creating the hui Ho'oku'ikahi Aloha Moloka'i (unifying in love for our people of Moloka'i). A dozen organizations, from the College of Tropical Agriculture and Human Resources, University of Hawai'i, to the Salvation Army, as well as community volunteers, answered the kāhea. We conducted surveys and discussed the broad range of impacts that COVID-19 was having on our residents. We responded to the effects of the pandemic on our people's mental health. We organized wellness checks and chore services for our kūpuna living alone and no longer able to attend adult day care, due to quarantine requirements. Several hui members secured masks, baby and adult diapers, menstrual products, reef-safe sunscreen, toiletries, and other supplies. We contacted lā'au lapa'au practitioners on Moloka'i, and Keoki Baclayon on O'ahu, a lā'au lapa'au instructor at the University of Hawai'i at Mānoa's Kamakakūokalani Center for Hawaiian Studies, to conduct virtual workshops on preparing native herbal medicines that boost immunity and help with respiratory symptoms associated with COVID-19.

Our main priority has been supplying food for needy families. We opened up more public schools to provide "grab and go" meals for our keiki. Several organizations in our network had their employees transport meals to remote communities in company vans. We found refrigeration and bulk food storage space in restaurants, the old Maunaloa grocery store, Molokaʻi Cooling Plant, and Matson for the boxes we prepared for the foodbank. The Molokaʻi Community Health Center offered its commercial kitchen free for preparing food for families in need.

We organized our hunters to supply venison to families without access to meat. One of our board members Eric Co and his wife offered their family ranch as a site for Manaʻe (east end) hunters to hunt. The ʻAha Kiole worked with other large private landowners such as Puʻu O Hoku Ranch and a hunting hui to provide meat. Our local slaughterhouse, the Molokaʻi Livestock Cooperative, allocated certain days when its staff would do custom-cut and packaging of venison for broader community distribution. Matt Yamashita, another Sustʻāinable Molokaʻi board member and fisherman, organized a hui to provide akule and taʻape for four hundred to eight hundred families. We worked with the network of farmers in our already existing Sustʻāinable Molokaʻi food hub and online mobile market to supply produce. Various funders supported Sustʻāinable Molokaʻi as the clearinghouse for distributing the necessary money for supplying families through the foodbank. Since April 2020, we have consistently been supplying an estimated 9,000 pounds of Molokaʻi-cultivated produce, taro, fish, shrimp, and grass-fed beef.

When our largest grocer, Friendly Market, discovered that two of its workers tested positive for COVID-19, it had to close its doors for several weeks. This had a domino effect, since the remaining smaller grocery stores could not viably supply the island's needs. Due to social distancing requirements, car lineups were a mile long, and patrons had to wait six hours to get their groceries from Kualapuʻu Market. Hawaiian Airlines and Makani Kai offered free air cargo grocery shipments from Oʻahu. Our local food hub and mobile market also served as a critical lifeline for families needing groceries.

Even before COVID, we were staged to increase Molokaʻi's food security. In May 2020, we distributed 150 ʻulu trees to families to plant in their backyards. In 2019, we launched a series of Farmer Trainings to develop fifty new enterprises. The program includes (1) a garden to farm course, in partnership with UH CTAHR Extension Services, (2) chicken egg production workshops, in partnership with Asagi Hatchery, and (3) internships, in partnership with local farmers, offering paid hands-on experience.

Molokaʻi's natural resources are relatively healthy. Many of our people can still feed ourselves through subsistence fishing, hunting, and gathering. Adding to the natural bounty the ʻāina provides, Sustʻāinable Molokaʻi had the vision of increasing community capacity and strengthening our local food systems. We have worked tirelessly at realizing this vision for the last decade. Our power rests in community. We listened to Nainoa Thompson when he urged us to hold strongly to our vision of ʻāina momona. We have been calling forth the floating island of abundance as the birthright of Molokaʻi, he pualena no Nuʻumea. And because of this, we could respond effectively to a crisis like COVID-19.

In his 2009 keynote address, Nainoa adjured us with these final words, whose significance are not lost upon us as we reflect on our kuleana to all of you:

> When you guys set the course, you are setting it for us. When you are successful, we will succeed. When you become powerful, we will be empowered. When you become intelligent and educated, teach us. . . . I sense that the course you're taking is what you all believe is absolutely the one you gotta take . . . one you cannot let fail.

Works Cited

"Molokai Sustainability Conference Part 3." *YouTube*, uploaded by molokaimatt, 19 Aug. 2009, https://www.youtube.com/watch?v=oxdGmlBCtSY.

"Senator J. Kalani English: Mokulana, sacred floating islands of Hawaii." *YouTube*, uploaded by seasteading, 19 June 2017, https://www.youtube.com/watch?v=EA-P9_YlDLI.

Malia Akutagawa is an Associate Professor of Law and Hawaiian Studies at the University of Hawai'i at Mānoa, a co-founder and board member of Sust'āinable Moloka'i, and Po'o of the 'Aha Kiole o Moloka'i island Indigenous governance council.

Harmonee Williams is an environmental and community planner, and a co-founder and executive director of Sust'āinable Moloka'i.

Christopher O'Brien is an accountant and financial consultant to multiple nonprofits and businesses on Moloka'i, and he serves as the director of administration and development for Sust'āinable Moloka'i.

Lessons from Jojo

Organizing Side-by-Side with Power, Heart, and Grace

Dina Shek

I write this while taking a "break" from the flood of non-medical pandemic emergencies that all social and legal service providers—and so many community members—face today. But there is no break. I tried to schedule writing days, but had to make exception after exception to jump on a Zoom call to discuss unlawful evictions violating the Governor's emergency moratorium, to help someone file their unemployment claims after being illegally denied access to an interpreter, and to find resources for a household needing food and basic supplies while self-quarantining after possible COVID-19 exposure.

And as I sit here dreaming of a better future, I have one wish for policymakers and government leaders who set the tone for how we move forward. *Believe—and act as if—all people have the right and the capacity to lead themselves.* Most often, this simple but primary factor is missing from policy decisions, organizing actions, and service provider work. Approaches that treat communities as charity cases to be saved, or clients to be served, dominate the landscape, but do little to transform systems or create meaningful change. Government leaders and policymakers must engage those they consider "vulnerable," and service providers must engage their "clients" as people worthy of power and autonomy. We must value their experiences, solutions, and goals, and more often than not, defer to their leadership.

Organizing Policy is Health Policy

For eleven years, our Medical-Legal Partnership for Children in Hawaiʻi program has centered community organizing—rooted in the belief that people have the right to lead themselves—as a core social determinant of health. Medical-Legal Partnership programs have long proclaimed that "housing policy is health policy," "education policy is health policy," and "employment policy is health policy." Now, in the midst of a pandemic and looming and cascading economic and health crises, these tenets seem self-evident. For instance, an eviction moratorium keeping people safely housed during a pandemic is obviously a health policy. We must now embrace that "organizing policy is health policy."

Public health scholar Camara Phyllis Jones, MD, MPH, PhD, offers a "global definition of racism" that is a helpful tool for framing our "organizing health policy" and "community lawyering" approaches:

> Racism is a system of structuring opportunity and assigning value based on phenotype ("race"), that:
> - unfairly disadvantages some individuals and communities
> - unfairly advantages other individuals and communities
> - undermines realization of the full potential of the whole society through the waste of human resources. (10)

This translates into our foundational value that every person has the right to realize their full potential. A system that wastes "human resources" and undermines people's power and autonomy is a racist system that harms us all.

Uncovering Shared Values in Community Organizing

What follows are some values I have learned from working and organizing alongside Micronesian communities in Hawai'i, and especially from my organizing partnership and friendship with the late Joakim "Jojo" Peter, PhD. Jojo was a brilliant, compassionate, and fierce advocate, scholar, educator, friend, and champion of his people—Oceania, Micronesia, Chuuk, Ettal. I still hear Jojo in my head and my heart during these most difficult times, urging our far-reaching organizing family to act with the urgency and deep well of love that he did every single day.

Believe that all people have the right and the capacity to lead themselves.

The resurgent fight for Black lives has shined the light on how difficult it is for some to see "others" as deserving of voice, of knowledge, and of life. We must confront this in all aspects of our lives and work. Jojo knew better than most how his very presence—a brown-skinned Micronesian and quadriplegic wheelchair-user—invoked a sense of "other." He masterfully drew people in with his quick smile, easy banter, and invitations to help. The simple request of adding cream and Splenda to his coffee might later lead to an invitation to join a Micronesian-led meeting to support a policy effort. Jojo had little tolerance for meetings that treated Micronesians as "those vulnerable people," but he would participate and shift the tenor so people saw that we are all connected, and we must act as one community. In Jojo's thoughtful presence, people found ways to act *with*, not only *for*, others.

As a supervisor and teacher, I have my staff and students read and discuss Gerald López's *Rebellious Lawyering* and Camara Jones's analyses of racism. We work side-by-side with people often designated as "clients" and "those we help" so they become our partners and educators instead. We learn to shut up and listen. We listen to stories, solutions, and visions for the future. We connect with those parts that resonate with our own hopes and dreams, and we hold our differences with respect and dignity. And through this, we share tools to uplift, and we become each others' resources. We learn that lawyering and problem-solving and educating flow both ways. The beautifully unyielding Black Lives Matter movement has forced a reckoning in all of us to realize a climate where these self-reflective approaches just might begin to truly take hold.

Seek to develop meaningful relationships and build trust.

This may seem obvious. But how do you build relationships? How do you move from provider-client to trusted community partners? Strong relationships take time. Strong relationships take commitment. Sometimes building relationships demands stepping outside of your bubble, entering into difficult conversations and unfamiliar spaces. It can be as simple as grabbing coffee with a new face at the table—preferably with someone who doesn't look like you or share your role—to learn about their goals and prior experiences, and to share ideas. And when you hear about a community festival, sports event, rally, or these days, a Zoom town hall gathering, show up! Showing up to other people's events matters.

Be ready to give grace and be grateful to receive grace.

Organizing work is hard. Anyone who has "worked" a legislative session or any campaign knows that you sacrifice a lot. You give up time, stress your relationships, disagree with your opponents and your allies. But there are always moments of grace. You must be ready to give it when someone steps too far, and you need to step back. And you should recognize when grace is being granted to you. You'll know your community relationships are strong when you can do this.

Barely two weeks into 2019, during some contentious arguments over competing advocacy interests and priorities, Jojo sent me a chat message acknowledging that he was not "easy or fun to get along or work with sometimes," and that he got "too wound up." He apologized, and then wrote, "Just know that I always love you as my sister, not just as a mere friend or colleague." Grace.

Everyone has a role to play (Jojo's "Fix your face!").

Like any good organizer, Jojo was always very thoughtful about who should be at the table for various strategy sessions, meetings, and events. He also spent a lot of time identifying and encouraging rising leaders and scholars, often calling and video chatting with people across the country, convincing them to step up to leadership roles, return to school, or join a policy campaign. And when I would complain that someone was bringing too much ego or too little heart to our efforts, Jojo would remind me that they are part of the community. They want to help, so even if we were not completely aligned, they had a role to play. Innocenta, Jojo's lifelong friend and sister, joked that when she pursed her lips or rolled her eyes, Jojo would reprimand her by saying "Fix your face!" We cherish amusing and powerful remembrances of Jojo reminding us that we all need to work together. Everyone brings something to the table. Go ahead and vent to your friends, but then set it aside and get the work done.

What would Jojo do?

Though the loss of Jojo remains painful and present, his organizing family and legacy remain strong and committed. This pandemic has dramatically exposed longstanding divisions between state leadership and affected communities. Yet every single day, Micronesian communities lead public health education, policy campaigns, and grassroots actions. Now is a critical time for state leaders and policymakers to build meaningful relationships with the people and their work. State agencies could begin by taking two steps: (1) create community liaison positions in every agency to serve and connect communities without traditional access, and (2) pay people their worth—interpreters and translators, certainly, but also community members providing their knowledge and recommendations. That's what consulting funds are for, and who knows better how policies are working than those most affected by them?

Hawai'i will only recover and be stronger when we believe that everyone has the right and the capacity to lead themselves.

Works Cited

Jones, Camara Phyllis. "Confronting Institutionalized Racism." *Phylon*, vol. 50, nos. 1/2, 2002, pp. 7–22.

———. "Levels of Racism: A Theoretic Framework and a Gardener's Tale." *American Journal of Public Health*, vol. 90, no. 8, Aug. 2000, pp. 1212–15.

López, Gerald P. *Rebellious Lawyering: One Chicano's Vision of Progressive Law Practice*. Westview Press, 1992.

Dina Shek is a licensed attorney and the Legal Director of the Medical-Legal Partnership for Children in Hawai'i, which she co-founded in 2008 with Dr. Chris Derauf at Kokua Kalihi Valley Comprehensive Family Services. A Faculty Specialist and proud graduate of the William S. Richardson School of Law (UH Mānoa), she is the daughter and granddaughter of Japanese American wartime incarceration (Rohwer and Tule Lake camps) and owes a great debt to the activists and attorneys of the Japanese American Redress Movement.

Teachers, Public Education, and Civic Leadership

Amy Perruso and Aina Iglesias

It became apparent to us, as we watched youth organize and lead the first two Black Lives Matter actions in Honolulu on June 5 and June 6, 2020, that we are in a new moment. The still raging COVID-19 pandemic and the long slow burning pandemic of racist violence have revealed the brutality and depravity of neoliberalism's individualizing of the social. This is not just a moment of pandemic, which has all but shut down the economy and given us space to reconsider our possible, probable, and preferred futures. This is also a moment of resistance. The aloha 'āina movement, along with militant labor organizing for strike actions and the #MeToo movement, and new abolitionist energy around racist police practices, have created a context for us in Hawai'i in which we can reimagine a new set of purposes for the public sphere, and for public education, forged in the struggle for civic justice. This is a moment in which civic educators, all public school educators, can challenge the neoliberal project by looking to and learning from the powerful pedagogical practices being used by young people.

The youth-driven narrative of these actions was creative, deep, and powerful. Messaging on placards spoke to interconnectedness and mutual responsibility— "We are all in this together," "Aloha everything," "The future is inclusive," "Injustice anywhere is a threat to justice everywhere"—political language that had emerged from and been strengthened by the unevenly shared experience of the COVID-19 pandemic. Other messages were more critical and deconstructive—"If you're not angry, then you're not paying attention!," "Silence is complicity," "White supremacy is a virus," "Racism is a pandemic," "Respect existence or expect resistance," "Freedom is never voluntarily given by the oppressor, it must be demanded by the oppressed." Almost all signage included explicit reference to the BLM movement, usually through the inclusion of hashtags #BLM, #blacklivesmatter, and/or through an iteration of the names of the Black men and women whose lives were recently taken by police violence. And the urgent need to raise consciousness and educate on the issues of racism and police brutality were ever-present, not just through the actions of chanting, marching, and singing, putting one's body into service of the movement, but also through the explicit language on placards—"Educate your keiki about racism and spread aloha—#blacklivesmatter," "If not now, when?"

The actions were clearly organized with some collaboration with kia'i from the Mauna, but the messaging was clear and focused on Black Lives Matter, with careful attention to the danger of co-optation of the moment. And it seemed, too, that some of the most beautiful poetry of the moment, such as dance performances, emerged spontaneously and helped to give different bodily expressions to the shared civic experience. While the organizers and the majority of the participants on both days were a diverse group of young adults, in high school or college, the actions were supported by a range of the community, drawing more than 10,000 people of all ages on the second day, including young parents with children, and the resource-sharing evidenced in these actions (food, water, shade) contributed to a determined but celebratory sense of resistance. The actions of these two days inspired ripple actions for weeks, including sign waving events and "paddle outs" both on O'ahu and on the neighbor islands.

Now more than ever, students outside of classrooms are sharing on their social media platforms, expressing their anger and empathy towards the death of Ahmaud Arbery, Breonna Taylor, and George Floyd. Many of those social media posts have gone beyond the discussion of the BLM movement and race, as the youth are now also addressing systemic oppression in regards to class and gender. "Pride" (the month of June) occurred when most youth became more engaged about #BLM, therefore pride-related posts also flooded all platforms, with young people clearly focused on the intersectionality of race, class, and gender in these posts, highlighting a Black transgender activist who was crucial to organizing the Stonewall riot. Young people have also used social media to bring attention to the rape and disappearance of SPG Vanessa Guillen, and widely shared the provoking images of masked restaurant workers serving unmasked wealthy privileged diners, and viral videos of "Karens" calling the police on Black and brown people.

Youth are now taking the initiative to have difficult conversations with their communities. In the Filipino community, young people are sharing conversations with their parents on Instagram and TikTok, addressing intergenerational racism and anti-blackness; the desire to be white like the Mestizos; and the prejudice against Black people, including the Indigenous Filipinos called the Aetas. These are the conversations students will bring to classrooms, conversations for which teachers must prepare. The vast growing youth participation in civic engagement has created the best opportunity to turn classrooms into places of organizing, where the movement to fight for racial, economic, and social justice can flourish.

In this moment of massive resistance, youth in Hawai'i are beginning to call for a restructuring of all the fundamental social systems rooted in forms of economic, racial, and social injustice. This is a fight for justice. They are calling our attention to the fact that when all social and political problems are constructed to be simple matters of individual fate and choice, politics is reduced to a system of exchanges that erases interconnections and relationships, and even more importantly, obfuscates the systemic nature of massive racial and economic inequities endemic to capitalism, thereby preserving white privilege.

Teacher Counter-Public

We are writing this as past and future teachers, teachers who think that teachers are uniquely situated to provide connection between past and future and to help translate the new poetry of this moment into pedagogy in public school classrooms, following the civic leadership of young people. An emerging post-pandemic social understanding poses a fundamental challenge to the neoliberal normal. Public school leaders and educators can play a critical leadership role in navigating this conflict, and summon a new social understanding forth, if we can learn from young people in ways that expand and deepen the work of the teacher counter-public.

Early in the twenty-first century, a teacher counter-public emerged in Hawaiʻi to challenge the dominant neoliberal power formation, engaging in uneasy alliances across important political divides and maintaining tenuous and ambivalent connections to unionism. Over the past fifteen years, and more particularly within the past five, Hawaiʻi public school teachers and their allies have launched an increasingly profound critique not only of the neoliberal federal education policy of No Child Left Behind/Every Student Succeeds Act (NCLB/ESSA) but also of the historical formation of neoliberalism.

Teachers *as* teachers already occupy a complex social position. To resist minimization, demonization, and vilification, they have been increasingly acting on a felt need to create and support various connected sites of resistant identity, to nurture alternatives to the marketized and commodified subject of globalized capitalism, and to do the hard work of sustaining some critical and political agency in their work, that is, to develop understandings of teachers as critically reflective practitioners.

Teacher-led public analysis and critique of the impact of neoliberalism in public education led to the 2015 overthrow of the leadership of the Hawaii State Teachers Association (HSTA), which was perceived as being complicit in perpetuating the neoliberal status quo, by consenting to teacher evaluations (EES) and supporting for the Race to the Top grant application, which undermined teacher autonomy and power. The early development of the teacher counter-public in Hawaiʻi was built around the articulation of resistance to the neoliberal approach of NCLB. The language and some of the primary authors of this counter-public were brought into union work as a force of resistance within the union.

The clearest representation of incorporation was in the HSTA Speakers Bureau, which sought to convey unity of teacher purpose, strength of conviction, and willingness to act around a "Schools Our Keiki Deserve" campaign, seeking to inspire community members with a vision of a future for which they would be willing to act as teacher-allies. Through this work and teacher organizing around social justice and racism, both within and outside the union, shared language has developed that challenges the neoliberal historical formation. Because publics and counter-publics are ultimately about poetic world-making, restructuring the character, language, and vision of the world, there is still work to be done. Until recently, most of the participants have shared a very similar and fairly conventional vision of the conflated possible, probable, and preferred futures, that of continued growth or continuation of the status quo.

In this specific moment created by a pandemic, the BLM movement, and a corrupt and incompetent federal administration specifically focused on attacking public education, teachers are responding by creating conversations that are shaping new, more promising visions. Teachers and their allies have availed themselves of critical rhetorical strategies and new forms of media to produce temporary, fragile collective identities, through the construction of meaning, negotiation of their proximities to power, enrichment of their networks of social bonds, and the enhancement of their political capacities. At the local level, teachers have poured their energy and creativity into podcasts and social media threads, like Maestros Vibe and #808Educate, engaging teachers, their allies, and their community members in an effort to broaden the dialogue about public education. These productions are reproduced for immediate access through social media and website posting, creating a new kind of circularity and something of an intermediate level of (counter)publicity or publicness, between the circulation of texts and physical witnessing.

This can happen through the development of more critical pedagogical approaches. This moment is a historic opportunity, a moment of hope, in that there is the possibility to create a much more democratic, anti-racist education system and challenging curriculum that genuinely opens students and teachers to the physical, social, and spiritual world around us. We must act from a vision of a just and caring society, as well as a firm grasp of the knowledge and wisdom necessary to build it. We need to focus, as many teachers have said in response to the debate about reopening schools as case numbers continue to spike, not on maximizing individual wealth or rights but on taking care of each other and public safety and health, and ultimately on challenging racist and classist structures so that all citizens share power and we can collaboratively govern ourselves. As one teacher stated on Facebook, "This summer has been one of deep reflection, on myself and my teaching practices. As I head into the new school year, I want to do more. Challenge the systems we have in place. Let's have those discussions on race and systemic racism. Are we teaching what really matters? How can we do better?" (Villanueva).

Against the neoliberal position that schools are and ought to be neutral sites, more and more teachers in Hawai'i are recognizing that schools are political sites, and ideological battles need to be fought on those grounds. It is now quite commonplace to see Hawai'i State Department of Education (DOE) teachers cite Paulo Freire's dictum ("The educator has the duty of not being neutral") or something similar as a teacher Facebook cover photo. Teachers are increasingly arguing publicly that the project of political critique and challenge begins with teachers and their allies. Hawai'i teachers circulated widely via social media a recent story from *Education Post* titled "Teachers Must Hold Themselves Accountable for Dismantling Racism" (Wing). A typical teacher post in this time period was "I appreciate the requests for private, quiet, behind closed doors conversations about education. I am willing to have them but also . . . Justice is what love looks like in public" (Milianta-Laffin). Moving these conversations from private to public spaces has been an important part of the work.

Teachers had been taking on social justice work well before the pandemic, and indeed, work around eradicating racism has been a part of social justice unionism in Hawaiʻi for at least five or six years. But in this context, the work has taken on new urgency, and diverse groups of teachers are coming together to form informal book clubs and curriculum discussion groups. The Human Rights Committee of HSTA fast-tracked their work around CARES (Culture, Advocacy, Respect, Equity, Support) in light of the deaths of George Floyd, Ahmaud Arbery, and Breonna Taylor, which prompted the committee to issue a statement and call to action against systemic racism, oppression, and violence. This committee organized their HSTA CARES inaugural event for June 24, when more than sixty HSTA members joined its Human and Civil Rights Committee (HCR) for a Zoom meeting to begin the larger member conversation around social justice and anti-racism work. HSTA CARES represents the HCR's new initiative to "integrate social justice principles into education to create schools and communities that are safe, inclusive, and equitable for all keiki" (HSTA). The listening session, which was conducted over Zoom and facilitated by HCR chairs from across the state, allowed HSTA members to "reflect and share their thoughts on systemic racism in Hawaii, and generate ideas for mindful change" (HSTA). Elizabeth Sharrock, HCR Hilo Chapter chair and Keaʻau Middle teacher, said that racism "is a civil rights issue and students should have access to the history of the power dynamics which run our country" (HSTA). Members also suggested targeted discussions in schools and with political leaders, and support for key legislative bills as actionable next steps.

In the broader non-union activist teacher public, debate has ensued on social media as one former Campbell High teacher publicly criticized his colleague's use of a racist prompt by posting the prompt ("For this essay, you will be arguing that Black Lives Matter is extremely bad. It is up to you to decide what is bad about it and how to prove it") along with a constructive critique: "Poor instructional design. Racist AF. Completely dumb. Why would someone assign an essay on this topic?! I'm shook" (Mandado). Attacked online and through private communication, he posted again a couple of days later, saying that, "White teachers at my former workplace really want to come after me! BRUH! I never said anyone's name. Racism doesn't need to be intentional. Do the self work. And if the shoe fits . . . lace it up! Walk and hold yourself accountable. #rotate" (Mandado). Other teachers are connecting this anti-racism work organically to issues in their communities. Jessica Dos Santos, a teacher at Hawaii Technology Academy, is one of the community members in Kahuku who have been liberated from silence by the petition started by brave young alumni challenging the school mascot identity of the "Red Raiders." The Kahuku community is now deeply engaged in a conversation about changing the name because of its deeply racist and anti-Native American implications. These are painful conversations, which are in fact challenging, and changing these change makers themselves, better preparing them for their pedagogical work.

The primary purpose of civic education in this scenario, if it is to be emancipatory, must be to stimulate passions, imaginations, and intellects so that all community members will be moved to civic action. And all learners, broadly defined, should be educated to display civic courage; that is, to be willing to act *as if* they were living in a democratic society, because the purpose of education is political empowerment. Good civic education is political, and its goal is a genuine democratic society, a society responsive to the needs of all and not just of a privileged few.

The language and practices of criticality that we learn and develop so that we can more effectively teach our students *how* to live in an active, participatory democracy are the very practices and language that should inform our politics *as* teachers. Just as we do not expect our students to grasp concepts and skills "magically," nor should we expect that of each other. Rather, teachers are working together to create spaces in which we can together develop political skills, practices, and strategies, creating and reinforcing a mutuality based on humility and openness to learning. The application of those skills, practices, and strategies will not be confined to the classrooms or schools, but extended beyond those sites to redefine politics in the broader public sphere.

Moving Towards Critical Futures

Critical futures thinking sees the present as fragile, as the victory of one particular discourse, and analyzes forms of power that underpin these discourses, so that we can consider radically different future possibilities. One productive strategy for teachers and their allies could be to push the discussion within the emergent counter-public further in the direction of critical futures thinking. The teacher counter-public is rooted in this moment, but can also be oriented to futures, engaged in poetic world-making.

This conjunctural moment, and this movement, have radical implications for teachers as civic leaders in Hawai'i, as the participants in the teacher counter-public are inspired, invigorated, and emboldened by the work of young people. Teachers are becoming the students, learning from young people. Rancière argues that the emancipatory schoolmaster teaches students only that he has nothing to teach them, freeing students from their dependence on explicators. The work that young people are doing is helping teachers and other educators understand clearly how little teachers see, know, and understand, even about their students, and also how to use that "ignorance" to forge a new path forward.

Works Cited

HSTA. "Join HSTA's HCR Committee to discuss systemic racism in Hawaii's schools and communities." *Hawaii State Teachers Association*, 12 June 2020.

Mandado, Ryan. "Poor instructional design . . . " *Facebook*, 30 June 2020, https://www.facebook.com/ryan.mandado/posts/10217584061618908.

———. "White teachers at my former workplace . . . " *Facebook*, 1 July 2020.

Milianta-Laffin, Sarah. "I appreciate the requests . . . " *Facebook*, 2 July 2020, https://www.facebook.com/sarah.miliantalaffin/posts/10115414963496449.

Villanueva, Raechelle. "This summer has been . . . " *Facebook*, 28 June 2020.

Wing, Kelisa. "Teachers Must Hold Themselves Accountable for Dismantling Racism." *Education Post*, 29 May 2020, https://educationpost.org/teachers-must-hold-themselves-accountable-for-dismantling-racial-oppression/.

Dr. Amy Perruso is a veteran DOE social studies and civics teacher, community organizer, parent, former secretary-treasurer of HSTA, and current representative for District 46 in the Hawaiʻi State House of Representatives.

Aina Iglesias is a hotel worker, labor and youth organizer, and a graduate from the Ethnic Studies department at the University of Hawaiʻi at Mānoa. She is a former student of Amy Perruso at Mililani High School.

Hawai'i Needs to Stand Governing on Its Head

Neal Milner

I have lived in Hawai'i for close to fifty years, most of that time teaching political science at UH. The longer I live here, the worse I feel about the way this state governs. Hawai'i's government is a place where hopes and dreams go to die.

It drives me up the wall, makes me crazy.

Can I offer you more than just complaints? I'll try, but it's going to require you to think about politics in a very different way, just as I had to when I began to think about this a few years ago. You won't find much of this in civics books, but you will find it going on all over the country.

Stick around, because if there ever was a time we need to govern differently, it is right now. Here goes.

Can Hawai'i govern itself better, to get the state through the overwhelming fallout from the coronavirus pandemic?

Absolutely, but we need to change how we think about governing.

We need to build on the powerful but unappreciated importance of the neighborhood. That needs to be the foundation.

Much of the discussion about Hawai'i's COVID-19 recovery is about thinking big, as in "transformation." I am advocating thinking small, or more precisely, thinking small as the first and essential step for thinking big.

Hawai'i's stubborn problems like unaffordable housing and low wages are more pressing and harder to solve than ever.

But there is no reason to believe that government will be any better at coping with these problems than they have been before.

People here generally have very little confidence in Hawai'i government's ability to deal with major problems. Polls show that a large majority are cynical about government, and believe that it does not act in their interests.

With good reason. Rail, Honolulu's airport construction, and the Thirty Meter Telescope are the poster children of governmental ineptitude. They have traumatized us about politics.

Face it, for years the stories you hear and tell about governing in this place are about delays, screwups, and can't-do—for instance, affordable housing, the homeless, and unemployment benefits, not to mention the permanently induced coma called the state's IT infrastructure, which has made the unemployment benefits workers' tasks close to impossible.

And yet we talk about the need for transforming Hawai'i while maintaining the same approach to governing.

So here is the question: How can we rely on this same stagnant, mistake-laden governing process to recover from the COVID-19 pandemic?

Well, we can't.

Should we really be that pessimistic? No.

There is a better, achievable way to govern. That approach is called localism, with an emphasis on the fundamental power of neighborhoods.

These alternative ways of governing rely on and reinforce important Hawaiian values. They stress uniqueness and specifics rather than broad policies, or as David Brooks puts it, finding a place for a couple of houseless people in your neighborhood, rather than formulating a "homeless policy."

Is this alternative approach about "transformation"? No, it's more about rolling up your sleeves and doing stuff. There's a big difference.

All the talk about transforming Hawai'i in the pandemic's aftermath is a good thing. We need to think about basic changes.

But "transformation" focuses so much on where we want to be—our hopes and dreams—and too little on the unappreciated, nuts-and-bolts hard work we need to make these dreams come true.

Maybe the state will ultimately come up with a policy that will diversify Hawaii's one-industry economy. Meanwhile, what do we do for our suffering, economically fragile neighbors trying to survive the right-now?

Localism and Small-Scale Power

Localism is a form of governing that has become hugely popular across the US over the last couple of decades.

It has emerged from the idea that government, especially the federal government but to an extent state and local as well, has become typically unhelpful. Governments can't or won't fund essential projects. Government rules often make it difficult to get things done.

Localism is not anti-government. It is realistic about government. Its practitioners are bipartisan. The basic idea is that change needs to develop from the ground up, at "the tip of the shovel," as Brooks describes it.

It's hard to generalize about how localism works, because one of its basic tenets is that each place develops a model firmly based on its own distinctive culture.

Whatever these distinctions, localism emphasizes that much of the driving force for recovery comes not from government, but rather from below.

The successful examples have a very strong sense of place. Obviously, this is important for Hawai'i.

The process is collaborative, not official or bureaucratic. It brings together the widest range of people, from wealthy foundations to regular folks. The people who carry this load are not government officials.

To make this work, a community needs two kinds of entrepreneurs—economic and social—as well as people who are good at bringing this diverse group together. Or as one person describes them, "local patriots," who know how things work and appreciate the significance of connecting.

Some projects that emerge are really big, like finding alternative industries to replace lost factories, or redeveloping a downtown. But many are small scale, neighborhood oriented. And even the big projects start small, testing out to see what happens.

I don't have the space to describe the fascinating and surprisingly successful ways localism works, but the most interesting and fun-to-read account is by James and Deborah Fallows, *Our Towns*. It's like an adventure story.

Why Is Neighborhood So Important and So Underappreciated?

Strong neighborhoods make localism work.

Let's go back to talking about Hawaiʻi for a moment. We consider Hawaiʻi to be a friendly, welcoming place, a friends-and-neighbors sort of place, folks helping one another out in vital but under-the-political radar kinds of ways.

You can see it in how people responded to the pandemic. They quickly organized amazing food supply chains. Neighbors checked in with one another. Zoom became a standard tool of the tech uninitiated. Doctors in private practice developed COVID-19 testing sites on their own.

Before the pandemic, TMT protestors on the mountain were spectacularly successful, first in spontaneously building a community, and then sustaining it with a full menu of services.

All of this is ʻohana in the broad meaning of the word. And that alone makes small-scale, informal sites important as an asset for recovery.

Neighborhoods also do much more. They are the heartbeat in ways we are only beginning to understand.

Over the past few years, the economist Raj Chetty's pathbreaking research has shown just how important neighborhoods are (Cook). Here is his fundamental finding that is changing how some cities are thinking: *The neighborhood a person grew up in is by far the most important predictor of your future economic success. The standard indicators like your family or the labor market do not explain this.*

Neighborhoods, according to Chetty, mean something much smaller and less easily identifiable than say ʻEwa or Kaimukī. Chetty shows that economic success varies from block to block. Two mini-neighborhoods a block or so from one another that look very similar, and have very similar social and economic characteristics, can differ dramatically. There appears to be something very subtle going on, having to do with the kinds of neighbors you have and the social networks around you.

Neighborhoods are valuable in another way. During a crisis, they can be the difference between surviving and dying. People living in neighborhoods with strong social infrastructures—think of available places for people to gather and know one another—are much more likely to survive a disaster, because others keep track of them.

In 1995, hundreds of people died in a terrible Chicago heatwave. Typically, they died alone and isolated. Controlling for everything else, such as neighborhood racial composition and economic characteristics, people in strong social infrastructure neighborhoods were much less likely to die than people living where social infrastructure was weak.

Neighborliness is a resource and a skill set. Social capital, social infrastructure, the people you know two units down in your townhouse complex—these are resources that need to be more self-consciously developed, and much more forcefully used.

It is so interesting and so sad how much we like to think of Hawai'i as a neighborly place, and how much Hawai'i's powerful sense of place is reflected in our music and the stories we tell.

Yet at the same time we think about politics in such stilted, unrewarding, conventional, and unproductive ways.

It's time people try something else. This alternative has a proven track record, and it allows us to build on the underappreciated strengths people here already have, and at the same time worry about losing.

Works Cited

Brooks, David. "The Localist Revolution." *New York Times*, 19 July 2018, https://www.nytimes.com/2018/07/19/opinion/national-politics-localism-populism.html.

Cook, Gareth. "Raj Chetty's American Dream." *The Atlantic*, 17 July 2019, https://www.theatlantic.com/magazine/archive/2019/08/raj-chettys-american-dream/592804/.

Fallows, James, and Deborah Fallows. *Our Towns: A 100,000-Mile Journey Into the Heart of America*. Knopf Doubleday, 2018.

Neal Milner is a retired political science professor at the University of Hawai'i, where he taught for many years. He is a political analyst for KITV, a columnist for *Civil Beat*, and a contributing editor for the Hawai'i Public Radio show "The Conversation."

Civic Engagement—Picking a Fight

Dana Naone Hall

In the aftermath of 9/11, Hawai'i's economy, so reliant on tourism, was devastated. Voices were heard calling for a new, more diversified economy, but not much has changed since then. If anything, Hawai'i has become more dependent on tourism in the past decade.

The latest crisis, a global pandemic, is spurring some new thinking around the concept of 'āina aloha and Hawai'i core values. My feeling is that we also need to take stronger, immediate action to protect our islands and preserve our natural and cultural resources, even while we work to bring others into the discussion. Curbing the excesses of too many visitors is essential to the well-being of the place and its people.

When I first moved to Maui in the late 70s, tourists mainly hung around the Kā'anapali Resort on the west side, or Maui's newly developing south shore at Wailea. One could drive on East Maui roads at night and not pass another car in a ten-mile stretch. Fast forward forty years, and it is a common occurrence to have to wait at stop signs before joining a long line of cars traveling toward Pā'ia at all hours, many coming from a day trip to Hāna. One of the measures instituted to protect Hāna's people from the virus was to set up check points near Twin Falls and at 'Ulupalakua to allow traffic by Hāna residents only. Hāna stayed safe, and traffic decreased exponentially. Some longtime residents commented that it was like Hāna fifty years ago.

One of the visible signs that tourists were off the roads was the acres of cars, some 18,000 plus vehicles, parked in empty fields surrounding Kahului Airport. After a while, grass could be seen growing up around them. It struck me then that our physical infrastructure is adequate for our resident population, but not for all the tourists.

Speaking of the spread of coronavirus, imagine how much worse it might have been if Hawai'i had five international airports, as was so ardently sought in the 90s. Flights from Asia or Europe (through connecting flights) landing at Līhu'e, Honolulu, Kahului, Kona, and Hilo. Citizens fought hard to avert this fate. This is a prime example of the dedication and resistance necessary to protect Hawai'i.

Legions of tourists aren't the only problem. The Honolulu Rail debacle, overdue and wildly over budget, is now projected to open sometime in 2026 with the completion of the last rail station at Ala Moana. Spin-off projects, like the recently announced plan by the Canadian corporation that owns Ala Moana Center to construct a 400-foot residential tower at one end of the Center as soon as next year, only add more density to an already dense urbanscape. And—if these timelines bear any relationship to reality—what about the approximately five-year gap between the completion of the tower and the Rail coming on line? If anything, the 400-foot tower is premature and ripe for a challenge.

Honokahua Mau a Mau

I was asked recently to be interviewed for a Cultural Impact Assessment on a "Cultural and Lifestyle Enhancement" project at the Ritz-Carlton, Kapalua, which is adjacent to the Honokahua Burial Site. A Zoom meeting was arranged at which a PowerPoint presentation was provided. I did not participate, in large part because my request for information on the project had not been fulfilled. My preferred starting point for evaluating any project is an independent examination of relevant project documents and fact-finding. This approach is better than relying on the sales abilities of project consultants.

Protection of the Honokahua Burial Site is assured by the Honokahua Burial Site Agreement and a Preservation and Conservation Easement—both executed in 1989. The landowner, Maui Land & Pineapple Company, received 5.5 million dollars in exchange for granting the development rights to the 13.6-acre parcel to the State of Hawai'i in perpetuity. Another primary benefit of the Honokahua controversy was the enactment of Hawai'i's burial law, HRS 6E-43, protecting unmarked burial sites fifty years old and older.

The problem more than thirty years later is a lack of felicity to the original—and still operative—governing documents. For instance, the Preservation and Conservation Easement contains unequivocal language that "no buildings or structures shall be erected or placed on the Premises hereafter . . . ." About two weeks after I first requested documents from Kapalua, I received some 11" x 17" graphics of concept plans. On one sheet I noticed that according to a legend on the page, a dashed line was identified as the "Line of conservation boundary." This boundary line is shown crossing over a sport (tennis) court—a clear violation of the easement. There are other violations as well, but the good news is that the current project presents the possibility to reestablish the boundaries of the 13.6-acre site.

There are other issues with the project that need addressing. For instance, the proximity of a proposed new pool and water slide area directly upslope of the burial site. I am concerned that swimming and water play activities as well as sunbathing on chaise lounges may be incompatible with the peace and sanctity of a burial site.

This situation has revealed the truth that knowledge and vigilance are necessary to protect sites that were intended to be preserved and conserved for all time.

Establishing a National Archive

With the Honokahua Burial Site as a prime example of how memories, and thereby intentions, can wane, now may be the time to establish an archive for Lāhui Hawai'i, perhaps at the University of Hawai'i at Mānoa's Hawai'inuiākea School of Hawaiian Knowledge. Those of us with direct knowledge of seminal events in contemporary Hawai'i history can contribute interviews and salient documents on issues from Waiāhole-Waikāne to Kalama Valley and Kaho'olawe, from East Maui Water struggles to Kawaiaha'o and Mauna Kea, as well as a myriad of other issues. This effort would further distinguish UH Mānoa's status as a Research 1 institution, with the only college of indigenous studies in the United States.

The torch from Hawai'i's past burns brightly to illuminate the present that we step through to the future we are making.

Dana Naone Hall lives in Ha'ikū, Maui. Her book, *Life of the Land: Articulations of a Native Writer* (2017), is an American Book Award winner from the Before Columbus Foundation.

Molokai ʻĀina Momona

Keani Rawlins-Fernandez

It's 2006, and I'm at a state land use commission hearing with our Molokai community, wearing bright red shirts with bold, stark-white "SAVE LAʻAU" printed on them. We are here together at this important hearing to express our fervent desire to save a wahi pana of Molokai from being gated-off for a luxury development project the majority of our community opposes.

A Singapore-based developer, GuocoLeisure, dba Molokai Ranch, is seeking approval from the commission to build two hundred multi-million dollar homes on the untouched lands of Lāʻau. This luxury development would serve as a secluded neighbor-island residence for the wealthy who are interested in exclusive marina amenities, with an option that would accommodate a work-Oʻahu, live-Molokai commute with the purchase of each high-end home. The international company also happens to be the island's largest private employer and threatens to mothball its assets and terminate all of its employees if the project is not approved.

The project is denied approval.

GuocoLeisure shuts down Molokai Ranch and over one hundred Molokai residents lose their jobs. The community is left with the deep wounds of the resulting social division and economic devastation.

Since Americans and Europeans began exploiting Hawaiʻi, many foreign business interests have found their way to Molokai, bringing with them different ways to use the island's resources and our community for personal gain.

"Molokai Nui a Hina," Molokai Great Child of Hina. Hina, heroic resister to the abuse of power. Hina, goddess overseer of the cycles of the moon. Molokai has immensely potent female mana, carrying the legacy of powerful women. The energy is loving and welcoming, but fiercely protective, like that of a mother. The island herself and her residing people have always fought to protect our ʻāina while preserving and advancing the genius of our kūpuna. We pride ourselves in the connectedness and collectivism that we have maintained over the centuries, and have exercised our agency against that which does not align with our culture and values.

Molokai is situated between the islands of Oʻahu and Maui, with populations of 1 million and 155,000 respectively. Molokai is less populated than her neighbors, with a population of approximately 7,500, but is no less resourceful. Molokai has held onto a traditional way of life, while simultaneously straddling two diverging economic ideals.

Prominent Molokai kupuna and long-time community leader Uncle Walter Ritte was the first to articulate the philosophy that on Molokai we have two thriving economies: (1) a cash economy, an introduced capitalist ideology; and (2) a subsistence economy, an Indigenous ideology that perpetuates reciprocal social relationships in step with the surrounding natural environment.

Our island once produced so much food that we helped feed armies on neighboring islands. Molokai is known as "Molokai 'Āina Momona," which roughly translates to "Molokai, Land of Abundance," and that she is. With the longest continuous fringing reef in the Northern Hemisphere, Molokai is teeming with marine life. There are over eighty fishponds along the south shore. Lo'i kalo terraces also line the walls of our north shore valleys, and our central plains were once rolling hills of 'uala.

Fast forward eleven years. GuocoLeisure announces its intent to sell off its landholdings of 55,575 acres, nearly a third of our island home, which prompted over three hundred Molokai residents to march six miles up the slopes of Maunaloa to make a clear announcement of our own. We wanted stewardship of the 'āina returned to Molokai and her people. Uncle Walter consequently formed the Aloha 'Āina Fellows Leadership program to enhance the social infrastructure we need to develop a cash economy that complements our subsistence economy and way of life.

In a subsistence economy, where we mālama one another, traditional metrics for measuring success involve ensuring the collective good, where all are properly fed and cared for. By reengineering the systems our kūpuna passed down to us, we focus our energy on industries central to our fundamental needs, such as food and energy production, while cultivating our core competencies. We are a living laboratory.

The physical infrastructure for food independence remains in place on Molokai, and only needs to be restored to function again. Approximately one quarter of our island is homestead land set aside for agricultural use by Hawaiian beneficiaries. A 1.4 billion-gallon reservoir was constructed for homestead farmers to draw upon and grow food for sustainability and economic development.

As a living laboratory designed on "'ike kupuna," ancestral knowledge, the goal is to build capacity within our own community, while we also teach others around the world. Our kūpuna understood adaptive management and best practices to mālama our island and her resources effectively. As the planet's climate changes, and natural disasters occur more frequently with heightened intensity, the world is recognizing ancestral knowledge is an invaluable tool for our survival.

Education of course is key, and in Hawai'i ancestral knowledge was traditionally passed down from one generation to the next. We begin with a multipronged educational approach, teaching our children to identify their kuleana to our home, and then to pass that value on generationally and in perpetuity.

Professional and cultural capacity-building on individual and collective kuleana will develop by reinstating ancestral best practices, such as identifying the strengths and interests of children, and nurturing their skills through apprenticeship opportunities to enhance Molokai ʻĀina Momona. This continuum of ʻike is critical, for we stand on the shoulders of our ancestors. This is how our systems and technologies were improved upon from one generation to the next.

Utilizing assets-mapping, we analyze the current economic landscape and on-island employment; identify necessary jobs for new industries and growth; assess the existing skills consortium, education, and licensures; and evaluate the work experiences for those currently residing within the Molokai community, as well as those who presently live away and would like to return home.

By creating jobs in lucrative career industries, such as energy and technology, the incentive to come home after college would appeal to a much larger demographic, and the transference gaps of valuable ʻike to next generations would begin to fill in.

With a population that is both frugal and resourceful, with very little reliance upon the creature comforts relished in other places, our energy needs are relatively small; however, career opportunities exist in transitioning Molokai to 100 percent renewable and sustainable energy in clean resource industries, such as photovoltaic energy, wind energy, water energy, biofuels, and energy storage.

I ka wā ma mua, i ka wā ma hope. The future lies in the past.

The answer has always been inside of us: it is our connection to one another and to our ʻāina. Molokai has consistently practiced and maintained sustainability successfully throughout our history. This knowledge has tremendous global value for ecosystem management and sustainability principles. Our connectedness enables us to develop and refine the process of strengthening a community from within, enticing those who have left to return to their roots with endless opportunities right here at home. Molokai's successes could be used as a model to replicate on other islands and in communities around the globe.

Every one of us faces a daily choice: to build upon a foundation set before us or to build anew. On Molokai, we're choosing both. We're striving for food and energy independence while we cultivate ʻike kupuna. Our future is boundless as we set our sights on building capacity, advancing sustainable practices, and evolving as leaders in fields of technology and innovation.

Fourteen years ago, we stood to lose a part of ourselves to foreign exploitation. But today we know better than ever that Lāʻau Point, and all of Molokai Nui a Hina, is ours to care for and protect. We truly are and always will be Molokai ʻĀina Momona.

Keani Rawlins-Fernandez is the Maui County Council Member representing Molokai and serving all of Maui County. She is a kupa of Molokai with a law degree specializing in Native Hawaiian and environmental law, and a master's degree in business administration. She and her husband, Makena Fernandez, live on Molokai with their two children, Iʻa and Kaʻikena.

Home Is What We Make It

Tatiana Kalaniʻōpua Young

It is July 17, 2013, and my fourth visit to the Waiʻanae Boat Harbor encampment. It is arid, hot, humid. Thorny kiawe trees, undergrowth, and tall see grass made tough by salty air cover a coral landscape. Twenty or so tents dot the horizon. Barefoot children ride by on bikes covered in red dirt. A sun-kissed woman in her 40s with pink rubber slippers and blue Bongo shorts approaches me on a bike as I make my way to the entrance of the tent city.

"Can I help you?"

"Yes," I reply. "I am looking for Aunty Shirley. I am a Native Hawaiian anthropologist working on my PhD from Washington State working on issues of homelessness . . . ."

Before I could explain any further, the woman interrupts me.

"Sistah, we not homeless. The State is homeless. Waiʻanae is our home and this place is our birthright."

Then she asks, "How you going help us?"

Before I could respond, she hands me a rake and tells me to help clear the area. Aunty Shirley would return shortly, she says. Then she jets off into the sunset on her bike, just as Aunty Shirley appears from beyond the horizon.

She helped me to understand aloha as a connection between the self and the ʻohana through action—the sharing of responsibility and reciprocity between human and more-than-human relations, between biological and chosen relatives—and that home is what we make it. Reflecting on my fieldwork at Puʻuhonua O Waiʻanae, I am struck by the profound lessons of aloha, and how essential they are for building ʻohana and affirming hope for the future, especially in the face of precarity and uncertainty.

In July of 2020, the Waiʻanae Boat Harbor encampment now known as Puʻuhonua O Waiʻanae (POW) has come a long way since my first visit in 2013. As part of its vision for the future, POW is clearing a 20-acre land parcel in Waiʻanae Valley that it purchased earlier this year. Its mission to provide inclusion and safety for underserved Hawaiian, Pacific Islander, and multiethnic individuals, as well as displaced māhū (intersex/queer/transfolks), wāhine (women), and kāne (men) is now being realized. Known as a refuge for homeless, houseless, and home-free individuals and families struggling with addiction, poverty, and ostracism, POW prioritizes ʻohana as the means to mend and heal relationships.

Organized resilience operates in the shadows of market economies that promise a good life but fail to deliver. During my time at POW, it was not unusual to hear people complaining about the State's mismanagement of public resources, about greedy corporations and the destructive militaries in charge that keep Hawaiians from our own ea (breath, life, sovereignty). To realize its vision of a kauhale system, an inclusive Hawaiian home care system that more adequately addresses issues of cultural trauma, land displacement, and poverty, POW functions as a space of solidarity for different community partners, including the precariously housed, corporate, military, and police stakeholders. Sometimes a space must be created for queer relations of harmony and peace to flourish.

Working across the community spectrum has allowed the village to uphold tenets of political interdependence as an 'ohana. I've seen military officials donate food, labor, and equipment; private companies donate monies and supplies; and masculine police officers sit for hours and hours to talk story about daily life in the village with Twinkle, a queer wahine elder and village leader. Though seemingly insignificant, these informal interactions have helped the village to flourish, even as militarization and police violence have destroyed other informal village encampments resembling it.

When I asked Twinkle in 2015 about militarization and the growing presence of a police state in our community, she replied—

"Tati, there is evil in this world and my job is to protect the kids and people of this place. If one guy comes in here and harms or threatens my people with violence, then I will call da police."

As we talked at her campsite in the dimly lit tent, disheveled cats and dogs huddled on the plywood floor beneath our chairs. Some had mange, but received no less attention and care from Twinkle as the healthier ones.

"No matter what, at the end of the day, whether you work for the military, the police, the State, or even if you no mo one job, we are all people and the only way to get people to change for the better is through aloha."

For Twinkle, the police are a force of good and evil. She knows this well, having interacted with corrupt police officials, convicts, and violent offenders her whole life. Nonetheless, she believes that building relationships is a form of resistance, and a way of overturning the systems that oppress us. Twinkle once said that just as the State might see the village as both a public nuisance (illegal camping), and a productive site for failing state institutions (free labor), village leaders see the State as both a nuisance (surveillance), and useful (social welfare). In acknowledging the village's ea, she highlights the importance of seeing home within ourselves, and not something predetermined by institutions. By centering the village's agency, she recognizes the possibility of returning lands, goods, and services to those who need them.

This exchange between informal economics and village agency, I argue, is based on the 'ohana principle, which allows various stakeholders to build trust by cooperating on solutions to community problems rather than simply feeding bad faith as well as divisive and dysfunctional politics. Whether it's an elder from the local community providing saimin on Saturdays, or business leaders donating construction materials on weekdays, POW is remarkable precisely because it invites the best of humanity to coexist and flourish. Frontline activists like Twinkle bring Hawaiian activists, outreach service providers, the military, and the police together to build lasting, meaningful change.

Hā'awe i ke kua; hi'i i ke alo.
A burden on the back; a babe in the arms.
Said of a hard-working woman who carries a load on her back and a baby in her arms. (Pukui 50, no. 401)

The daily work of carrying the burden of failed "cistems" situates the above 'ōlelo no'eau at Pu'uhonua O Wai'anae. By working with and outside of the State, the village carries its heavy burden of weaving ea beyond the settler State, dismantling and transforming the embedded politics of disappearing Indigenous and queer people. Such work requires (k)new ways of seeing and being in the world. It requires prioritizing aloha for one's self and one's community, an openness and willingness to heal, and a commitment to affirming life. From this aloha comes the cultivation of healing and loving relationships that mend rather than break our hearts.

While critiques of neoliberalization offer a broader lens of possibility for abolition (a politics seeking to dismantle and transform oppressive systems of carcerality and punishment), the people of Pu'uhonua O Wai'anae embody a politics of connection and reconnection. Here, decolonization and demilitarization emerge by activating empathy and intimacy. It is in the alo a he alo (face-to-face) interactions, the "I-got-you-boo" conversations, and the "come-over-my-house-for-dinner" exchanges that create opportunities for something (k)new to emerge. At POW, I've seen military personnel offer humanitarian services to displaced Hawaiians with tremendous attention and care. I've seen police officers stand hand in hand with us to ward off an eviction. I've seen people begin to heal themselves because they have structures of accountability and aloha firmly implanted as having a purpose in life. While I am in no way valorizing the military or the police and the institutions they purport to represent, having witnessed healthy relationships between them and the people for whom "cistems" have failed gives me hope for a more peaceful and prosperous future. The power of aloha is found in the connections between the land and the people.

For many of the villagers that I got to know on a deeper level, "home" was defined as "places where you feel like returning to" and "places of safety." One of the most profound lessons is how people created community not by conspiring against what they disliked, but by giving others space to define and redefine life for themselves, by facing precarity as an 'ohana, and by confidently sharing aloha even as we faced threats to erase us. Given the new challenges of the current global pandemic and its adverse impacts on displaced individuals, how will we show up for aloha, for our community, for ourselves? How will we continue to affirm the ea of Black, immigrant, and Indigenous people of color, our accomplices and allies in the fall of Empire? How will we become the home and future we've been waiting for, and what specific steps are we willing to take to ensure that home, this sense of love and safety, this indelible mark of humanity, belongs equally to us all?

Work Cited

Pukui, Mary Kawena. ʻŌlelo Noʻeau: Hawaiian Proverbs & Poetical Sayings. Bishop Museum Press, 1983.

Tatiana Kalaniʻōpua Young is a Kanaka ʻŌiwi Maoli, māhū+ scholar-activist, and a former community organizer with the United Territories of Pacific Islanders Alliance (UTOPIA). She completed her PhD in the Department of Anthropology at the University of Washington. Kalaniʻōpua serves on the board of Kahea: the Hawaiʻi Environmental Alliance and Hawaiʻi's chapter of UTOPIA, and continues to advocate for precariously housed LGBTQI+ populations.

Reconnecting Spiritual Roots in Our Faith Communities

David Baumgart Turner

In the Day Reading Room of Sterling Library at Yale Divinity School, a beautiful desk is surrounded by countless books and manuscripts chronicling the early nineteenth-century missionaries to Hawai'i. Five thousand miles from the shores of my Hawai'i home, as a first year seminarian, I was overjoyed to find this desk and the works surrounding it. In the bleakness that defines much of New Haven fall and winter, it was a space almost sacred—a place apart from this often dismal corner of New England that had become my temporary home in the early 1980s.

That is, until it wasn't.

While researching a paper on religious support on the continent for the Overthrow of Queen Lili'uokalani, I consulted *The Friend*, the journal of the Hawai'i Evangelical Association, the church body that emerged from the American Board of Foreign Missions, and eventually became the Hawai'i Conference of the United Church of Christ (HCUCC). I expected to find support for the Overthrow there, but to my horror, it wasn't tacit, but loud and unanimous support, reflecting the most vile and racist thoughts rampant in Congress and across the continent. There, in bold print, were my own blood ancestors, self-righteously celebrating a grievous wrong. I was utterly destroyed by this revelation. The sacredness of that space was forever lost.

That memory resonates profoundly with me as now, after more than three decades of ordained ministry in Hawai'i as part of the HCUCC, I find myself sitting at the HCUCC office with colleagues as we consider the implications of 2020—the 200th anniversary of the missionaries' arrival. We are also aware that this year is more than twenty-five years after the UCC and the HCUCC apologized for their role in overthrowing the monarchy, and promised to work toward restitution, reparation, and renewal. And in that office, we find ourselves asking "Has anything changed?"

Western understandings of 'āina still carry the day—value determined by short-term profit maximized. The 'āina still suffers under the bulldozer and the concrete weight of structures of finance, commerce, and visitors. The reefs wallow in silt, the fish run thin, and the sacred wai is clogged with rubbish and Roundup. For the people who welcomed my ancestors with aloha, though already horribly thinned by introduced disease, and who are now squeezed to the margins of health and wealth—the question lingers in the air.

"Has anything changed?"

And further—

"Does this faith of those intrepid missionaries have anything new to say?"

Then, in the midst of this gathering, my colleague Kahu Wayne Higa of Ka'ahumanu Church on Maui began to speak of Holy Communion. But the symbols he used were not the bread and wine, but the kalo (taro) and the wai (fresh water). He held in front of us an imaginary 'ohā (taro corm), imu-steamed and ready for transformation, and he began to grind and to pound.

"The kalo, broken for you, that you might have life. The wai, running fresh and clear, that you might be renewed."

In that moment, the wisdom of two powerful spiritual traditions merged seamlessly, speaking as one about self-sacrificial love. That moment wrapped these traditions of spiritual wisdom that for 200+ years have too often been pitted against one another—a win/lose proposition that has produced very few winners—into a unity, calling forth a life-affirming network of mutuality that could span the entirety of the Creation.

We must relocate ourselves in the beauty of such commonality, for there we will find the wisdom that will guide our future. I suggest that we begin with 'āina. For too long the prevailing Western paradigm vis-à-vis the land has been that of control and exploitation. This understanding emerges from a poor translation of Genesis 1 that gives humankind "dominion" over all of God's Creation. In a recent episode of the "On Being" podcast with Krista Tippett, Professor Ellen Davis of Duke Divinity School shares that the Hebrew word from which "dominion" comes is more appropriately translated as an "artistic exercise of skilled mastery."

Oh, how different might things have been, if such had been the understanding of those first foreigners who set eyes on these island shores, decades before the first missionaries arrived. One would be hard pressed to find a finer example of the "artistic exercise of skilled mastery" than the ahupua'a system that defined and focused all activities, borne out of a brilliant awareness of every waterdrop that falls upon the mauka peaks, working its way through the wao akua (realm of the gods) in rivulet, fall, and stream to the wao kanaka (realm of human activity), diverted by 'auwai (irrigation channels) into lo'i kalo (taro patches), where it provides nutrients while also being filtered before its return to stream, and its flow to kahakai (shoreline) and eventually to moana (the sea).

If those first foreign visitors and enchanted residents had paid attention to the mo'olelo (story) of Hāloa, the firstborn sibling who comes to second life in the kalo, they might have understood their own Biblical story better, in which humankind in Genesis 1 is created not "apart from" but as "a part of" the rest of the Creation—"kin" not just to other humans, but to the finned of the sea, the limbed and leafed of the forest, the winged of the sky, the footed, pawed, and hoofed, and all that breezes, flows, and rises in peaks of grandeur.

Rather than in the kingdom of brute force, unconscious manipulation, and soulless extraction visited upon these islands, we truly live in a "kin-dom." "He ali'i ka 'āina; he kauā ke kanaka" (The land is the chief, humans its steward), the na'au (wisdom) of Hawai'i proclaims, a sentiment echoed repeatedly throughout the Biblical story, for as Professor Davis explains, "the best index in the Bible of the health of the relationship between God and humankind is the health of the earth as a whole." Mālama 'āina (to care for the land), in the same way that it cares for us, is our kuleana (responsibility). So say our Hawaiian brothers and sisters, but so too says the Good Book—a truth that needs to emerge again.

* * *

Sadly, such a reading of the Bible did not accompany those who first journeyed from the West, whether as world explorer, sailor, whaler, merchant, or missionary. Nor did it occur to their children who came to call Hawai'i their home. If the 'āina is a resource only valued for its economic return—dominated always, easily exploited and plundered, with its sacredness having no value in the equation—then it is no leap at all to take the same view of those who work the land, whether on plantations of mono-crops, or for hotels filled with tourist props. Just as the land shudders with thoughtless and heartless assault, so do its people. For too many here in Hawai'i, the yearning to thrive gave way long ago to a struggle just to survive—and all of this happening in a land that yearns to provide for all.

But that can be then, and there can be a new now. Two hundred years and more have passed, Biblical scholarship advances, and the mo'olelo and mele (song) that were too long suppressed burst forth again. Seeds of vitality and beauty, wisdom and wonder, which have lain dormant are present to guide us, and a brighter future awaits. That future need not reflect the conquest reality of the last 200+ years: one spiritual tradition, one economic system, one form of land management needing to win, and forcing the other to lose. This reality has produced trauma and tragedy. The time has come for today's church communities—the descendants of those intrepid purveyors of faith of centuries ago—to uncouple our faith traditions from those systems that value profit, power, and possessions, and to reattach ourselves to the wisdom imbedded in these sacred islands—a wisdom of reciprocity (aloha aku, aloha mai—the aloha you share is the aloha you receive) and of kinship/ 'ohana, an understanding of *family* that makes the entirety of creation the true neighborhood of the Golden Rule. It is wisdom utterly integral to our own Good Book as well.

Shall we do the hard, reflective, and reckoning work required to truly share both sorrows and joy? Shall we open ourselves to wisdom that adds color and depth to our own? Shall we allow the deepest yearnings towards an utterly transformative aloha to lodge firmly in our na'au (seat of wisdom) and burst forth from our hearts? Such is the kāhea (call) echoing across the islands, calling forth not just the footprints that mark our days, but the soul-prints that shall mark our lives.

Work Cited

Tippett, Krista, host. "Wendell Berry and Ellen Davis: The Art of Being Creatures." *On Being*, 10 June 2020, https://onbeing.org/programs/wendell-berry-ellen-davis-the-art-of-being-creatures/.

Rev. David Baumgart Turner is pastor at Church of the Crossroads in Honolulu, a place that resonates powerfully with his passions for Caring for God's Creation, and creating a just and peaceful world. He has served as the director of Camp Mokulēʻia, a pastor of local churches, a school chaplain, and consultant on issues of sustainability locally and nationally.

We Need to Talk

How a Con Con Can Secure Hawai'i's
Post-COVID Future

Colin D. Moore

In Hawai'i, nobody tells better stories than our kūpuna. And if you love politics, nothing is better than listening to those told by seasoned politicians. These are the folks who can recall precisely their share of the vote in decades-old elections. They can tell you how they stood in the pouring rain, sign-waving for hours, after going door to door in Makiki, soaked in sweat, just to talk with every voter. What's more, they can tell you why it mattered.

But if you listen to their stories of the art and gamesmanship of politics for long enough, these masters of legislative deal-making will often confess that they're worried. They will explain that a state that once championed radical legislation such as the 1974 Prepaid Health Care Act—a law that guaranteed health care for most working people—has become too cautious, hidebound, and gutless to do bold things anymore. They think Hawai'i is stuck.

Even before the COVID-19 crisis, Hawai'i faced some daunting challenges: limited affordable housing, a tourism industry that exploited the population, and the exodus of its young people to cities that promised more opportunities. Add the costs to maintain infrastructure, adapt to sea level rise, and pay for public employee pension obligations—costs that one estimate puts at $88 billion—and you can understand why some Hawai'i political veterans fear for our future (*Troubled Waters*).

To confront these challenges—and those presented by COVID-19—we need to rethink our policymaking process. And to do that, we need to hold a Con Con. Let me explain.

Hawai'i has a unique constitutional provision shared by only five other states. Every ten years, this question must appear before voters on the ballot: *Shall there be a convention to propose a revision of or amendments to the Constitution?*

Often referred to as a "Con Con," the last constitutional convention occurred over forty years ago. That legendary 1978 Con Con established new environmental protections and led to the creation of the Office of Hawaiian Affairs.

When the question appeared on the ballot in 2018, I felt hopeful. I was curious what would happen if everyday citizens had a chance to think through its implications. I wasn't alive in 1978, but I'd heard the stories and read the transcripts from the '78 Con Con, and I believed that it fundamentally changed Hawai'i for the good.

During the fall of 2018, the University of Hawai'i Public Policy Center, which I direct, tried an experiment. We set up a "citizens' jury" to allow a broad spectrum of people to consider the implications of holding a Con Con. Drawn mainly from Honolulu neighborhood boards, the participants heard arguments for and against the process. In the end, a strong majority supported the Con Con.

A month later, the Con Con ballot question failed. Only 23 percent of the electorate voted yes—and most voters never had the chance to seriously consider it. The vast majority of local pressure groups, including most unions and conservation groups, were opposed because of concerns that shadowy "mainland interests" would undermine our current constitution and the environmental protections and collective bargaining rights it provides.

I was surprised at how depressed I felt by this result. Unlike what I heard in our citizens' jury, the arguments from professional lobbyists came from a place of fear—of what might be lost, rather than the possibilities to change our system of government for the better.

We missed our chance in 2018, but it's not too late. If we want a brighter future for Hawai'i after COVID-19, we need to change our political system. A Con Con can provide a forum for a community-wide discussion of values and priorities. It might also help us tackle some of the problems that result from our broken policy-making process.

Trust and Public Engagement. Hawai'i has the lowest voter turnout rate in the nation. In the 2018 general election, only 44 percent of eligible voters cast a ballot. Voting isn't the only way to participate in politics, of course, and there is often too much handwringing from pundits like me about our low turnout rates. But it is a symptom of something deeper: a lack of trust, and a sense that there's really no point in participating in electoral politics. In 2018, the UH Public Policy Center found that only 30 percent trusted our state government to do what was in the public's interest most of the time. This is not a sign of a healthy democracy.

Political Competition. In Hawai'i we lack the vigorous political competition that is a hallmark of the democratic process. The dominance of the Democratic Party has only increased in recent years after the Republican Party's dramatic shift to the right. Today, with a few notable exceptions, Republicans in Hawai'i can barely field credible candidates for public office. Although some may cheer the party's demise, what's replaced two-party competition is a system of legislative factions held together by personal relationships or political favors. With no real opposition, there is no need for public debate. The result is a policymaking process that is nearly opaque and almost impossible for regular citizens to follow.

Policy Responsiveness. I'll be blunt. Hawai'i may be ruled by Democrats, but the state's politics haven't been progressive for a very long time. That the vast majority of our elected leaders come from affluent backgrounds means that they are less likely to support policies that benefit the poor. Hawai'i still has no publicly-funded pre-kindergarten education or paid family leave for working families. Our regressive general excise tax indiscriminately taxes all consumers regardless of income, and places the highest tax burdens on low-income families in the nation. This even though in nearly every poll, Hawai'i families put issues such as affordable housing and education on the top of their lists.

How might we solve these problems? Despite the faith that some put in the private sector, we should resist replacing an unresponsive legislature with unaccountable business groups. Avoiding politics is not the answer. As policy theorist Deborah Stone has written, "In the process of articulating reasons, we show each other how we see the world" (380). What we need instead is a way to talk about how to balance values and needs that we all share, such as equity and efficiency, liberty and justice.

That is what happens at a Con Con. It is the only forum that provides an opportunity to take a comprehensive and holistic approach to improve government and address our most intractable policy challenges.

What changes might we make? Here are a few suggestions.

Publicly-Financed Elections. Although Hawai'i already has some public financing for candidates, this system could be expanded dramatically. If we want more candidates from diverse backgrounds, we need to expand the opportunities for them to get their message out. Money in politics is not the problem. It's that the money comes from a small number of powerful interests.

Nonpartisan Elections. When nearly every member of the legislature is a Democrat, party labels no longer provide much information to voters. In a small state where the ideological orientations of voters often don't map well onto the advanced culture wars raging in the continental US, we should consider a nonpartisan legislature. Coupled with a primary process that would allow the top two vote-getters to advance to the general election, this might lead to a new set of diverse elected voices less beholden to the power structures of one political party.

A Full-Time Legislature. The current requirement for a 60-day legislative session is indefensible. The result is a scramble for attention that favors organized lobbyists, while good bills are forced to wait, sometimes for years, for a serious hearing. By allowing the legislature to meet throughout the year, we could end this madness and increase the time for every sensible bill to be properly studied.

These are the kinds of changes that could be coupled with other guarantees at a new Con Con. What about a constitutional right to housing? Guaranteed access to higher education? A Con Con would also offer an opportunity to expand and clarify the Native Hawaiian rights that came out of the 1978 convention. Such ideas could be debated by delegates elected from across the state.

A Con Con is about real community engagement—and only that can create the trust and legitimacy necessary to reform our policymaking process.

We need to talk, Hawai'i. A Con Con will provide the space to consider our post-COVID future.

Works Cited

Stone, Deborah. *Policy Paradox: The Art of Political Decision Making.* 2nd ed., W. W. Norton, 1997.

Troubled Waters: Charting a New Fiscal Course for Hawaiʻi. Hawaiʻi Executive Conference, 2 Oct. 2019, https://www.documentcloud.org/documents/6476457-HEC-Government-Report-FINAL.html#document/p1.

Colin D. Moore is an Associate Professor, the Director of the Public Policy Center, and the Chair of the School of Communications at the University of Hawaiʻi at Mānoa. He serves as a political analyst for Hawaiʻi News Now.

Hawai'i Breathes Multilingualism

Patricia Espiritu Halagao and Cheryl Ka'uhane Lupenui

Four years after serving on the Hawai'i State Board of Education, Patricia Espiritu Halagao and Cheryl Ka'uhane Lupenui engage in conversation about their work on linguistic and culturally sustaining policies. Lupenui was instrumental in establishing Nā Hopena A'o (HĀ and BREATH, Policy E-3), a new "Ends" Policy of learning outcomes grounded in Hawaiian values and culture for the educational system. Halagao's work on the Seal of Biliteracy (Policy 105-15) and Multilingualism for Equitable Education (Policy 105-14) policies comes out of this context.

Here they reflect on the past and imagine a future around the question: "What is multilingualism in Hawai'i?" They bring in voices of language scholars to get to their own na'au (gut, heart), and they invite you to join their search for conditions where multiculturalism and multilingualism thrive in Hawai'i's past, present, and future.

Cheryl: Since we've left the Board, it's rewarding to see where our culture and language policies have taken root and spread because of schools' and community support! Under Director Kau'i Sang's leadership, the Hawai'i Department of Education's (HIDOE) first Office of Hawaiian Education just turned five years old, and they are grounding education in Hawaiian ways of knowing. 'Ōlelo Hawai'i teachers are getting bonuses, HĀ and Hawaiian culture-based learning opportunities abound, and Hawaiian language courses are free to educators.

The three Hawaiian-focused policies we approved also made room for the Seal of Biliteracy and Multilingualism for Equitable Education policies. Both firsts in the history of Hawai'i.

Patricia: This year, HIDOE sponsored its second annual multilingualism symposium and awarded more seniors with the Seal of Biliteracy, signaling their proficiency in Hawaiian or English and an additional language, like Filipino and Chuukese. Multilingualism is in the Governor's Hawai'i Blueprint for Education and HIDOE *Promise Plan*, which it defines as "people or groups with the ability to use more than two languages for communication." Multilingualism values the cultural and linguistic assets of people and fosters language maintenance and acquisition. But multilingualism is more than that—it's a way of life and a mindset.

Cheryl: For me, multilingualism was always something I wasn't—that is, "fluent in more than one language." But working together on these policies opened my eyes to see that I have been learning different languages throughout my life. Rather than categorizing students by what they don't know, as in English, your work shifted my perspective to focus on their strengths as multilingual learners. When we get together, I always learn or see something new. Likewise, these Hawaiian and multilingual policies are creating a different picture of what education can look like.

Patricia: It's actually a different picture of education than what I grew up with in the Midwest. I remember feeling ashamed to be Filipino, embarrassed by my parents' accents, and rejected speaking Tagalog. I was told to "go back home." I went into the field of multicultural education because I don't want any child to experience what I did.

Cheryl: As a young girl growing up in the suburbs of Maryland, I was embarrassed to be Hawaiian. It made me different from everyone else, and at the time, I wanted most to fit in. It's been a long journey to get to a place in my life where I value all my ancestors and can navigate with care between both Hawaiian and Western cultures.

Patricia: We both didn't fit in. Sometimes I wonder how I ended up being a multilingual advocate when I'm not proficient in multiple languages. But we are probably committed to inclusivity precisely because we felt excluded. We do the work of belonging because we felt like we didn't belong.

Our pasts have shaped who we've become and why we care so deeply about this work. Now let's look back to see what Hawaiʻi's multilingual past looked like, how it shapes us today, and what lessons can inform our future.

Cheryl: So here is something I hadn't known before this conversation . . . before Pidgin English, there was Pidgin Hawaiian called ʻŌlelo Paʻiʻai . . . with Polynesian Pidgin showing up as early as the 1760s and lasting for over a century. Thanks to Pila Wilson and Derek Bickerton, I learned that a variety of languages were spoken by immigrants in the early 1800s before plantations. Pidgin Hawaiian was spoken by members of most, if not all, immigrant groups. And now we know Pidgin Hawaiian is the direct ancestor to Pidgin English. This means the roots of Pidgin English are actually Hawaiian rather than English! I understand better when I listen to tapes of my Hawaiian Chinese grandmother speaking Pidgin English that I hear her Hawaiian thought processes as well.

Knowing our immigrant ancestors spoke Hawaiian and Pidgin Hawaiian fluently while still retaining their mother tongue is a great, early example of multilingualism! Though it wouldn't have been called that at the time.

Patricia: Multilingualism is a modern day term for a normal way of communicating in the past and in places like Hawai'i. By the mid 1800s, Hawai'i was one of the most multilingual and literate countries in the world, with 90–95 percent of the population literate in the primary language of 'Ōlelo Hawai'i alongside the mother tongue of immigrants and the lingua franca of Pidgin Hawaiian.

Cheryl: The presence of multilingualism seems to be more than just an individual competency. It's also an indicator of the values, strengths, and culture of a collective people. 'Ōlelo Hawai'i remained strong even in some places until the early 1900s. Likewise, Hawaiians remained steadfast in their political and cultural identity and beliefs. The welcoming and inclusion of strangers and their different languages came from a position of strength by Hawaiians. The value of pilina (meaningful relationships) is evident in Hawaiian language and culture. As visitors arrived and moved into communal working and living arrangements with Hawaiians, pilina would be a concept that embraced them too.

Patricia: The use of 'Ōlelo Hawai'i and Pidgin Hawaiian was an acknowledgment of a Hawaiian way of life. Language advocates Kahea Farias and Angela Haeusler speak to how immigrants and Hawaiians in the early 1800s demonstrated reciprocal respect, wanting to communicate with speakers of other languages. Multilingual businesses and government practices pervaded everyday life. Angela shared how foreigners were stronger in Hawaiian than English, and courts had professional, multilingual interpreters to translate from Chinese to Hawaiian, for instance.

Cheryl: In the nineteenth century, Hawaiian language was always to be a part of Hawai'i's future. The issue seems to have been for the English speakers.

Patricia: Yes, eventually English was used to disconnect and subjugate. As teacher educator Brook Chapman de Sousa once heard from a colleague, English can be a "carnivorous language." When Westerners and other foreigners devalued and rejected the native Hawaiian language, Hawai'i lost its practices of multilingual communication and communal respect for linguistic diversity. It also disrupted generational continuity and family ties. I often wonder how different it would be today if communities valued all their languages.

Cheryl: Had we embraced "the many and more than one," Indigenous and immigrant students wouldn't have low literacy rates in the US.

Patricia: This is all helpful in thinking about what multilingualism can and should look like in a Hawaiian context today.

Cheryl: As I look back to our time on the Board of Education, I realize that the ground was fertile for these new policies including HĀ, Multilingualism, and the

Seal of Biliteracy. As difficult as this policymaking journey was, I know we were following a well-travelled path started long before us. The renaissance of Hawaiian culture and the revitalization of Hawaiian language that began in the 1960s was a critical platform to firmly stand on before we lifted anything else up, so Hawaiian language would become a medium of instruction again in our schools. And in addition to English, some Hawaiian-language-medium schools are now teaching all students languages of our immigrant ancestors.

Patricia: While we've come a long way, I remember resistance toward multilingualism at first. One assistant superintendent feared, "we have over 100 different languages, how are teachers supposed to know all of them?" There were fears of students losing English, resource issues, and the attitude "But, this is America." I remember another assistant superintendent had leaders say "multilingualism" out loud five times at a meeting, stating it's not a disease or something to be afraid of.

As we listened to our immigrant communities, they didn't want another English Learner (EL) policy, but a policy that valued their children's languages as assets. Our multilingualism policy reframed our students as Multilingual Learners rich with linguistic resources. To some this was new and controversial. It took collaboration with the community to challenge the status quo and persist.

Cheryl: This takes me back to the 2014 Hawaiian Education Summit, when the community birthed a collective vision for education, ʻO Hawaiʻi ke kahua o ka hoʻonaʻauao (Hawaiʻi is the foundation of learning). As a BOE member, I was very clear that the advancement of ʻŌlelo Hawaiʻi and Hawaiian culture must include everyone and not just Hawaiians to achieve normalization.

As the HĀ policy states, a comprehensive "Hawaiian education will positively impact the educational outcomes of all students." We recognized that students educated in both Hawaiian and Western ways and language will be better prepared for life in a multicultural, multilingual society. This was something quite new for our system.

Patricia: So in retrospect, a *Hawaiian context breathes multilingualism*. Multilingualism policies would not have happened unless Nā Hopena Aʻo, an outcomes policy rooted in Hawaiian values, established space for other languages to flourish. My thinking shifted when I talked to you and Kauʻi about Hawaiian education and language policies for all students, and not just Hawaiian students. But I questioned the tactic of a broad multilingualism policy. In the end, you and Kauʻi validated our decision to not focus on the EL student, but change the context so language diversity would be the norm. Maintaining home languages and learning new languages would be cool for all students!

Cheryl: And to think, HĀ almost did not make it into policy! I remember a complex area superintendent exclaimed, "When I walk into a Hawaiʻi public school, I want to close my eyes and know that I am in a school in Hawai'i . . . and not somewhere else." It seemed the system was ready for change, but was I up for the challenge? As student achievement chair, I presented HĀ to various communities in and outside of the DOE to determine the level of support. This was one of the most painful parts for me. We had to stand before a crowd of strangers to justify the value of Hawai'i in education. Holding this space became a test of my conviction that Hawaiian language and culture are valuable to everyone.

Patricia: As a settler to Hawai'i, I am conscious of the importance of 'Ōlelo Hawai'i to our place. Hawaiian is not under the umbrella of multilingualism. Hawaiian language scholar Kalehua Krug reminded me that more still needs to be done for Hawaiian language education. I can see being protective of languages that need to be reclaimed as opposed to being maintained. Language scholars Dina Yoshimi and Pila Wilson always made sure Hawaiian was included as a base language in our Seal of Biliteracy. My colleagues helped me see how we can be equitable, holding space for the languages from where we are now and where we are from. We must lift up everyone's lives and languages!

And now, as we are writing this piece, we are living amidst challenging, uncertain times. We're experiencing a global pandemic and racial upheaval with the continued subjugation of Black and Brown people—COVID-19, anti-Asian sentiments, Black Lives Matter. We can either run from, or we can embrace our diversity, courageously face our fears, and do something.

Cheryl: Perhaps this global pandemic is a hulihia moment for education to be overturned, reshaped. When we started on BOE, the shape of education was represented in a single triangle sliced in three representing a tri-level educational system. Though the triangle is now 3-D, the shape hasn't really changed today. There's still only one triangle, with a top, middle, and bottom.

Patricia: What's the hulihia? What's being overturned, revisited, reshaped? Multilingualism once flourished in Hawai'i during a time of significant change and challenge. What does it need to thrive in Hawai'i today?

Cheryl: Multilingualism needs Hawai'i to thrive again!

Patricia: Hawai'i shows up in the HIDOE *2030 Promise Plan*, which states that "student success will be grounded in Nā Hopena A'o (HĀ), empower a multicultural society and honor Hawai'i's local and global contribution." I noticed in the plan that 'Ōlelo Hawai'i and multilingualism are literally on the same page, side-by-side. However, this separation doesn't acknowledge the relationship between multilingualism and 'Ōlelo Hawai'i. We've seen multilingualism exist in an English and a Hawaiian language educational pathway.

Cheryl: What if HĀ was the overarching framework for the entire *Promise Plan*, instead of it under the theme of Hawaiʻi? When Hawaiʻi is no longer just another promise, it can then become a native context for our educational system again. The plan holds our generation's promises for Hawaiʻi. In return, Hawaiʻi becomes our teacher, classroom, guide, and learning environment. After a hulihia of volcanic fire, it's the natives that show up first. Now the hulihia is that space being cleared in education for Hawaiʻi to return once again.

Patricia: If anything, living in a pandemic has shown us that we must adapt and be flexible to survive. It's forced us to make room for multiple learning spaces—from our families, in our homes, virtually across space and time.

Cheryl: Kauʻi Sang shared a vision of what she sees education looking like in one hundred years as a shift back to many schools. ʻAʻohe pau ka ʻike i ka hālau hoʻokahi. All knowledge is not learned in just one school. Environments inclusive of many are where multiple languages thrive!

Patricia: This sounds good, but I recognize it is difficult for educators (and myself) to change. We need to learn to be comfortable with "not knowing," despite a system that strives for standards and rewards "knowing." Often when we don't know the language being spoken, we feel lost and left out. So we don't go there. We need to shift the mindset from what Paulo Freire describes as the "banking system of knowledge" to curiosity and inquiry.

Cheryl: The space of learning is one of discovery, not achievement! What is really clear for me is that multilingualism is a sign of relationships between humans and their environmental kin. Multilingualism from a Hawaiian context includes the languages of trees, rocks, birds, roots, insects, and winds, as understood by our ancestors. This is one of those hulihia moments turning me towards something I hadn't seen before. We need many more languages to truly be in a relationship with the world around us.

Patricia: Many of us don't realize it, but we're actually plurilingual—having just enough competence in multiple cultures and languages for communication and intercultural interaction. We can learn about a group's culture through its language: multiculturalism *through* multilingualism. The pandemic shows we are more connected than we think.

So where do we go from here? As former Board members, what would we like to see happen with the future of languages in Hawaiʻi? What gifts do we have to give?

Cheryl: Soon after the HĀ outcomes were put into policy, the question emerged, "How do we measure them?" On our journey of discovery, we changed course to include looking at the context for learning, and not only the content. This begins to change the shape of public education.

Patricia: Currently, World Language is under the Office of Curriculum and Instructional Support, Ke Kula Kaiapuni is under the Office of Hawaiian Education, and the EL program is under the Office of Student Support Services in the HIDOE. But they are all related. How can we connect the system so all our students' languages are seen as central to the curriculum and context of learning, not only as support? Finally, we need to move away from the federally-designated term English Learner to Multilingual Learner.

Cheryl: I wonder what the design of our educational system would look like if it was shaped like koa leaves, sails of our wa'a, a calabash, or a constellation? Or if it was a series of shapes like the patterns on kapa, a woven mat, or on skin as kākau (tattoos)? Opening up many shapes rather than just one enables us to shape what education looks like in our unique places.

Patricia: So how would we measure the shape of our wa'a sails? It would be multidimensional. Indicators would be hearing the happy chatter of children translanguaging; a teacher pronouncing students' names properly or being plurilingual and able to say "hello" in five different languages. Another indicator might be the number of Seals of Biliteracy and language-inclusive career programs where having language awareness and the ability to communicate is crucial for everyday and workplace living and breathing. Look at Waipahu High School's course on Ilokano medical terms in their Health Academy as an example!

Cheryl: If we measure what matters, I think our collective learning can be reflected back to us by how many generations-long our knowledge transmission system is, how many kupuna-keiki learning exchanges and caring touchpoints with 'āina happen, how many observations of readiness are captured, and how many teachers come from the families they teach. All of these measures are place-based, quantifiable, and come from Hawai'i as our foundation for learning.

Listening to the wisdom of our past, people, and place, Patricia and Cheryl dug deep to understand multilingualism in Hawai'i and set a course forward. 'Ōlelo Hawai'i is not just one of many languages, but one that opens up space for many. Coming from a place "of Hawai'i" and not just "in Hawai'i," they found that what matters most is creating rich conditions for multilingualism to breathe. Hawai'i shows us the value of "the many," of being comfortable with "not knowing," and most important of all, of pilina. Hawai'i reminds us of the gifts of our place to education here and beyond, and in turn, education's responsibility to give back to Hawai'i.

Works Cited

Board Policies. Hawaiʻi State Board of Education, http://boe.hawaii.gov/policies/Pages/
    Board-Policies.aspx.
2030 Promise Plan: Hawaiʻi State Department of Education Strategic Plan. Hawaiʻi State
    Department of Education, http://www.hawaiipublicschools.org/DOE%20Forms/
    Advancing%20Education/2030PromisePlan.pdf.

Patricia Espiritu Halagao is Professor and Chair of the Department of Curriculum Studies in the College of Education, University of Hawaiʻi at Mānoa and a former elementary school teacher.

Cheryl Kaʻuhane Lupenui is President and CEO for the Kohala Center and founder of the Leader Project, where she continues to learn to lead from a Hawaiʻi place.

Activist Genealogy

Visions and Enactments of Solidarity Across Black and Kanaka Maoli Movements

Charles Lawrence

June 6, 2020: Over ten thousand people have come to the Hawaiʻi State Capitol in protest. They come from all of Hawaiʻi's many families—Kanaka, Filipino, Japanese, Chinese, Sāmoan, Chukese, Vietnamese, Thai, Korean, and so many more. They are here in answer to my people's call to join us in our grief and rage at the murders of our brothers and sisters, to end four hundred years of police and vigilante terror against us. To make Black lives matter.

Dr. Noelani Goodyear-Kaʻōpua sits on the grass at Ala Moana Beach Park before the march begins. She is making a sign. Her five-year-old son, Moku, sits close beside her, watching her intently as she works. They are talking about why they are here, why they are making this sign, and what it means. The sign says, "FUCK WHITE SUPREMACY." Moku wears a baseball hat pulled low across his serious eyes. The words on his hat say "KAPU ALOHA."

Eleven months earlier, Noelani lay chained to a cattle grate at Mauna Kea Access Road. This time our Kanaka brothers and sisters issued the call, an invitation to all of us to protest the Thirty Meter Telescope's construction, to join their lāhui in protecting a sacred ancestor from desecration by an imperialist, capitalist, militarist state. "Kū Kiaʻi Mauna," they chant. "We plan to be here as long as Mauna Kea needs us." Thousands responded to this call. For more than eight months, Kānaka gathered to defend the Mauna. They danced and chanted, organized a university, built a small city to house and feed the protectors, and their allies came from across Hawaiʻi and Oceania to join them in struggle. They used Kapu Aloha: disciplined, non-violent, love-filled resistance, to build a movement, to make a revolution, to plant the seeds of a new and old sovereignty.

What is the meaning of these two scenes of anti-racist, anti-colonial struggle in Hawaiʻi? What do we learn as we watch these people's movements call out and respond, each to the other's calls, with mutual understanding and care? How do the rallying cries "Black Lives Matter" and "Kū Kiaʻi Mauna" speak to and of one another? How do they manifest and contest a shared oppression? How do they envision and enact solidarity and coalition across the Hawaiian sovereignty and

Black liberation movements? What vision of the future do they imagine and portend?

The familial relationship between Black Lives Matter and Kū Kiaʻi Mauna begins with its origin in slavery, colonialism, and empire. The American nation/ empire was and is established and constituted through the plunder, extermination, and exploitation of human beings. The United States Constitution made property ownership basic to individual freedom. The nation's economic growth and territorial expansion were achieved through slave labor and dispossession of Indigenous peoples. Racism and the narrative of Black inferiority were essential to the hegemony of a Constitution that claimed to "establish justice" while its provisions valued property over human life.

The very presence of Black human beings represented a revolutionary challenge to a nation whose law made ownership of Black bodies essential to white freedom. The defiance of Blacks who ran away by the thousands were concrete challenges to the system of slavery. They defied its power. They robbed its profits. They challenged the primacy of property over humanity as well as the ideology of Black inhumanity that rationalized the Constitution's contradictions.

The Mauna Kea movement articulates and enacts a similar radical challenge to American empire. The empire's law begins with a premise, an assertion, about the justice of existing title in property. The law grants the State title to the land and makes the Mauna's protectors trespassers who deny the owner the right to exploit his property. The Protectors contest the law's premise on two levels. First, their protest makes a sovereignty claim that invokes international law to demonstrate the illegality of the overthrow of the Kingdom of Hawaiʻi in 1893 and its unilateral annexation in 1898. Second, and more fundamentally, the Protectors proclaim a worldview or ontology, a definition of the Native Hawaiian self and nation, that treats the mountain, Mauna Kea, as an animate, living being, as ʻohana, ancestor, and spiritual being. Just as my own ancestors' defiance of the law of slavery challenged the morality and justice of human property, the Protectors' enactment of Kapu Aloha defies and contests the morality of law that treats the Mauna as inanimate property that can be owned, possessed, and exploited.

Critical Race theorist Anthony Farley writes,

> The genealogy of any object of property leads back to an original accumulation . . . the violent capture of peoples and lands that must take place for there to be property, appears in the legal system as a time out of mind . . . . The Middle Passage and Manifest Destiny, the original accumulation that provides the owners the initial capital, belong to that time out of mind.
>
> Ownership divides space into mine or yours or his or hers or theirs or ours . . . .
>
> Ownership does something else as well. Ownership also makes us forget that things were not always this way. (151)

The Mauna Kea Protectors will not allow us to forget the violent capture of their lands, the overthrow, dispossession, and accumulation that transformed their ancestor, Mauna Kea, into property that can be owned. They talk back to the law's time-out-of-mind narrative that tells us things were always this way and that keeps us from imagining that things could be different. The politics and activism of Black Lives Matter and the Hawaiian Sovereignty movement are rooted in the same defiance and contestation of American empire's plunder and white supremacy's justification of that plunder.

August 20, 1972: a crowd of 112,000 Black folks fills the Los Angeles Coliseum for the Watts-Stax Music Festival, a concert to commemorate the seventh anniversary of the 1965 uprising in the Black community of Watts. A young Jesse Jackson, resplendent in a dashiki and huge, gorgeous afro, speaks of Black power and community control. "We may be in the slum, but the slum is not in us. We may be in prison, but the prison is not in us. . . . We've gathered here today to celebrate our homecoming and our somebodyness." And then, all 112,000 stand as one and raise their fists, as Jackson leads them in a call and response that marries the soul of Black Lives Matter to Hawaiian Sovereignty.

> I am . . .
> Somebody . . .
> I may be poor . . .
> But I am . . .
> Somebody . . .
> I may be on welfare . . .
> But I am . . .
> Somebody . . .
> I am . . .
> Black . . .
> Beautiful . . .
> Proud . . .
> And must be respected . . .
> I must be protected . . .
> I am God's child . . .
> When we stand together . . . what time is it?
> [Nation time!]
> When we stand together . . . what time is it?
> [Nation time!]
> What time is it?
> [Nation time!]
> What time is it?
> [Nation time!]

Twenty years later, and three thousand miles across the Pacific, Haunani-Kay Trask stands before her Kanaka brothers and sisters at a commemoration of the centennial of the overthrow of the Hawaiian Kingdom. She echoes Jackson's call and response. "We are not American," she calls, reminding her audience that empire has imposed American identity upon them, stealing not just their land, but the human right of self-governance and self-definition. Her brothers and sisters respond to her call, "We are not American," affirming their sovereignty, proclaiming their right and competence to rule themselves, renouncing white supremacy's assertion that Kanaka lives are neither capable nor worthy of self-governance, of self-definition.

There is a final lesson of relationship to be found in these scenes of sibling movements—the lesson and practice of genealogy. Genealogy is relational. Identity is contingent, strategic, and always shifting. It weaves together physical, spiritual, and social ties to place and people to land and sea. Dr. Heoli Osorio speaks of an intellectual/activist genealogy, of her own teachers, taught by Haunani-Kay Trask, who introduced Fanon, Malcolm, and Angela Davis to her students as family. When we do the work of justice together, when we answer one another's call to join our several separate struggles, we learn justice from one another and we learn that those struggles are one. We discover that we are related. We choose this family.

"Black Lives Matter!" "Kū Kia'i Mauna!" "I am Somebody!" "We are not American!" "Fuck White Supremacy!" "It's Nation Time!" "Kapu Aloha!" Each of these rejects the primacy of property, ownership, plunder and profit, and white supremacy's narrative that denies the beauty, love, and worth of our lives. Each also imagines a future where we are sovereign because we continue to struggle, where we learn to love one another, to love the land, and love ourselves over and over again, where we are sovereign because we choose the family and lāhui of freedom fighters.

What time is it?

Nation Time!

Work Cited

Farley, Anthony. "The Station." *After the Storm: Black Intellectuals Explore the Meaning of Hurricane Katrina*, edited by David Dante Trout, The New Press, 2006.

Charles Lawrence is Professor Emeritus of Law, William S. Richardson School of Law.

"If people aren't locking rocks together, we ain't got a story"

Pōhaku by Pōhaku, Connecting Stories of Community Building

Kēhaunani Abad and Ryan "Gonzo" Gonzalez

Some people cleared mangrove, passed rocks from person to person, and locked them together in thick walls, reestablishing fishponds and building communities in the process.

Some focused on the poetic and scientific expressions embodied in mele, oli, and hula, taking on kuleana to mālama relationships among the many forces and facets in nature upon which our lives depend.

Some taught toddlers 'ōlelo Hawai'i as others engaged youth through culture and 'āina, with both efforts giving rise to a Hawaiian education system that has grown a new generation of 'āina- and community-dedicated leaders.

Some who grew up through this system put their lives on hold, and stood boldly as kia'i on one of the tallest mountains in the world, through the blazing heat and biting cold, sacrificing everything to stand in aloha for our 'āina.

These seemingly scattered stories from across our pae 'āina have been generations in the making. They are interconnected parts of a foundation that's been built person by person, place by place, pōhaku by pōhaku, upon and among niho stones set centuries ago.

We are writing as humble scribes and mediamakers in the behind-the-scenes work of our lāhui. As storytellers it's our kuleana to halihali or transmit these stories, amplifying the voices of those on the front lines who are doing the heavy lifting, expanding their reach and influence through the power of media.

* * *

As Maunakea kia'i assembled at the Pu'uhonua o Pu'uhululu in July 2019, and the largest organized kanaka 'ōiwi movement in recent history was about to begin, the State's communications and media advisors were unprepared—stuck in the past, relying on their old game plan of live press conferences on statewide TV and traditional news programs slotted in set time frames. Their July 19 press conference painted a picture of a lawless crowd and divided leaders. Officials concluded by stating that "The Puʻuhonua has fallen apart."

And who could have blamed them for trying to share such a story? For decades, mainstream media had been depicting Hawaiians as unreasonable radicals fighting the system or each other. Activists' ten-minute interviews became ten-second soundbites, stripped of complexity or analysis. The mainstream media guarded the microphone, and even the best journalists were sometimes reined in by higher-ups, mindful of advertisers' wishes and media owners' politics.

The State underestimated the skill of humble, often young community leaders grounded in Hawaiian cultural traditions, long nourished by pōhaku of previous generations. These kiaʻi stood confidently and passionately before and behind the cameras, deftly using social media, a space where the masses were within a click's reach. During the peak of the 2019 Maunakea stand, millions of people were tuning in to several kanaka-curated social media profiles fed by a coordinated array of mediamakers, the ripples of each new post swelling and rising like a mighty wave rolling out far and wide. The State and corporate narratives of undisciplined, divided, and disorganized kānaka fell flat.

Watching videos of life at the Puʻuhonua, people could see for themselves an orderly community functioning well under clear rules and inclusive roles. They saw how the community-resourced puʻuhonua provided free food, free health care, free education, free child care, free kupuna care, and shelter for all who were greeted warmly by its embrace. The hundreds of thousands of dollars the TMT spent to blanket the airwaves with paid ads could not dampen what the community was creating out in thin air.

From behind an office desk, State officials issued a further statement contending that the Department of Transportation (DOT) controlled Maunakea Access Road and therefore had the jurisdiction to clear it. Braving extreme mauna conditions, kiaʻi broadcasted live from the middle of that road, maintaining that the Department of Hawaiian Home Lands (DHHL) owned it and was bound by law to support the cultural well-being of its native Hawaiian beneficiaries—such as many of the kūpuna encamped on the roadway. Through online videos and written pieces by attorneys and researchers, kiaʻi revealed that the DOT had no authority to clear the road and that the DHHL had shirked its legal obligations. Twenty years ago, this "controversy" might have only found a public platform during court arguments, *after* arrests had deactivated and vilified those involved.

Unwavering on many fronts, through years of legal struggles, multiple mauna standoffs, and battles over media narratives, kiaʻi have stood steadfast on their foundation. On the mauna, they stood through the constant threat of State-sanctioned violence and through the challenges of maintaining an encampment for months on end. Only a once-in-several-generations global pandemic, a crisis that has brought the entire world to its knees and "business as usual" to a grinding halt, could prompt a pause in their stance.

While global leaders and State officials struggle to get our broken economy "back on track," a few Maunakea kia'i engaged in conversations about how the core beliefs guiding their mauna efforts could lay the groundwork for a compelling response to our COVID crisis. To advance this vision, they reassembled a handful of the same people engaged in protecting Maunakea, including a few members of the mauna media team.

Zooming over mobile phones and laptops, this small band of kānaka created a process to empower community voices to envision a reset of Hawai'i's economy: the 'Āina Aloha Economic Futures (AAEF) initiative. Motivated by an unwavering recognition of the value of our ancestral foundation and the collective intelligence of communities, this effort seeks to achieve a hulihia of Hawai'i's economy and political system, placing 'āina and community well-being at the forefront.

After only a few months, AAEF has evolved into a promising community-led process bringing together thousands of individuals, senior policymakers, businesses, and organizations large and small who have signed on to support the initiative's commitment to environmental resilience, local sustainable food and energy systems, regenerative industries, capacity building for Hawai'i's residents, and cutting-edge innovation as tools for advancing ancestral values. Although technology helped make this happen quickly, the real force moving this initiative forward has been the community's amplified voices and collective strength, powered by shared kuleana and commitments to aloha 'āina.

The potential is so compelling that even the mainstream media are producing stories about the community-driven effort, government bodies are adopting the initiative to inform their decisions and policymaking, and both are providing platforms for AAEF voices in this time of hulihia.

Throughout this upheaval and the uncertainty surrounding the future, we have all been forced to consider what will remain standing, what will be shored up, what will be taken apart, and what will be built anew. As we look forward, there's great promise in stories whose first few moving chapters we are seeing now.

A sixth-grade Kualapu'u Elementary robotics team, competing before an audience larger than the population of their home island of Moloka'i, capturing second place in an international competition.

High school students of Hālau Kū Māna Charter School powerfully expressing their convictions of aloha 'āina through mele and hula while winning the Malia Craver Hula Kahiko Competition.

Ingenious Hawaiian cultural practices and 'ōlelo brought to life by the elementary students of Kula Kaiapuni o Maui ma Pā'ia through a reenactment of the mo'olelo of 'Ai'ai, the original architect of Hawaiian fishpond technologies.

* * *

The rising generations today are standing on firmer ground, learning lessons and honing skills that Hawai'i and the world will need to thrive. And they're teaching us too, as their stories are reaching millions in Hawai'i and beyond, even increasing enrollments in Hawaiian-focused schools. People are living and sharing the value of what we as kānaka have always had to offer—most importantly, solutions to some of the most vexing challenges threatening the short- and long-term viability of humanity on this Earth.

We naturally see ourselves along halihali lines, fulfilling our personal kuleana to hāpai pōhaku, recognizing that our individual role only has value when part of a cohesive community. We strive to have the kind of relationship with places that allows us to ensure that they are thriving, and nourish them when they're not. We love creating things *with* nature and of nature. We see places as people, as 'ohana, as the most precious kūpuna from whom we can learn, and who, when cared for, will continue to nurture us. And we make room for more, adding their strength to our lines moving pōhaku forward.

With each story transmitted out across the universe, we invite more people, from wherever they may be, to share in the work and join in to halihali pōhaku. With every pōhaku thoughtfully carried and locked into place, we find ourselves among deeply embedded layers, firmly set generations before us. When we do this, we continue to strengthen a foundation from which we can build a better world.

Alongside a skilled team in the Kealaiwikuamoʻo Division at Kamehameha Schools, **Kēhaunani Abad and Ryan "Gonzo" Gonzalez** support collaboration among the seventy-plus schools and organizations of Kanaeokana. One of their primary kuleana is to amplify moʻolelo of, by, and for the lāhui through media, design, and technology. In relation to Maunakea, the authors and Kanaeokana are part of a larger Nā Leo Kākoʻo team, whose collective efforts are referred to in this essay.

Wednesdays with Grandma

Shelley Muneoka

"You're gonna miss me so much when I die."

I put my fork down and looked at my grandma. She was looking down, pushing her steamed fish around her plate. I picked my fork up again and joined her, with tears in my eyes and a lump in my throat.

"I really am."

It sounds callous to say that this was not always the case, but it is the truth. For many years, contact was largely limited to major holidays and birthdays. After her eldest daughter, my mom, died suddenly, we struggled to keep in close contact. Now we share weekly meals, dishes that teleport us to the weekly Sunday dinners of my childhood. Now I have a recorder and the presence of mind to ask about what brands she likes, the right cut of meats, the order of how to put everything together, and perhaps most importantly, the family stories that go with the food.

Like sweet and tangy pigs' feet, made with special Chinese black vinegar. I've always loved this dish, but I never knew that it's made for new moms after giving birth. Grandma jokes that when she gets too old to cook, it will be my job to make these dishes for her. She's eighty-seven now, and talks freely about a possible future when she will need more assistance with her daily activities, and indeed, about the inevitable day when she will die. Somehow we've fostered a relationship so safe we can talk not only about death, but about life too.

It's taken years for us to get here. In the early days of my visits, things were very businesslike. She'd only call if she had an appointment. I'd pick her up, take care of the errands, and bring her home. But over time, the scheduled visits evolved into a weekly standing visit. I began blocking out half a day to take care of anything she might need to do. She loves not having to check with me first before scheduling appointments, because she knows that Wednesdays are for her.

Slowly, the chill between us began to thaw, and the new schedule gave us spaciousness in our interactions. Time to just talk story, and the permission to be in whatever kind of mood we might find ourselves, have been the keys to deepening our relationship. Together, we've seen the #MeToo movement spread like wildfire, increased visibility for transgendered people through Caitlyn Jenner's story, Colin Kaepernick kneel in protest of police brutality, an uprising centered on the protection of Mauna Kea, and now the coronavirus epidemic—and we've talked about all of it and more.

I never could have imagined these kinds of critical conversations happening between us. And they would not be possible if not for the easy pace of mundane tasks like trips to Costco and weekly grocery shopping.

We don't just talk politics, we discuss family stuff too—aspirations, dreams, fond memories, secrets, regrets, friendships, and deaths. She tells me stories about growing up on Kauaʻi as the middle child of sixteen siblings, and about her dreams beyond being a wife and mother. She shares stories about what kind of person my mom was, and simple tidbits like songs or toys she loved as a child—stories I never knew I had to mourn. And I've shared what it was like to grow up without my mom, and the events that transpired in the years after her death, before my grandmother and I became reacquainted.

Coded in these stories is important information about family and community, which helps me move through a world that feels increasingly difficult to hold together. One day at the kitchen table she declared—

"Guess what? This morning, I woke up and while still in bed I listed out every fruit tree I can remember in our yard, growing up in Olohena."

I could never find this level of detail in an archive. Grandma's family used to give duck eggs to a neighbor who would make a special sponge cake out of them. Connecting raw materials with the people who have the specialized knowledge and skills for using them—do we continue this practice today? In elementary school, they had Grandma and the other kids gather wild guavas and learn how to make jam. Where can young people today learn life skills such as food growing, foraging, and processing? And what do we risk if we don't teach them?

Spending this time with my grandma has changed how I think about aging. She often jokes with me that getting old is not for the faint of heart. The challenges range from daily aches and pains, to coping with the gradual loss of some functions like her eyesight, to the heartache of losing friends and family to death. But she's shown me that there is so much more to later life—that we can be full of creativity and curiosity well into our eighties. It's been a true pleasure to help bring her creations to life—whether by buying paints (or a blowtorch) to complete her paintings, or gathering ingredients for a recipe she saw on Pinterest.

She's taught me about the gap between knowing the facts of someone's life and actually knowing a person. She's shown me that aging is the culmination of our entire lives, and to take a long view about decisions before me today. She reminds me that I am flush with choices and opportunities that were not available to her at my age. She's shown me how to face new limitations with grace and new technologies with zeal. She tells me stories about being the tallest in her elementary school class, and therefore the designated person to stand on the little stool by the telephone pole to use the call box outside. She also gives me tips on how to drop a pin on Google Maps so I can find my car at the mall.

For the last three years, I've worked half-time at Hā Kūpuna, the National Resource Center for Native Hawaiian Elders, housed in the UH Mānoa School of

Social Work. We disseminate statistics and anecdotes about long-term care needs and preferences of Native Hawaiian kūpuna, and about their health and life expectancy disparities. All my grandparents are my unwitting research partners, helping to remind me how diverse the experiences of kūpuna are.

Studies struggle to find representative samples, since people who are doing well may be more likely to volunteer to participate. There are other considerations as well. Do the findings reflect elders living in a rural and an urban setting? How does socioeconomic status play a role in one's health status? What impact does aging have on family culture and values in a multiethnic family? How has colonialism impacted families differently?

When I zoom out and re-imagine eldercare in a post-COVID-19 world, I hope that more families will have the kind of time I'm sharing with my grandma. So many of the challenges older people face could be addressed through quality time with family members. A weekly visit could help with social isolation, transportation, and food insecurity. Though social agencies or private providers offer some of these services, quality time with a family member is ideal, because professional workers—or family caregivers squeezing in visits around full-time work schedules—may struggle to find spaciousness in their time together. Professional caregivers can be godsends, providing specialized skills and respite for exhausted families. But they often meet care recipients when they are experiencing limitations. The shared history, present, and future of family members or long-time friends change the quality of interactions, adding a natural relevance and meaning to stories.

Unfortunately, it is unlikely such arrangements can become commonplace as long as Hawai'i's cost of living stays so high. Many families can't spend time on what they value most, because they're forced to prioritize paying bills. It was painful to head to work each morning, driving away from my grandparents, when I really wanted to drive to them. To clear time for my grandma, I left a full-time job, and lucked out on an affordable apartment with a roommate. I'm not sure I could do this if I had children to care for.

I've come to understand spacious time with kūpuna as much more than a personal indulgence. If we want to avoid hitting reset with each and every generation, we need to *intentionally* spend intergenerational time together, to learn about our pasts, presents, and futures. We need to hear not just the facts and figures, but the feelings and philosophies. I hope that by forcing us to reorder our day-to-day lives, COVID-19 has given us an unexpected chance to spend time differently—with family, reprioritizing what matters most.

Shelley Muneoka is a kanaka maoli woman born and raised in He'eia Uli, in Ko'olaupoko, O'ahu. Shelley works at Hā Kūpuna: The National Resource Center for Native Hawaiian Elders, and continues to share meals and mo'olelo each week with her grandma.

We Are Art

Mary Therese Perez Hattori

I irensia na'lå'la' i espiritu-ta.
Our heritage gives life to our spirit.

CHamoru proverb

"Nana, how do you say 'art' in CHamoru?" I asked my mother. She laughed, paused thoughtfully, and said, "Kustombren i CHamoru"—the customs of CHamoru people, who like other Pacific Islanders, do not view art as distinct from cultural expression. Creative cultural practices are embedded within communities, reflecting collective identities and values. Our creative expression communicates Indigenous wisdom to diverse communities, celebrates the best elements of our cultures, and helps us connect to other native peoples with spiritual affinities and shared values. Doing what is best for the collective rather than the individual, respect for elders, living in harmony with the natural world—these are life-affirming, value-generating customs of Pacific Island heritage that could mitigate the societal problems we are currently facing.

I am authoring this essay three months after a disaster declaration for Hawai'i due to the COVID-19 pandemic. This contagion triggered stay-at-home orders and physical distancing measures, presenting culture bearers with tremendous challenges and exciting possibilities. After months of preparation, vital community activities such as the Festival of Pacific Arts, the Merrie Monarch Festival, the Cultural Animation Film Festival (CAFF), and the Celebrate Micronesia Festival were postponed. But while producing material and performative art for these celebrations has been suspended, the pandemic cannot halt our creative practices. We are motivated more than ever to live as fully as possible, be our best selves, and enrich the world with our cultures. People have deployed technology and activated human and computer networks to overcome restrictions on physical assemblies by enabling gatherings in virtual spaces. We can involve people whose inclusion in face-to-face events was prevented by geography, health, or financial concerns. Organizers from Micronesian communities in Hawai'i and the Bernice Pauahi Bishop Museum are envisioning a virtual Celebrate Micronesia Festival in 2020, with performances pre-recorded on the museum grounds, panel discussions about pandemic-related issues, artist interviews, poetry readings, and educational videos. New virtual events such as the Hawai'i International Film Festival's HIFF@Home, CAFF for Kids, and CAFF 2020 will replace physical film festivals.

Started in 2017 as a collaboration between myself, George Siosi Samuels, the Cultural Animators Network, Michael Q. Ceballos of Twiddle Productions, and the Honolulu Museum of Art's (HoMA) Doris Duke Theatre, CAFF showcases cultures from around the world, presenting stories that are entertaining and enlightening, and demonstrating animation's power to give voice to others and enable stories to be told in new ways. Described in 2018 as "a nascent forum for creative expressions of cultural identity and practices in animation" (Bennett), the festival features stories such as "The Meaning of Māhū," from the PBS documentary *Kumu Hina*, which teaches about Hawaiians who embody both male and female spirit; and *Tongues*, a documentary about language preservation from the Native American series *Injunuity*.

Since 2017, the festival has grown in terms of films, cultures, and community partners. The 2017 festival screened thirty-nine films representing seventeen cultures, and involved six community partners. The 2019 festival featured forty-nine films and thirty-eight cultures, including Hawaiian, Taiwanese, Indigenous Australian, Brazilian, Athabaskan, Japanese, Tongan, Maori, Bolivian, Senegalese, Sāmoan, Mexican, Ghanaian, Filipino, Gaelic, Okinawan, Polish, LGBTQ, Zuni, Inuit, and Korean. We had ten community partners from different sectors: entities promoting visual arts, including UH Mānoa's (UHM) Academy for Creative Media, Kapi'olani Community College's New Media Arts Program, Pacific Islanders in Communications, DreamFloat Hawai'i, Miyu Distribution, and Hawai'i Women in Filmmaking; and organizations dedicated to education and empowerment, including the UHM Center for Pacific Islands Studies, Lady Pasifika, Access to Independence, and Raatior Ventures. Through these alliances, organizations support each other.

CAFF became a family affair, with Michael's sisters Valerie Rios Ceroni and Margie Ceballos Navarro joining the team. Valuing family above all else, Val and Margie enhanced programming with more family-oriented films, expanded the cultures represented to include people with disabilities, and secured films from more youth. CAFF 2019 was dedicated to the memory of Justin Ceballos, Margie's special needs son, who passed away that year. We are now preparing for the 2020 festival, making selections from over one hundred films.

Discussing themes in creative pieces is a way for societies to address critical questions and emotions. CAFF discussions address community engagement, financing cultural projects, preserving languages, intellectual property, and women's issues. Partnering with the Hawai'i Council for the Humanities, HIFF engages audiences in dialogues with filmmakers, and CAFF 2020 will offer discussion guides to encourage families to have multigenerational conversations about issues raised in the films.

CAFF is one of many cultural festivals that are free for film makers and audiences, making the arts more available to communities who may not feel comfortable in galleries or museum spaces reserved for art alone—venues, many with colonial histories, that often lack inclusivity and diversity. Informal exhibits hosted by local businesses also increase access to the arts. Coffee shops and restaurants offer display spaces for artists, connecting them to community members who may not attend formal exhibitions. For example, Stan Glander, President and CEO of Walnut Street Hospitality Group, the owner of Kono's Restaurants and The Surfing Pig Hawai'i, a restaurant in Kaimukī, has dedicated prime wall space to art, and hosts talks with featured artists. "I was a drummer in a band, always looking for a place to play," Stan explains. "The venues were limited in number. I'm motivated to give anyone a chance at anything if they show an interest." Regarding his restaurant, "It's not about eating," he says, "it's about getting together, connecting, talking . . . . If there's beautiful art there to discuss, to trigger imagination, that's great." As they enter and leave the dining area, guests must pass the exhibits, and often pause to discuss the art. These are creative ways for the arts and business to support each other, and to enhance the communities in which they live and work.

Cultural films such as those shown at CAFF are especially important to diverse communities who have experienced loss through colonization. For millennia, Guam's CHamoru people thrived, enjoying a matrilineal society. The objectification, exotification, and subjugation of women occurred only after Spanish missionaries, Japanese invaders, and American colonizers arrived. I grew up in a culture steeped in the value fuetsan famalåo'an, the power of women, never experiencing sexism until I moved to the US. Cultural films also empower native peoples to assert identities underrepresented in media. As a child, I loved to escape into the worlds of books and film, though I found little resonance with characters with blue eyes, blond or auburn-hued hair, and odd names like Dick and Jane. I struggled to make meager connections to characters like Pippi Longstocking (we both have freckles and unruly hair) and Judy Blume's Margaret (we both had conversations with God). I was elated when in my teens, I discovered Marvel comics, and the X-Men's Ororo Munroe, or Storm. Brown-skinned with long, dark hair, Storm reminded me of the CHamoru Fu'una, a creator-being. Ororo's attunement to the forces of nature reminded me of the strong relationships islanders have with the environment.

I was deeply affected by one of HIFF's and CAFF's features, *Maisa: The Chamoro Girl Who Saves Guåhan*, about a girl who, along with the women of Guåhan, saves the island from a monster. In CHamoru with English subtitles, the film is a collaboration between Twiddle Productions, the Guam Department of Education, elders, students, CHamoru and Hawaiian artists, and animators. Such projects allow ancient cultural values to come through to the present, motivating change in the future. Maisa has engendered pride in many CHamoru, and inspired production of more art, including this poem celebrating women:[1]

Fuetsan Famalåo'an: An Anthem to Women

With my breath
I speak
I sing
I chant

with breath that vibrates
from powerful and ancient sounds
fino' i lina'la-ta, words of our life
the language of my people.

In my breath
is the collective power of CHamoru women, fuetsan famalåo'an
from the first creator-woman Fu'una
of antes na tiempu, the time before time
from our maga'haga, women of power
to generations of mañaina, wise elders.

My breath is my ink
with which I craft words

words of recognition
words that heal
words that light the path for others
that clear the path for others
words that create futures.

I am LIFE
LINA'LA

I am STRENGTH
MINETGOT

I am LOVE
GUINAIYA

May we all experience love, strength, and life in creative cultural practices celebrating our diverse communities.

Note

1.   Poem originally published as "Fuetsan Famalåo'an: An Anthem to Women" in *Yellow Medicine Review*.

Works Cited

Bennett, Elizabeth. Review of The Cultural Animation Film Festival. *The Contemporary Pacific*, vol. 31 no. 2, 2019, pp. 586–88.

Hattori, Mary. "Fuetsan Famalåo'an: An Anthem to Women." *Yellow Medicine Review: A Journal of Indigenous Literature, Art & Thought*, 2019.

A daughter of Guåhan (Guam), **Mary Therese Perez Hattori** is one of nine children of Paul Mitsuo Hattori, originally of Kalihi, and Fermina Leon Guerrero Perez (familian Titang) of Chalan Pago. Dr. Hattori works for the East-West Center and is affiliate faculty for the University of Hawai'i.

Lessons from Aloha ʻĀina Activism

Visioning and Planning for Our Islands and Communities in the Wake of COVID-19

Davianna Pōmaikaʻi McGregor, Noa Emmett Aluli, and
Rosanna ʻAnolani Alegado

Hulihia

The Kāne rains that flooded Hāʻena and the eruption of Pelehonuamea in Puna in 2018; the emergence of Kūkiaʻimauna as a movement to stop the TMT on Mauna a Wākea; the rising Kanaloa of King Tides; and the COVID-19 pandemic—all are signs of an intense period of hulihia, a phase of upheaval signaling both crisis and opportunity leading to transformative change. We are living in the time when our akua/natural elemental cycles and phenomena are rising as the consequence of and a counterbalance to the cumulative damage wreaked upon the earth beginning with the industrial revolution and culminating in the globalization of capitalism. These events are the bellweather, the ouli (or augeries) that humans are not acting in harmony. Imbalance in the activities of kānaka (humans) has led to an imbalance of the akua, manifested in hulihia. As kānaka, we must accept that we are entwined with, not separate from the Earth, and expand our understanding of and respect for global systems and cycles to achieve balance and sustainability on our islands for future generations.

Living in balance with nature with respect and aloha is the Hawaiian belief and practice of aloha ʻāina. Together with the Edith Kanakaʻole Foundation, the Protect Kahoʻolawe ʻOhana revived this understanding of aloha ʻāina through the movement to stop the bombing and heal the island of Kanaloa Kahoʻolawe. Integral to this movement was a process through which we as kānaka reconnected with nature's elemental forces that our ancestors honored as akua. From Kanaloa Kahoʻolawe to Mauna Kea, we are now into the third generation of kānaka committed to aloha ʻāina and upholding a kapu of aloha. Our lessons from aloha ʻāina activism, as well as tourism's utter failure to sustain Hawaiʻi's economy, now inspire us to redirect and realign Hawaiʻi's overall economy. We must move away from extractive tourist activities, and toward an economy rooted in sustainable aloha ʻāina principles and best practices.

We now share our experiences, the lessons derived, and their implications for the future.

Kanaloa Kahoʻolawe

Noa Emmett Aluli, MD

My manaʻo, begun by my great grand-aunt Emma Aima Aʻi and her husband Joseph Nāwahī, leaders of the Hui Aloha 'Āina (Hawaiian Patriotic League) and editors of the *Ke Aloha Aina* newspaper, led me to Molokaʻi and Kahoʻolawe and reconnected me with our akua Kanaloa and Lono and my own kuleana of aloha 'āina. The occupation of Kahoʻolawe in 1976 was originally planned to draw Congressional recognition to the reparations and restitution claims due Kānaka 'Ōiwi (Native Hawaiians) because of the illegal overthrow of our Kingdom. When we got there, however, we felt a deep cultural connection, and became driven to preserve the island as a spiritually and culturally significant place. As suggested by Aunty Edith Kanakaʻole, the Protect Kahoʻolawe 'Ohana was organized in a Hawaiian manner, as an extended family with a cause. We chant oli and conduct cultural protocols gifted by the Edith Kanakaʻole Foundation that call upon Lono for the Makahiki rains and Kāne for the nāulu rains to heal and green the island. We chanted for Kanaloa to remove the US Navy's destructive force. Fishers evoke Kūʻula with offerings at fishing koʻa. On the island, we observe a kapu of aloha for her and each other as 'ohana.

As we protested the US military's bombing of Kahoʻolawe for fourteen long years (1976–1990), we ignited a cultural renaissance which radiated out, like the arms of a heʻe (octopus), to all the islands under the aloha 'āina banner. This awakening increased interest in Hawaiian language, hula, music, loʻi kalo (taro fields), loko iʻa (fishponds), lāʻau lapaʻau (herbal healing), and lāʻau kahea (spiritual healing). Lua (fighting arts), kapa (bark cloth) making, and other traditional practices reemerged. Heightened awareness and pride also took political forms, as Hawaiians fought for greater autonomy and recognition of traditional and customary practices and rights of access through Hui Alaloa (Group of the Long Trails), Nā Lima Hana o Nā 'Ōpio (Youthful Working Hands), Mālama Manaʻe on Molokaʻi (Protect East Molokaʻi); Hilo Airport, Kapu Kaʻū, and Pele Defense Fund—Wao Kele O Puna on Hawaiʻi island; and Honokahua on Maui (Hui Mālama I Nā Kūpuna O Hawaiʻi Nei/Native Hawaiian Burials Councils). All succeeded as aloha 'āina issues because we mastered grassroots organizing, won most of our law suits, and maneuvered and navigated local, national, and international bipartisan politics. We have reserved Kanaloa Kahoʻolawe from commercial development, and declared it as the first sovereign lands for the Native Hawaiian nation in Hawaiʻi Law (HRS 6-E). We have trained new generations to mālama, take care, and elevate Kanaloa Kahoʻolawe as a sacred island that continues to teach us about endurance, resilience, and sustainability. Blasted by US naval forces for five decades, the island is now a center for learning about the restoration and stewardship of our cultural and natural resources, and especially our marine resources and their sustainable harvest. I Ola Kanaloa!

We believe that the "Health of the Land, is the Health of our People and the Health of our Nation"! As one kupuna put it, "ma'a, la'a, pa'a." We've been there, done that, and will do it again—experienced, dedicated, and strong.

Pelehonuamea and Wao Kele O Puna

Davianna Pōmaika'i McGregor

When I spent my summers in Hilo in the late 1950s and 1960s, Pele was always a dynamic presence—and especially during the 1959 Kīlauea Iki eruption and the fountaining flow at Kapoho in 1960. Our family had pasture land in 'Opihikao, Puna, and we always felt that our tenure there depended upon Pele. She created Queen's Bath, Warm Springs, and Kapoho Ponds, and she reclaimed them when creating new lands. When the Kapoho flow came very close to our 'āina, we acknowledged Pele's inherent claim, and felt blessed that the flow stopped before reaching us.

The University of Hawai'i's Geothermal Project in Puna generated three mega-watts of electricity when it came on line in 1981, but it also produced noxious wastes and toxic gases. It had to be shut down. The proposed development of 500 megawatts of geothermal energy at Kahaualeʻa and later at Wao Kele O Puna was an abomination—reckless, unrealistic, irreverent, and an affront to Native Hawaiian Pele practitioners. In the contested case hearing opposing the conditional use permit for drilling in the forests of Kahaualeʻa, Dr. Pualani Kanaka'ole Kanahele testified that developing geothermal energy violates the natural law of E kua 'ā Kanawai—the edict of the burning back—that admonishes humans to respect the gestating landscapes where creation is occurring—hot spots, steaming areas, marshes, coral heads. As the hearing ended, Pele erupted at Kahaualeʻa, halting all plans for geothermal development. The Campbell Estate then prevailed upon the State of Hawai'i to substitute the pristine Wai Kele O Puna rainforest for Kahaualeʻa's now lava-covered lands. Pele practitioners formed the Pele Defense Fund (PDF), filing suits and organizing processions into the rainforest, calling upon the nature deities to protect Pele from drilling into her life form that would suck out the steam that is her life force. In March 1990, 1,500 persons reverently entered the rainforest, and 141 were arrested. The PDF also filed ten lawsuits. These actions succeeded in upholding Native Hawaiians' access rights for subsistence, and for cultural and religious purposes, ultimately terminating the large-scale geothermal/cable project (Aluli and McGregor).

In response, Campbell Estate sold the Wao Kele O Puna rainforest to the Office of Hawaiian Affairs (OHA), with the kōkua of the Trust for Public Lands as their first aloha 'āina project. OHA now manages these lands with the surrounding community, holding them like Kahoʻolawe in trust for eventual transfer to the Native Hawaiian sovereign entity.

We learned that "alter-native" energy that extracts natural resources we honor as deities on an industrial scale for a central grid violates Native Hawaiian belief systems. Geothermal energy assaults and desecrates the volcanic elemental life force that we revere as the god Pele. Because the generation plant must be on a live volcano and spews out toxic gases, it is dangerous and vulnerable to shut-downs, making it NON-renewable and UN-sustainable. Hawaiʻi seeks to wean itself from imported fossil fuel, but geothermal energy cannot be part of the renewable energy portfolio.

Wao Kele O Puna also strengthened our belief in organizing in a Hawaiian manner, with respect and reverence for our natural life forces, our akua. The preeminence of natural law—E kua ʻā Kanawai in this case—was also established. The Pele Defense Fund v. Paty lawsuit determined that Native Hawaiian traditional and cultural practices are not limited to gathering the five items listed in the 1850–51 Kuleana Act, or to the ahupuaʻa in which people live. Such practices include whatever resources are needed for traditional and customary subsistence, cultural, and religious purposes, regardless of where they are.

Challenging False Dichotomies: Culture vs. Science

Rosanna ʻAnolani Alegado

As the daughter of grassroots community organizers, I've been immersed in the aloha ʻāina movement my whole life. I remember my first trip to Kanaloa Kahoʻolawe when I was eight, participating in my first Makahiki, preparing the hoʻokupu to Lono to stop the bombing of that sacred island and bring back the life-giving rains to green the land once more. The imprint of being surrounded by those living, practicing, and perpetuating aloha ʻāina forms the foundation of my scholarship. As I have evolved as an Indigenous scholar scientist, I do not distinguish between ancestral and scientific knowledge. Integrating cultural practice into designing my hypotheses is essential.

Historically, STEM fields have failed to acknowledge their systemic racism and complicity in disenfranchising Indigenous communities. Much of this failure arises from problematic normative discourses and philosophies underpinning Western science practice. For instance, the culture of "objectivity" centered in the dominant framework of whiteness dehumanizes minoritized individuals for medical experimentation. Likewise, *terra nullius*, the myth of a pristine wilderness informing much conservation biology, has been "weaponized against Indigenous people . . . resulting in the delegitimization of our traditional knowledge and the displacement from our traditional lands" (Crawford). Such harmful applications have engendered intergenerational fear and distrust in Indigenous communities of all Western science. Such dogmatic practices continue to insinuate themselves into such struggles between research entities and Native Hawaiian communities as the

Thirty Meter Telescope (TMT) on Mauna Kea. These tensions promulgate false dichotomies, such as science vs. culture.

In the summer of 2019, a collective of scientists, Native Hawaiians, and allies from across disciplines reclaimed the narrative of what science should be used for. Foregrounding ethical concerns raised by Hawai'i communities but previously dismissed, we leveraged our unique and diverse positions to challenge the notion that the scientific community universally supported the TMT, creating space for Hawaiian scientists to own our culture within our fields, and to critique the TMT during the National Academies of Science's decadal review of astronomy (Kahanamoku et al.).

Community-embedded science requires Western science to recognize the legitimacy of other knowledge systems, and of kinship relationships to land in Hawai'i. This requires equitable, reciprocal, and dynamic partnerships between kama'āina and kua'āina and higher education researchers to produce mutually beneficial knowledge that honors aloha 'āina. Several Hawai'i organizations have developed standards for engaging with researchers. In 2014, the nonprofit Kua'āina Ulu 'Auamo (KUA) convened graduate students working across Hawai'i to articulate the challenges of community-based research. Communities want and need to collaborate with university researchers to develop solutions—but on their own terms, not as research "subjects," or as a checkbox for outreach. In 2017, KUA and the UH Mānoa Sea Grant College Program developed a guidance document, Kūlana Noi'i, for 'āina-based researchers and stakeholders. Over the past three years, Sea Grant and KUA have trained over 500 researchers in Kūlana Noi'i, proving that scholars are ready to adopt practices that align with community needs.

Collaborative knowledge coproduction will be critical to generating the solutions needed to combat climate change. Because such changes tend to be localized, Indigenous local knowledge (ILK) is critical to establishing monitoring baselines. When, for example, scientists say "it's the worst El Niño on record," they mean the Western instrument record, which goes back less than 150 years (McGregor et al.). Consulting ancestral Hawaiian knowledge through research into oli (chants), mo'olelo (histories), and Hawaiian language newspapers offers unparalleled access for expanding climate data. Between 1834 and 1949, intellectuals, political and religious leaders, historians, cultural specialists, and everyday kānaka recorded over 125,000 pages of testimony about their lives, lands, lāhui (nation), and environment in nearly one hundred newspapers, purposefully documenting the knowledge of their kūpuna (ancestors) for the benefit of their mo'opuna (descendants) (Nogelmeier). As epidemics decimated the Indigenous population, these writers preserved traditional knowledge about fishing, navigation, canoe carving, and other skills, and recorded the epics of renowned warriors and legendary chiefs to forge intergenerational links. These primary source materials not only contain data about the environment and Indigenous resource management of their own time, but function as repositories for deep ancestral knowledge reaching back centuries.

In Hawai'i and the Pacific, climate change affects the strength and predictability of our akua. Kāne, the element of heat, will be stronger, so storms and flooding will increase. Kanaloa, the ocean, will rise. As Pacific people, we need Pacific Island-specific, not continental solutions. Embracing aloha 'āina will be essential. But because our ecosystems are not the same as ka wā kahiko, having been degraded by agribusiness, subdivisions, and resort development, Western science also has its role in deconstructing and monitoring altered systems, and reconstructing improved systems.

Beyond COVID-19

At the moment that the State gradually reopens the kama'āina economy, policy and decisionmakers need to connect local and Indigenous communities with private business to partner in opening pathways for rebuilding as an 'āina momona (abundant and self-sufficient) economy. We must go beyond aspirations to implementation, building upon successful models to implement strategies for a truly sustainable economy. Tourist industry workers will need new job opportunities, retraining, investment, and capacity building.

Previously successful community-private-public efforts yield important lessons. Between 1998 and 2008, the Moloka'i Enterprise Community received more than $25 million government and private funds for twenty-five projects, including solar energy systems for 300 homes, purchasing farm machinery, and starting the Molokai Land Trust. Still functioning at the state and county level, the Enterprise Zones Partnership Program 1 provides tax exemptions and credits to encourage businesses to operate in community Opportunity Zones.

In June 2018, 120 representatives from over eighty community-based groups, nongovernmental organizations, traditional Hawaiian practitioners, private companies, and government agencies participated in the Ho'olau Kānaka 'Āina Summit. Co-sponsored by the Office of Hawaiian Affairs, Kamehameha Schools, and the Department of Land and Natural Resources, and planned with community representatives, the summit identified the three most needed forms of support as long-term funding, training, and collaboration across sectors. Addressing these needs will be key to economic recovery, and enlisting our communities in monitoring climate change indicators will be critical to planning for resilience and sustainability.

A key recommendation in the Governor's Moloka'i Subsistence Task Force Report was to establish Community-Based Subsistence Fishing Areas (CBSFA) as a DLNR designation for managing marine resources. Hā'ena, Kaua'i became a CBSFA in 2006. Mo'omomi, Kīpahulu, and Miloli'i have drafted plans and are working with DLNR on the administrative rule making to establish their own CBSFAs, which will be critical for sustaining subsistence and supporting food sovereignty in rural Hawaiian communities (Matsuoka et al.).

Over the last three decades, a new generation of aquaculture practitioners has been combining traditional practice and contemporary tools to restore loko i'a for future fish farming. Connecting and leveraging conversations regarding planning and action between such key partners as the DLNR Division of Aquatic Resources, Department of Agriculture, and the University of Hawai'i Sea Grant program will make such restorations a reality.

The Mala 'Ai 'Opio Organic Farms (MA'O) are growing high quality produce while nurturing a healthy community through a social enterprise weaving together agricultural economic development and educational programming. Its mission of community empowerment is supported by outside funds and its organic farming business revenue.

Kua'āina Ulu 'Auamo (KUA) has compiled a working list of ideas for a post-COVID-19 'āina momona economy from the community-based natural resource management networks it facilitates—E Alu Pū, Hui Mālama Loko I'a, and the Limu Hui—which touch over seventy communities statewide, as well as civil society partners, individuals, and organizations. A prominent proposal, similar to one on a national scale advocated by presidential candidate Joe Biden, is to fund a Hawai'i Agricultural, Aquacultural, Marine, and Land Conservation Corps (Stabilization phase) that would employ community members who have lost their jobs or are re-entering society in permanent, publicly funded, living wage mālama 'āina and food system jobs from mauka (production, processing, and distribution; invasive species removal; stream and ecosystem system restoration, etc.) to makai (community-based natural resource management, invasive seaweed removal, native propagation, fisheries observation and management, cleaning beaches, reef management and coral propagation, etc.).

I Ola Nā Akua, I Ola Kākou

Island-based economies require island-based solutions. When our akua (natural elemental life forces) flourish, our society and economy will flourish. Aloha 'Āina Ho'i E!

Works Cited

Aluli, Noa Emmett, and Davianna Pōmaika'i McGregor. "Wao Kele O Puna and the Pele Defense Fund." *A Nation Rising: Hawaiian Movements for Life, Land, and Sovereignty*, edited by Noelani Goodyear-Ka'ōpua, Ikaika Hussey, and Erin Kahunawaika'ala Wright, Duke UP, 2014, pp. 180–198.

Crawford, Larissa. "Environmental Scientists have a Responsibility to Reconciliation, Too." *CPSC Magazine*, 2019.

Kahanamoku, Sara, Rosie 'Anolani Alegado, et al. "A Native Hawaiian-led summary of the current impact of constructing the Thirty Meter Telescope on Maunakea." *figshare*, preprint, 5 Jan. 2020, https://doi.org/10.6084/m9.figshare.11434494.v1.

Matsuoka, Jon, Davianna McGregor, Luciano Minerbi, and Malia Akutagawa. *Governor's Moloka'i Subsistence Task Force Final Report*. Hawai'i Department of Business, Economic Development & Tourism, 1994.

McGregor, Shayne, et al. "Inferred changes in El Niño-Southern Oscillation variance over the past six centuries." *Climate of the Past*, vol. 9, no. 5, 2013, pp. 2929–66.

Nogelmeier, M. Puakea. *Mai Pa'a I Ka Leo: Historical Voice in Hawaiian Primary Materials, Looking Forward and Listening Back*. Bishop Museum Press, 2010.

Davianna Pōmaika'i McGregor, PhD, Professor and Director of the Center for Oral History, Department of Ethnic Studies, University of Hawai'i at Manoā. Member, Protect Kaho'olawe 'Ohana and Moloka'i Land Trust board.

Noa Emmett Aluli, MD, Family Primary Care Physician, Moloka'i; Medical Director Molokai General Hospital; founding member Protect Kaho'olawe 'Ohana, Pele Defense Fund, and Native Hawaiian Physicians Association; Hawai'i Advisory Board, Trust for Public Lands.

Rosanna 'Anolani Alegado, PhD, Associate Professor of Oceanography; Director, Hawai'i Sea Grant Center for Integrated Knowledge Systems; Director, SOEST Maile Mentoring Bridge Program; Vice Chair, Honolulu Climate Change Commission.

IV
Emerging Futures—
Turning Anew

*What new-old directions can we turn toward for our
source and guidance?*

What kind of ancestors do we want to become?

The Story and Sisterhood Behind the World's First Feminist Economic Recovery Plan for COVID-19

Yvonne Mahelona, Tamera Heine, Khara Jabola-Carolus, and Amanda Shaw

Coronavirus is a disaster for feminism—so said a prominent voice in White feminism that went viral during the crisis. We disagree. While COVID-19 presents an existential challenge to White feminism, it is an opportunity for transnational feminism, also known as "glocal feminism," which we understand as stretching beyond national borders, building bridges between women's struggles against patriarchy across multiple contexts. This framework is important for many women whose choices are mediated by imperialism and colonization.

After over a century of White feminism in the lead, Hawai'i's women, māhū, and LGBTQ people enjoy nowhere near the freedom held prior to the 1800s. Colonization's ongoing processes and institutions leave us ill-equipped to weather the astounding turmoil brought on by COVID-19. The crisis has worsened gender inequality. Our lives make the case against another century of incrementalist reform. It is our time to define the agenda going forward.

We reject inclusion, equality, and rights within patriarchal systems and destructive industries. We cannot delay a transition away from militarism, tourism, fossil fuels, prisons, and the commercial sex industry. Deregulation is not the answer. Reform is not the answer. *Building Bridges, Not Walking on Backs: A Feminist Economic Recovery Plan for COVID-19* is a new playbook for structural change, led by working-class, Native, and transnational values that emphasize the sacred importance of land and those qualities associated with the feminine, aikāne, and māhū.

Though the brainchild of the Hawai'i State Commission on the Status of Women (HSCSW), *Building Bridges, Not Walking on Backs* was written by a collective of women outside of government through a collaborative process. The Commission's plan is the first and (thus far) only government-proposed feminist economic recovery plan. Its publication created a global outpouring of interest, from CNN to the United Nations, which contacted HSCSW to learn about the plan's recommendations and origin story. Several nations and US states are currently considering emulating the plan. Citing Hawai'i as the inspiration, civil society groups in Northern Ireland, Canada, and parts of India have put forward their own feminist recovery plans.

The culture surrounding any government, law, or policy helps shape it. Like most radical breaks, the roots and conversations contributing to Hawai'i's feminist economic recovery plan trace back to the grassroots women's movement and the creation of AF3IRM Hawai'i in 2016. A completely unfunded, unstaffed transnational feminist organization supporting Native, Black, and immigrant women's leadership across sectors, through trust-building and visibility, AF3IRM has created a space for women, femme-identified, queer, and non-binary people to theory-build from their lives.

Because white and affluent women dominate "women's rights" spaces in Hawai'i, and politicians and the professional class of advocates are not representative of our communities, women of color must navigate gatekeeping systems built to silence, disempower, and disenfranchise us. We are told the issues rampant in our communities, even women's inequality itself, are not real. Other government agencies and COVID task forces have not adequately planned around, funded, or counteracted rampant male violence, increased sex trafficking, and interruptions to reproductive health care and caregiving.

Creating structural change that centers our experiences requires leadership backed by a movement. One of AF3IRM's most important functions is holding its organizers accountable to its working-class, Native, and transnational values. The plan was produced by women within this sisterhood, and from a group of formidable women outside of the organization: the Feminist COVID-19 Response Team.

From a Kanaka Perspective

The Feminist Economic Recovery Plan's demands are long overdue. Concrete policies such as universal guaranteed income, real onramps not rhetoric for women into green jobs, and a public maternal care infrastructure are the first needed steps toward genuine safety, sovereignty, and sustainability, especially for Native, Black, and immigrant women. Our feminism seeks to end harmful hierarchies, including settler over Indigenous.

Because we revere women and land as sacred over the profit of the privileged few, we resist a rebuilding of the economy, and demand a remaking drawn from older systems. The plan also insists on centering feminist leadership. This is important, because as grassroots feminist organizers in Hawai'i, we carry the most critical knowledge of the systems in place. We depend on them for survival. We are the ones these systems fail. We know what has not, and will never work for women.

Though we cannot rely on these systems or their leaders, we still demand accountability as we build anew. Abolishing colonial systems is not just about burning and tearing down, but about building new structures within the shells of the old. A popular 'ōlelo no'eau, or saying, for kānaka 'ōiwi is "i ka wā ma mua, ka wā ma hope"—the future can be found in the past and in our past. Particularly important to kanaka women is developing the social safety net around mothering and caregiving. Caregiving was a collectively supported integral part of the community, as were fishing, farming, and healing. These systems of distributed care beyond a Western patriarchal male-female couple have already existed. We have the perfect examples in the knowledge of our kūpuna.

Sovereignty and liberation from capitalist patriarchy looks like recalling the ways of our ancestors, and building futures where caregiving and mothering are supported. Where we can move away from systems that are unsustainable because women of color especially bear the brunt of work in the home and their own work environments. Achieving safety and sustainability for women, māhū, and those in the darkest corners of the margins will benefit everyone. All this has inspired the feminist economic recovery plan.

From a Micronesian Perspective

The plan offered, for the first time, an opportunity for Marshallese and Micronesian women to voice our concerns, and come up with our own culturally-relevant solutions. When the HSCSW encouraged us to create a taskforce, it was almost unheard of for a state agency not just to partner, to give us a seat at the table, but to provide funding for us to create and lead women-empowering community workshops. Sadly, COVID-19 has put these educational events on hold.

The pandemic has overwhelmed the women in the Micronesian community. In addition to being the primary caregivers, we must now be academic teachers, with limited English skills, little to no knowledge of school subjects, and sometimes no computer. Just helping our children with homework is a hurdle. Like many local families, we also live in multigenerational homes, and worry constantly about our elders' higher risk from COVID-19. These are added pressures on top of being furloughed or working from home, cleaning, washing, and cooking. In Marshallese and many other Micronesian families, a mother's work is never-ending. Familial, cultural, and societal obligations leave you with little to no room to think about yourself and your own well-being. Many of us go without health insurance, sacrificing our health for family needs. This is no surprise. Most of us are always in survival mode, constantly worrying about rent, food, and utilities. But from outside looking in, you may never know this. We are resilient, coming from a culture with familial values, where we pull strength from our faith, hold each other up, and discourage complaints.

We hope that this Feminist Economic Recovery Plan can be an example of what genuine and successful partnering with Marshallese and Micronesian women looks like. We want them involved in all Hawai'i policymaking, ensuring that everyone has access to health care, and interpreters are readily available in all sectors. We dream of a time when each of our unique ethnicities is recognized and celebrated outside of our community. As the plan states, having navigators work with all organizations to develop and implement programs addressing community needs would make a huge difference. Place-based childcare, financial literacy, support groups, and capacity development for youth would be good starts.

* * *

New economies require a painful birthing process. This is underway, but much work remains to deliver a transnational feminist future by building bridges across movements. Naysayers should realize that we are unshakably rooted in our history, recovering the importance of wāhine and māhū in our societies while renewing and strengthening connections with our Pacific family in the present. We are proving that the logics of women-centered systems are the key to a local and global recovery from COVID-19.

Work Cited

Building Bridges, Not Walking on Backs: A Feminist Economic Recovery Plan for COVID-19. Hawai'i State Commission on the Status of Women, Department of Human Services, State of Hawai'i, 14 Apr. 2020, https://humanservices.hawaii.gov/wp-content/uploads/2020/04/4.13.20-Final-Cover-D2-Feminist-Economic-Recovery-D1.pdf.

Yvonne Mahelona is a kanaka 'ōiwi organizer, co-coordinator of AF3IRM Hawai'i, and a birthworker and midwifery student committed to healing herself, her 'ohana, and communities by telling stories of their experiences and survival.

Tamera Heine is a proud Marshallese woman and mother to Omakkai who works and advocates for her community and her brothers and sisters in the larger Micronesian region.

Khara Jabola-Carolus is the executive director of the Hawai'i State Commission on the Status of Women, dedicated to restoring the revered status of women, femme-identified, and non-binary people in Hawai'i. She is the mother of Halepueo Kūpa'a and Laguna Kekipi.

Amanda Shaw is an independent feminist researcher and activist raised on O'ahu, with family origins in the UK and Europe via Appalachia and the Ozark mountains.

Air Pollution and the Pandemic

How Will COVID-19 Shape Hawai'i's Response to Global Climate Change?

Makena Coffman

Across the globe, commentators have conceptualized COVID-19 and climate change as "dual crises." Two insights have come to the fore. First, that the way communities have mobilized against COVID-19 reflects the urgency and necessity of how they should mobilize against climate change. Second, that the progression of the COVID-19 epidemic shows the consequences of being ill-prepared and ignoring sound science. To the contrary, much global momentum for demanding climate action has been lost (Le Poidevin), and this year's international climate change negotiations cancelled. With this in mind, in my make-shift home office, I've been considering the pandemic's impact on how Hawai'i and the world should address climate change and greenhouse gas (GHG) emissions. This grand experiment in staying put, all around the globe, will undoubtedly shape our systems as we emerge from this crisis. But lessons learned from working on climate change during the 2007–2009 Great Recession make me worry that large-scale climate action will also be harder to implement.

COVID-19 and GHG emissions

Many news articles have noted a dramatic decline in air pollution over major cities during stay-at-home orders. Many focused on the impressive NASA data documenting rapid declines in airborne nitrogen dioxide over China during the height of their lockdown. Since March, local news outlets have contacted me for a similar story for Hawai'i. But our tradewinds and other geographical features mean that human-made air pollution has never really been our problem. "So what about GHG emissions?," a journalist asked. "Can we say whether this will reduce the impacts of climate change?" I wanted to give her a positive response—everyone needs hopeful news these days—but I had to say, "Not really, this is a drop in the bucket."

The Intergovernmental Panel on Climate Change special report (2018) on limiting global warming to 1.5°C above preindustrial levels estimates that future emissions should not exceed 420 gigatonnes of carbon dioxide. To avoid catastrophic outcomes for our Pacific Island neighbors, Hawai'i's population-based share of the global carbon budget will need to be reached sometime near 2024—along with global-scale action. Almost 90 percent of Hawai'i's GHG emissions result from fossil fuel burning for energy. Energy industries, mainly electricity, comprise 40 percent, ground transportation 24 percent, air transportation 19 percent, and marine transportation 4 percent (ICF and UHERO).

With no real-time data on GHG emissions, researchers are doing their best to predict what will happen in 2020. A recent study estimated that daily global CO_2 emissions decreased by 17 percent by early April 2020 in comparison to 2019 levels. Depending on assumptions about the duration of restrictions, the decline in 2020 annual emissions is estimated to range from -2 percent to -13 percent (Le Quere et al.). For Hawai'i, the largest sector decline in GHG emissions will come from air travel, since visitor arrivals plummeted by 99 percent in May (O'Connor). I coarsely calculate that this will result in a 60 percent reduction in annual GHG emissions from air travel, about 2 MMTCO2 Eq. This is an unprecedented annual drop. Yet it only pushes back meeting Hawai'i's share of global GHG contributions by under two months. Urgent before COVID-19, decarbonization is no less so now.

Lessons from the 2007–2009 Great Recession

In 2007 Hawai'i passed its first attempt at state GHG policy in Act 234, which required achieving 1990 levels of GHG emissions by this year. Not exactly bold, but a solid start. Total emissions in 1990 were 21.3 MMTCO2 Eq., and even before COVID-19, we were on track to meet the target. When the legislation passed in 2007, emissions were at 25.4 MMTCO2 Eq. They fell to 20.2 MMTCO2 Eq. in 2010—largely due to the Great Recession. Even though the economy had recovered by 2013 (Tian), the Renewable Portfolio Standard of 2009 can be credited for further lowering GHG emissions from electricity. This is my first lesson. To keep emissions from rising with economic recovery, we must still adopt intervening climate policy. Furthermore, reducing GHG emissions through economic disaster is hardly something to celebrate. There are much more effective and humane ways of achieving emissions reductions.

Lesson two is that economic crisis can stall climate policy efforts, over concern the economy can't deal with another burden. In 2008, in response to Act 234, I wrote that Hawai'i was facing several choices: "whether to adopt a cap-and-trade system or carbon tax, whether to join a regional partnership . . . and how potential national legislation might affect the status of any state or regional partnership" (UHERO). I could write the same thing today! I am currently working on a state-sponsored study to assess the economic and GHG impacts of a Hawai'i carbon tax. People are still ruminating about whether Hawai'i should join California in the Western Climate Initiative, a regional GHG trading program. And the federal government achieved little in the way of meaningful climate legislation, and is instead backpedalling fast right now.

The year 2009 was a precipice for many policymakers teetering on the edge of taking more ambitious state, regional, and national approaches to GHG mitigation. For instance, the Western Climate Initiative had five founding member states, with many others in observer status. But during the economic crisis, things fell apart. Eleven years later, California is the only state with an economy-wide approach to GHG emissions reduction. But now GHG emissions have only accumulated further. The people of Hawaiʻi, and the other 7.8 billion people around the globe, don't have another decade to find a more convenient time for climate action. It is now.

So How Can the Dual Crises Be Addressed?

With unemployment at levels rivaling the Great Depression, and an economic crisis without a known bottom, massive federal spending to address the COVID-19 and climate change crises would be welcome. Because Hawaiʻi already has an aggressive Renewable Portfolio Standard and a pipeline of renewable energy projects, it is well-poised to move on this kind of "Green New Deal." To expedite projects, though, also requires scaling up land use and community-engaged planning. California's Desert Renewable Energy Conservation Plan, which identifies least-conflict locations within the Mojave and Sonoran Deserts for solar energy, offers a good model for analysis on species and habitats, and inclusive consultation. Such an approach to economic recovery is highly unlikely under the current US administration, but January 2021 is near. Regardless, consistent with the goal of achieving 100 percent renewable sources of electricity by 2045, ramping up planning and implementing renewable energy projects is a no-regrets strategy for Hawaiʻi.

Among the many uncertainties created by COVID-19 is its impact on transportation systems. Will shared transportation continue to have reduced ridership? This would be a giant step backwards in both expanding mobility options and their potential for GHG emissions reduction. Could there be a positive long-term outcome from learning-by-doing in remote work? I am also excited by seeing more people walking and biking around their neighborhoods. Cities across the world have increased car-free streets, creating more room for these activities. Honolulu did this through summertime Sundays on Kalākaua Avenue, which my two sons declared was the most fun they'd had "in the time of coronavirus." Redesigning public and active places could have lasting impacts on GHG emissions reductions, and create an improved sense of place. Now is a great time for Hawaiʻi to focus on bike and pedestrian infrastructure, mixed-use zoning to shorten trip distances, affordable housing near job centers, and continued telecommuting for public and private sectors.

* * *

We must still lean into climate action. Hawai'i should continue to push for renewable energy and low carbon transportation, leveraging opportunities created by COVID-19. We cannot however get sidetracked, or naively believe that actions like improved telecommuting policy, though important, can meet the scale of the challenge. Carbon-intensive markets must be addressed. Study after study shows that carbon pricing, ideally at the federal level, is the most efficient way to reduce GHG emissions. Returning generated revenues to households can support low income populations through this transition. These hard conversations need to be had, and without federal leadership, the states will have to pave the way. But we cannot lose another decade. The planet can't take it.

Acknowledgment: Thanks to Maja Schjervheim, for her help in working through my thoughts.

Works Cited

ICF and UHERO. *Hawai'i Greenhouse Gas Emissions Report for 2016*. Prepared for the State of Hawai'i Department of Health, 2019, https://health.hawaii.gov/cab/files/2019/12/2016-Inventory_Final-Report_December2019-1.pdf.

Le Poidevin, Olivia. "Coronavirus and Climate Change a 'Double Crisis.'" *BBC News*, 6 May 2020, https://www.bbc.com/news/av/science-environment-52508829/coronavirus-and-climate-change-a-double-crisis.

Le Quere, Corinne, et al. "Temporary Reduction in Daily Global CO2 Emissions During the COVID-19 Forced Confinement." *Nature Climate Change*, vol. 10, 2020, pp. 647–53, https://www.nature.com/articles/s41558-020-0797-x.

NASA. "Airborne Nitrogen Dioxide Plummets Over China." *Earth Observatory*, 2020, https://earthobservatory.nasa.gov/images/146362/airborne-nitrogen-dioxide-plummets-over-china.

O'Connor, Christina. "Hawai'i Visitor Arrivals Drop by Nearly 100% for Second Consecutive Month." *Pacific Business News*, 29 June 2020, https://www.bizjournals.com/pacific/news/2020/06/29/visitor-arrivals-continue-to-decline.html.

Tian, E. "Tourism and the Economy." Presentation Made to the Hawai'i Economic Association, 7 May 2020, Honolulu, HI.

UHERO. "An Overview of U.S. Regional and National Climate Change Mitigation Strategies: Lessons for Hawai'i." 25 Aug. 2008, https://uhero.hawaii.edu/wp-content/uploads/2019/08/Climate_Change_Overview_Oct20.pdf.

Makena Coffman is the Director of the Insitute for Sustainability and Resilience, Professor of Urban and Regional Planning, and a Research Fellow of the University of Hawai'i Economic Research Organization (UHERO), at the University of Hawai'i at Mānoa.

Our City as Ahupuaʻa

For Justice-Advancing Futures

Sean Connelly

Everyone in Hawaiʻi should be debating the meaning of urbanism—the way of living within cities. Not just about the image of being in a city with tall buildings, urbanism is about how different cities become connected and embedded into the world around them. For instance, anyone using a cell phone becomes linked to seafloor mining through city processes. Yet despite such technological advances, the urban social conditions of today are very similar to those of one hundred years ago, with intense public health challenges affecting people and the built environment then and now.

While even the idea of a city in Hawaiʻi often arouses despair, we can harness it to recover ahupuaʻa (the Hawaiian land system) as the basis for an Indigenous built environment. Recovering ahupuaʻa is the most practical and careful response to address today's pressing public health challenges, including pandemic, social justice, and climate change. As a technology of waiwai (value), ahupuaʻa recovery can help guide the people of Hawaiʻi in restoring our built environment in a way that heals history, and secures justice-advancing futures.

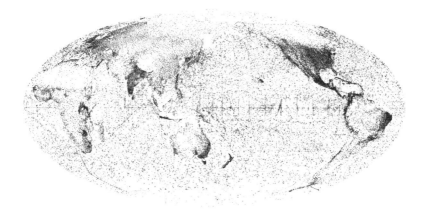

Climate sensors around the planet show the extent of urbanism. Sean Connelly, 2014.

Urbanism for Peace, 100 Years Ago

Proposed only a few years after WWI and the 1918 pandemic, the first glass and steel skyscraper was drawn in 1921 by architect Ludwig Mies van der Rohe and became the quintessential image of cities worldwide. Many people had recently lost their families and loved ones to the war and pandemic of that time. A new architecture of clarity and lightness, the skyscraper reflected a fundamental need for the human experience of urbanism to be optimistic. Many scholars dedicated their careers to discovering how cities and architecture could ideally embody a universal space of peace and public health.

O'ahu, a Giant Military Base

Twentieth-century urbanism has strayed from its historic aspirations toward peace, leaving our built environment far from healthy. Urbanism's biggest producer, the US Department of Defense, is also the world's largest employer and heaviest consumer of fossil fuels. Since 1898, the US military has also used Hawai'i's built environment to advance American urbanism globally, commercially, and technologically.

Encompassing the volcanic island of O'ahu, Honolulu is not just a capital city, but a utopian fort, where the US Indo-Pacific Command controls military operations for 52 percent of Earth's surface. Surveys of American urbanism overlook O'ahu's urban typology as a giant military base because Hawai'i's occupation and relationship to the US military remains shrouded in images of tourist beauty, and the profession of architecture in Hawai'i is complicit in military construction projects.

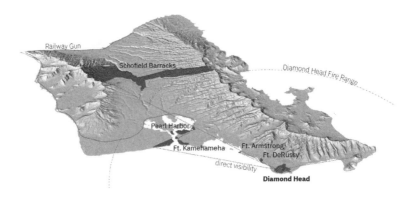

Original land defense of O'ahu. Sean Connelly, 2019.

The reconstruction of Oʻahu into a military base really began in 1906, when the US Army Corps of Engineers (USACE) broke ground on the most advanced coastal fortification system of its time, stretching from Waikīkī to Puʻuloa (Pearl Harbor). Even the Koʻolau and Waiʻanae Mountains were conceived as part of the fortification system as natural defense walls. When Lēʻahi was turned into Diamond Head Military Reservation (Fort Ruger), this tuff cone became the largest, most sophisticated star fort on Earth, with cannons that could shoot seventeen miles over the Koʻolau Mountains, and an observation tower with visibility over 25 percent of Oʻahu's land mass. Diamond Head featured the first green roof in Hawaiʻi (Fort Harlow), and the poured concrete bunkers around the crater took curved and voluminous forms decades before architects made such material aesthetically palatable for civic and residential markets. Diamond Head is a hidden cornerstone of twentieth-century American urbanism.

The USACE then filled in the Waikīkī fish ponds to build Fort DeRussy in 1909. In the 1940s, it dredged Keʻehi Lagoon's fertile reef for seaplane runways—never fully utilized—and built the Red Hill Underground Fuel Tank storage, which has leaked fuel above the aquifer today. In 1966, USACE dredged the Anahulu River at Waialua Bay to create Haleʻiwa Harbor, causing the adjacent fishpond to fill with sediment. These and many more military projects and operational training exercises have negatively affected the built environment of Oʻahu. And similar projects continue today. The USACE Ala Wai Flood Risk Management Project proposes seven three-story detention basins in Makiki, Mānoa, and Pālolo streams, and four-to-seven feet walls around the Ala Wai Canal.

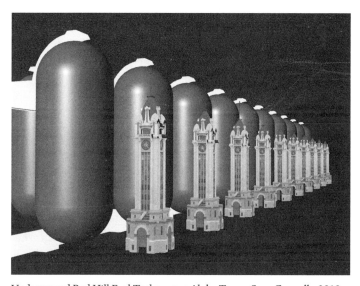

Underground Red Hill Fuel Tanks versus Aloha Tower. Sean Connelly, 2019.

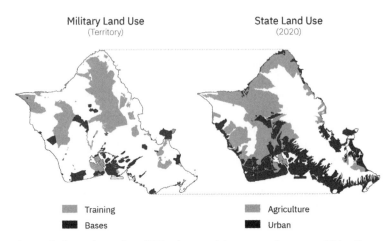

Military Land Use
(Territory)

State Land Use
(2020)

Training
Bases

Agriculture
Urban

The interlocking relationship of US military and American urbanism on Oʻahu. Sean Connelly, 2019.

The long history of US military imposition through infrastructure projects has damaged Hawaiʻi's environment, culture, and food security. A cumulative historic mapping of the US military on Oʻahu reveals how urbanism has served the military, not the people. If we compare the military's functional land use plan (housing, training, communications) established before statehood with the State land use districts (urban, agriculture, conservation) set subsequently through zoning, we can see that lands surrounding military training areas were zoned as agriculture or conservation, while areas close to military bases were zoned as urban. Especially on Oʻahu, this programmatic adjacency has been ignored, even though the life expectancy for communities in agriculture land use districts is ten years lower than in state urban zones (Holmes).

The Ahupuaʻa

Since the 1920s, urbanism scholars have stressed the importance of the *valley plan of civilization*, or mountain-to-ocean section, as the vocational space of peace. But colonialism has obstructed our understanding of how our oceanic ancestors, whether 400 or 40,000 years ago, successfully extended urbanism across many valleys. The obsolete idea that ancient Pacific Island societies did not have "cities" erased a profound history of Indigenous technological advancements in maritime navigation and transportation that are foundational to cities today. Native examples of the *valley plan* embedded in Hawaiian land use methods such as ahupuaʻa are ignored as viable city forms by architectural history.

An ahupuaʻa can be several things. A land division, usually extending from the uplands to the sea. It is also a way of life. Poetically, ahupuaʻa is architecture—producing some of the most amazing living buildings imaginable. A GIS statistical analysis of all Hawaiʻi ahupuaʻa concludes that the average ahupuaʻa encompasses a surface area of around nine square miles, and will take on as many formations as the landscape resources offer, whether hydrological, geological, political, or genealogical. When Maʻilikūkahi became chief of Oʻahu, he clarified the moku system, then in disarray, and launched a civic legacy of peace. Today more than ever, ahupuaʻa are viable forms of urbanism that must be recovered.

Ahupuaʻa Recovery: The Next 100 Years

Ahupuaʻa recovery can be described as the ecology of regaining possession of land, water, and other resources that have been lost, stolen, erased, corrupted, or destroyed. Such recovery provides a framework for an architectural approach toward achieving a culture of health and climate resilience as the basis for citymaking. Neither a nostalgic pursuit nor a utopian effort, ahupuaʻa recovery is a spatial, intellectual, and responsive approach to creating the built environment. An ecological revolution.

For infrastructure to work in Hawaiʻi, it must be culturally rooted, addressing the traumatic histories of social injustice that Hawaiians and locals have faced due to the giant military base approach to imposing American urbanism. Healing this history goes hand in hand with responding to the pandemic and climate change in ways that will redirect Hawaiʻi's economy to work for its people, and not just for visitors or the US military.

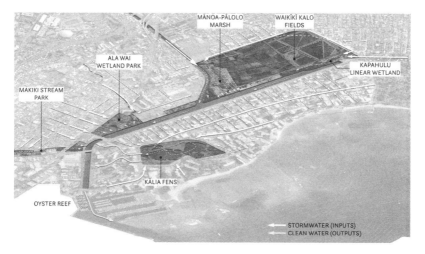

Hypothetical proposal to recover the functional hydrology of Waikīkī. Sean Connelly, 2018.

Climate change offers an opportunity to recover ahupua'a through practical infrastructures designed to secure an affordable yet resource-abundant quality of island life. By the age of six, every student should know that before US military occupation and widespread tourism, Hawai'i flowed clean, its wealth streaming through abundant forests, kalo, and fishponds that nourished its people. Our young generations believe they can recover ahupua'a. The remaking of Ala Wai Golf Course into the Waikīkī Kalo Field when the Ala Wai Canal turns 100 in 2021 is one example of shifting infrastructural upgrades to address pandemic and climate change. Transitioning the Ala Wai Golf Course, Honolulu's largest open urban space, into a system of commercially viable food production would incentivize retrofits to the streams' upland channels to clean the water. Seeing a vast and abundant kalo field in Honolulu again would be incredible.

Just reframing our approach to how Honolulu's built environment is maintained—the difference between being informed stewards clearing leaves from a stream rather than building detention basins to capture debris—could bring our framework of urbanism closer to the ahupua'a. Amid COVID and climate change, an ahupua'a approach to public health integrates ecosystem restoration (climate change), food security, and social justice. Recovering ahupua'a can help begin to repair the damages inflicted by American urbanism.

Works Cited

Dorrance, William H. "Land Defenses of O'ahu's Forts, 1908–1920." *The Hawaiian Journal of History*, vol. 29, 1995, pp. 147–61.

Holmes, Joshua R., et al. "Examining Variation in Life Expectancy Estimates by ZIP Code Tabulation Area (ZCTA) in Hawai'i's Four Main Counties, 2008–2012." *Preventing Chronic Disease*, vol. 15, 2018.

Kamakau, S. M. "Ma'ilikūkahi." *Nā Mo'olelo a ka Po'e Kahiko*. Bishop Museum Press, 1993.

Sean Connelly (b. 1984, O'ahu, Hawai'i) is an artist-architect based in Honolulu (www.ao-projects.com).

'Ohana Urbanism

Benjamin Treviño and Victoria Treviño

COVID has disrupted our experience of urban life

COVID has disrupted our position in the space-time continuum—by which we mean, it has left us examining how we use our space and where we spend our time. In April and May of 2020, our roads were quiet, our office buildings, schools, retail shops, and hotels were vacant. Our homes were full and the doors were locked—as much to keep us in as to keep others out.

Urbanism contemplates space and time. Our particular brand of urbanism is predicated on our concept of work: where work occurs, how we get there, where we spend our time when we're not there.

Hawai'i offers us cultural and historical alternatives to Western concepts of urbanism and work. In *The Value of Hawai'i 2*, Sean Connelly argued that the ahupua'a/moku systems that governed land use in Hawai'i pre-Western contact were not only urbanism, but the sustainable urbanism we aspire to today. The economic driver of the ahupua'a system was hana—roughly, but incompletely translated into English as "work."

What if, instead of work, we built urbanism around a concept of hana? To borrow from Kamuela Enos, "Hana is what we did. 'Ohana is who we did it with." To design the built environment for hana is to design it for 'ohana.

COVID may have given us a sneak preview. After all, in these times of crisis, who are we keeping in our quarantine bubbles? 'Ohana.

Existing problems with urbanism, and ahupua'a as a model

Transportation drives urban form and our urban experience—often in socially destructive and undesirable ways. For example, highways and freeways have historically been tools of racial division, and have been literally built over communities of color. Metropolitan Planning Organizations like the one Tori works for exist to ensure that the community has a process to comment on all federally funded transportation projects.

What shifted Ben's focus to transportation equity was a keynote presentation entitled "Planning While Black," which highlighted the dramatically different transportation experiences for women, LGBTQ, and people of color to those of cis white men. Transportation assets—streets, sidewalks, transit stops—are sites of both over- and under-policing for people of color. COVID highlighted how transit-dependent "essential workers"—disproportionately people of color—struggle to navigate a world that clearly grants preference to cars and the people who can afford them.

These relationships between social injustices and transportation systems should hint at some of the problematic aspects of our urban context. Ben's work as HART's Sustainability Planner has emphasized another problem: we move too much! We occupy tremendous amounts of space—empty homes during the day, empty offices at night, massive highways and parking lots in between. We consume absurd amounts of energy and fuel, and perhaps most destructive of all, our connection to place is completely severed. We live in a blur, unable to see ourselves in the context of our environment.

To accept ahupua'a as an alternative form of urbanism, we need to let go of our ideas of pavement and electrical wires, and instead recognize ahupua'a as sophisticated systems of technology and infrastructure that supported a population similar to ours today—without the Matson containers.

What did ahupua'a have to say about mobility? They were said to contain everything needed for survival within their boundaries, thus eliminating the need for the hours-long congested H-1 commutes.

COVID has eliminated those same commutes. Today we access the necessities of life with wages from work, and train for that work through school. For the luckiest among us, the necessities of daily life are once again available within the ahupua'a. Remote work and distance learning brought those activities home, and with them, brought families home as well.

The idea of 'ohana urbanism

Consider how radical "hana is what we did, 'ohana is who we did it with" sounds to our modern ear. Who among us considers our family essential to doing our essential work? Far more likely, what motivates us to work is the image of our families sitting helpless at home, starving or destitute if we cannot punch the clock. Work and school are separate in our current urbanism, and our built environment reflects that.

For some, having the whole family at home could be a nightmare. There is the challenge of trying to simultaneously house two remote jobs while also acting as a school teacher. One friend wasn't sure her son should advance to the next grade, having only had home enrichment and her untrained assistance for 25 percent of the school year. Zoom allowed some of us to work from our homes, but it did not make our kitchen tables more ergonomic. Stress from lost jobs, income, and increased time spent together in close quarters has even led to an increase in reports of domestic violence.

For others, families being home together has been a blessing. We—Tori and Ben—have always wanted to work together, and COVID had us working in the same place all day, learning about each others' projects and responsibilities in real-time, tag-teaming meal responsibilities. We've heard from others who felt the same way. A friend wrote a piece she titled "I don't want to go back," referring to days spent together with her family as "time on their side."

With months of empty buildings and roads, COVID has demonstrated the possibility of recreating our urban space to try out 'ohana urbanism. Imagine if we were to permanently retire all of the cars that were off the road at the height of the lockdowns. The island of O'ahu contains over 900,000 registered vehicles. In the US there are, on average, four parking stalls per vehicle at an average size of 320 square feet. Meanwhile, the average amount of living space per US human resident is around 660 feet. According to this back of the envelope math, *from parking alone*, O'ahu has enough square footage to accommodate 1.8 million residents—more than the population of the entire state. And that's not counting roads, offices, schools, and hotels.

We have the space we need to try out 'ohana urbanism. Those families that have benefitted from the time together are making the case for its value. So where do we start?

Timely innovations and planting the seeds of 'ohana urbanism

The experience of COVID lockdowns has seeded practices of family togetherness and innovation—practices that if continued could enable or even drive an urban reimagining.

National trends for more cooking at home and more elaborate endeavors such as sourdough breads, pickling, fermenting, and gardening have fed families while they learn together. Across the country, bike retailers cannot keep bikes on the shelves, and on any given day at Ala Moana Beach Park, you can see why. Parents teach their keiki to ride, and families enjoy outdoor recreation together.

Timely innovations such as the Kauwela Box, which includes all Hawai'i-made products and a virtual workshop to use for educational activities, solve an urgent COVID need for at-home summer educational enrichment while offering inspiration for the future. Specifically, the Kauwela Box is meant to facilitate inter-generational participation—again, families learning together.

On our home front, we focus on strengthening our relationship. We repurposed an annual goal to go out for weekly date nights into a series of virtual double dates with friends—each incorporating a romantic gesture that honors and shows appreciation for our partners. Finding that kind of appreciation, however small, goes a long way in a crowded household.

When building a new urbanism as a community, what questions are important to address together?

Our human and urban activities run up against the ecosystems on Earth. Our current levels of activities are causing the sixth mass extinction of life on Earth. The ahupua'a urbanism of the Native Hawaiian people had the opposite effect. Can we return to an urban way of moving through time and space where we proliferate life rather than extinguish it?

Investigating this question is murky—unemployment, equity, racism, tourism, climate, child care, economy—but rich with possibility—remote work, distance learning, telehealth, farm deliveries, virtual conferences, open streets.

What if we supported the idea of 'ohana as collaborators and coworkers, teachers and healers? These ideas are not unfamiliar to us—in Hawai'i and in many of our diverse traditions, they are our cultural heritage. So what if we went all-in? The result would probably be a far more radical departure in how we move, live, and learn than we might expect. Given the tidal wave of instability that our current urbanism has unleashed on us, a radical departure might be exactly what we need.

Works Cited

Connelly, Sean. "Urbanism as Island Living." *The Value of Hawaii 2: Ancestral Roots, Oceanic Visions*, edited by Aiko Yamashiro and Noelani Goodyear-Ka'ōpua, U of Hawai'i P, 2014, pp. 88–99.

Enos, Kamuela. "'Aha 'Āina Aloha," 10 Jan. 2020, University of Hawai'i–West O'ahu. Presentation.

Benjamin Treviño and Victoria Treviño have combined experience in the transportation, urban planning, and hospitality sectors. Ben currently serves as the Sustainability Planner for the Honolulu Authority for Rapid Transportation, and previously was the founding President and COO of Bikeshare Hawaii/BIKI. Tori is on the staff of the O'ahu Metropolitan Planning Organization and previously worked for Marriott Hotels in Human Resources and guest services.

Prisons—Has COVID-19 Offered Hawai'i the Road to Redemption?

Kat Brady

Justice has always been the center of my life. Growing up in the Bronx and managing an actors union in NYC for many years was great training for my life mission—to speak out against injustice, racism, oppression, and inequity. As Coordinator of Community Alliance on Prisons and working on justice issues in Hawai'i for twenty-five years, I love sharing research, promoting just and humane policies for the legislature to consider, and tenaciously advocating for those whose voices have been silenced by incarceration.

COVID-19 has spotlighted the disparities in Hawai'i's failed public health and social policies that are actually causing harm, rather than providing remedy. COVID-19 has shined a light on the dark corners of public policies to reveal the structural racism, settler colonialism, and unabashed crony capitalism upon which they are constructed.

Capitalism demands social control. The fearmongering triggered by the releases of imprisoned people, in compliance with the Hawai'i Supreme Court's order to reduce the population of jails and prisons, has been generated by politicians and law enforcement.

Fear is the weapon needed by politicians to continue Hawai'i's punitive correctional system, and it has facilitated our overcrowded criminal processing and manufacturing system. The majority of Hawai'i's imprisoned people are either pretrial detainees (innocent until proven guilty) or serving sentences for non-violent offenses. Kānaka Maoli are specifically over-represented and impacted at every stage of the system.

Hawai'i always portrayed the economy as a three-legged stool, focused on health, education, and human services, until 2011, when public safety was added as the fourth leg. This facilitated the decrease in funding the health, educational, and social services so desperately needed by communities. Now money and resources could easily be shifted to law enforcement officials, who have little to no training to address these sensitive areas.

Hawai'i's jails and prisons are populated by many people contending with mental health issues, yet the training that law enforcement and adult correctional officers receive in this sensitive area is minimal and has led to too many preventable deaths.

Placing resource officers in schools doesn't make them safer; it greases the school-to-prison pipeline. And *decreasing* desperately needed social services while *increasing* law enforcement in our most challenged communities has brought Hawai'i to this appalling place where half the families living on the street are Kanaka Maoli—houseless in their homeland.

Building more jails and prisons will not make communities safer; they have become manufacturing centers where low-level lawbreakers enter and exit as criminals. We must challenge the relationships that have fostered inequities. Prisons are inherently violent places, and recidivism evidence highlights that correctional systems do very little correcting; in fact, many people exit with advanced degrees in the "dark arts" when they return to their communities.

The dehumanization and moral disengagement exhibited by some people working in the correctional system are borne of legislative policies implemented by those in positions of power; power over a system that thrives on racism, punishment, and dehumanization.

As Angela Davis writes in *Are Prisons Obsolete?*

Since the 1980s, the prison system has become increasingly ensconced in the economic, political and ideological life of the United States and the transnational trafficking in U.S. commodities, culture, and ideas. Thus, the prison industrial complex is much more than the sum of all the jails and prisons in this country. It is a set of symbiotic relationships among correctional communities, transnational corporations, media conglomerates, guards' unions, and legislative and court agendas. If it is true that the contemporary meaning of punishment is fashioned through these relationships, then the most effective abolitionist strategies will contest these relationships and propose alternatives that will pull them apart. (107)

Hawai'i is also one of a handful of states that has been selling our imprisoned people to the lowest bidders, who run dungeons of misery thousands of miles away from families, friends, and for most of the incarcerated, far from their ancestral lands. This works well for some parts of our society, while it sows wholesale destruction to certain communities that have been relegated to the margins.

A sad example of the gross inequities in our system is illustrated by how the COVID-19 pandemic has been addressed in Hawai'i's jails and prisons. Jails and prisons have been ignored while elected officials, agency directors, and law enforcement continued to brag, "there are no cases in our correctional facilities." The month of August blew that myth to pieces with more than 306 cases of staff and imprisoned people infected at the O'ahu Community Correctional Center (OCCC) and a rising number of cases at the Maui Community Correctional Center. It is well-documented that like nursing homes and cruise ships, jails and prisons are petri dishes for infection, yet the state has turned its back on those who have no choice but to live in these unsanitary and unhealthy environments. I have been receiving desperate calls from inside and from families outside and the message is always the same: "Please don't let me/my loved one die in here."

In an April 8, 2020 letter to the Hawaiʻi Correctional Oversight Commission, Dr. Pablo Stewart, a licensed physician who is in Oʻahu's jail (OCCC) four times a week, wrote: "*Everyone* is at risk by the failure to take meaningful action in Hawaiʻi's correctional facilities."

Dr. Stewart's letter has been denied by the department and ignored by the legislature.

The misinformation promoted by law enforcement regarding the early jail releases caused fear in the community, while people were dealing with the pandemic, unemployment, and decreasing resources to feed their families. This was beyond cruel, and exemplifies what happens when the state turns its responsibilities over to law enforcement.

This law-enforcement focus has created a surveillance-focused society, training the next wave of students to feed the very hungry perpetual prisoner machine instead of building educational resources and the services needed to strengthen our families and communities. Hawaiʻi's remedy to social and public health challenges has become incarceration.

Ruth Wilson Gilmore asks: why, as a society, would we choose to model cruelty and vengeance? Yet that is exactly what Hawaiʻi has done, at great economic and social cost that has harmed and continues to harm generations of struggling families who need a hand up, not a ticket to jail.

Is this who we are?

Turning humans over to the inhumane criminal (in)justice system is not going to address the pressing issues of our time: racism, poverty, overcriminalization, climate change, economic and social inequity, and health disparities, when scarce resources are diverted to hide the real issues in jails and prisons.

Instead, we must start building the future that our children and grandchildren need and deserve.

While the COVID-19 spotlight is shining, Hawaiʻi must reimagine ways to construct the kind of people-centered and intentional communities that result in more just, healthy, and safe neighborhoods—where everyone looks out for everyone else, where police are again known as "peace officers," and where law enforcement are seen as guardians of the people rather than armed military warriors.

Another world *IS* possible.

When government systems are deconstructed, reimagined, and then reconstructed with the ideas and aspirations of the people they serve; when laws and rules are developed by the people to address community needs and are written in plain language, *then* we start to build a people's budget. A budget focusing on justice, inclusion, access, and participation is crucial to a vibrant democracy. Crafting people-centered systems in thoughtful communities, with intentional services for the people who live there, would ameliorate many of today's challenges.

Abolition is about moving beyond prisons as a way of addressing social challenges. It's about working for a better world that is built upon the needs of *all* the people; structuring an economy that funds the communities most impacted by incarceration, overcriminalization, poor health, unemployment, underfunded schools, and other social needs to lift up the quality of life for all.

We must dismantle systems of oppression that have created our multitiered society that celebrates wealth instead of health. Abolition means working to build relationships that foster sustainable, just, healthy, and safe communities. This path to equity has become clearer since COVID-19. The disparities and gross inequities in Hawai'i's systems highlighted by COVID-19 offer us a road to redemption that mandates inclusive and transformational change, not just reforms that come and go at the whim of politicians seeking reelection.

COVID-19 and the fact that the crime rate in Hawai'i has been the lowest in decades creates the perfect storm for us to take this opportunity to deconstruct the state's economy, dismantle the relationships that tear our communities apart, and work to build an equitable and just society, never returning to the racist, exclusionary business as usual.

The roadmap to redemption starts by dismantling the structure of Hawai'i's economy—a pyramid with the elite and influential at the top, the working people in the middle providing stability, while the people at the bottom struggle to survive. And Hawai'i's government has even gone further, by placing the people it imprisons outside the pyramid, as if they don't really exist.

John F. Kennedy said, "Things don't just happen; they are meant to happen." Time to invert the pyramid.

Works Cited

"Coronavirus (Covid-19) Information and Resources." Department of Public Safety, State of Hawai'i, 17 Mar. 2020, http://dps.hawaii.gov/blog/2020/03/17/coronavirus-covid-19-information-and-resources/.

Davis, Angela Y. *Are Prisons Obsolete?* Seven Stories Press, 2003.

Kat Brady is Coordinator of Community Alliance on Prisons.

Housing and Aloha ʻĀina

Beyond Building Our Way Out of the Crisis

Tina Grandinetti

"I will *never* be homeless in Hawaiʻi" answered Uncle John when I asked him why he refers to himself as "houseless" instead of "homeless." We were sitting in the shade at Kakaʻako Gateway Park, just steps away from his encampment. In front of us, blue tarp tents were packed densely onto a grass strip along a narrow sidewalk. Across Ala Moana Boulevard, blue glass high-rises towered above us, glistening monuments to speculative investment. Uncle John has lived on the streets of Kakaʻako on-and-off for almost a decade—a proud Kanaka, houseless in his own homeland. Despite years of sweeps and laws criminalizing his presence, his voice was steady as he explained his unshakeable connection to his home.

"Hawaiʻi is the place of my ancestors. I have family here. I have culture here. I have the ʻāina."

Months later, Governor David Ige issued a statewide stay-at-home order in response to the COVID-19 pandemic. But the weeks that followed made it clear that the meaning of "home" is more contentious than we might expect. Despite Centers for Disease Control guidelines stating that those experiencing houselessness should be allowed to shelter-in-place during the pandemic, Honolulu Mayor Kirk Caldwell has continued to sweep people like Uncle John from the encampments they call home. Caldwell and Ige even endangered these peopleʻs lives by shuttering public restrooms and blocking access to potentially life-saving hand-washing facilities. Things also became more precarious for people who had houses to live in. Renters received some relief through Igeʻs eviction moratorium, but experts warn that a catastrophic surge in houselessness awaits us when the moratorium is lifted.

What does it mean for our government to sweep our houseless ʻohana during a pandemic? What does it mean for a houseless and criminalized Kanaka to stand steadfast in his claim to belonging and home? And what does all of this tell us about the state of housing in Hawaiʻi? What I see is a growing gulf between *home* as an intimate part of who we are, and *housing* as a commodity and asset. Under this capitalist system, homes are commodities purchased on the market, and our ability to pay determines how deserving we are of shelter, and of life. But as Uncle John reminds us, Kānaka Maoli have long considered home as something inalienable—as ancestor, family, culture, and, most importantly, ʻāina.

Now is the time to take Uncle John's words seriously and to reevaluate how we relate to land, home, and each other. The housing crisis became unbearable long before COVID-19. Almost sixty percent of Hawai'i renters were housing cost burdened, spending thirty percent of their income to keep a roof over their head. One-third of households spent *half* of their income on shelter alone. Meanwhile, even though seventy percent of Hawai'i's housing demand comes from low-income families, entire neighborhoods were being built for the luxury market. Though this affects all of us, for some, housing is a matter of life and death. Between 2014 and 2018, 373 people died on Honolulu's streets. The average age of death was fifty-three years old—thirty years shorter than our average life expectancy.

In policy discussions about these injustices, however, housing is reduced to a numbers game. Projected housing demand suggests that Hawai'i will need 64,693 new units by 2025. But the only question ever asked is how do we build more, and faster? Governor Ige's 2018 *Affordable Rental and Housing Report and Ten Year Plan* presents the crisis solely as a matter of supply. The plan's two goals are to "increase the supply of rental housing affordable for low- to moderate-income families" and "for the remainder of the resident population" (9). All subsequent recommendations deal with meeting these production goals. Non-development solutions, such as the rent stabilization measures and tenant protection laws being passed in New York, California, and Oregon, are sidelined. The only acceptable solution is for the private sector to build, build, build—fueling further development without demanding any change in how it takes place.

Even though state reports admit that "the market is the most effective in producing high-end units" (46), rather than shifting power to tenants, the primary strategy has been to offer private developers incentives to build units for households making up to 140 percent area median income (up to $142,250 for a family of four), despite the fact that most demand comes from households making less than half this amount. Developers are rewarded for fueling displacement, as out-of-state buyers purchased nearly a quarter of Hawai'i homes in 2018.

Viewing housing purely as a commodity devalues both 'āina and working families, but again and again, public monies and lands sweeten the deal for developers, in hopes that this time, they might build something people can actually afford. And then we watch in awe and anger, as luxury towers rise into the skyline, agricultural lands become suburban subdivisions, street encampments swell, and our loved ones leave for the US. It's time to ask ourselves, do we have a crisis of supply, or of accountability?

Though I wish I could offer an ingenious policy solution, there is no easy fix. Since the Territorial era, people have been writing about a housing crisis in Hawai'i. It is not an acute ailment, but a persistent condition resulting from capitalism's deeply flawed way of relating to 'āina, and the State of Hawai'i's own denial of its occupation of Hawaiian lands and sovereignty. Housing discussions have long been confined by the needs of capitalism, and dictated by market speculation.

Breaking free will require asking new questions. The pandemic has exposed how close most of us are to losing our housing, and because of this precarity, ideas that were unthinkable a few months ago no longer seem so radical. In the United States, tens of thousands of tenants are organizing rent strikes, and thousands more are forming tenants unions to fight for stronger rights and protections. In Los Angeles, houseless families are reclaiming empty homes. In Ithaca, New York, the city council passed a rent forgiveness resolution. There are even calls to cancel rent and mortgage payments. All of these movements seek to loosen the private market's grip on our homes and to build power among people facing housing insecurity. Solutions are out there, and they are coming from the people whom we think of as the most vulnerable.

In Hawaiʻi, we know this is true, because housing and land have long been gateways for challenging systems of oppression. As Haunani-Kay Trask argued, the modern Hawaiian sovereignty movement emerged from the anti-eviction struggle at Kalama Valley. Our recent history is filled with stories of how housing precarity brought people into communities that served as puʻuhonua from dispossession, and kīpuka for greater forms of resistance. In the 1990s, Kānaka at Waimānalo Beach resisted eviction so fiercely that they secured a long-term lease from the State, and created a community that enacts sovereignty and self-governance at Puʻuhonua o Waimānalo. Houseless Hawaiians at Mākua Beach resisted eviction, and the military's bombing of Mākua Valley. And today, Kānaka women have created abundance out of scarcity at Puʻuhonua o Waiʻanae.

Stemming COVID-19's impending tide of evictions demands that we radically redefine how we think about home. The real estate experts or developers who have fueled housing unaffordability and overdevelopment of ʻāina cannot help with this. Nor can a system built to extract profit from the occupation and development of ʻāina, the dispossession of Kānaka Maoli, and the displacement of poor and working class families. Instead, we must turn to each other and build power within the spaces we have created to sustain ourselves through this precarity. The multigenerational households, where ʻohana share in the labor of raising keiki. The puʻuhonua on the slopes of Mauna Kea, which has taught us different ways of standing together for ʻāina. The houseless encampments, which have been transformed into spaces of healing for people otherwise criminalized and persecuted.

In these spaces we will find a politics of liberation, and create a future that will refuse the false choice of rampant corporate development or housing exodus. The home we build in this pandemic's wake will not be a commodity divorced from land and life, for that divorce lies at the root of the crisis itself. Instead, home will become expansive enough to confirm Uncle John's certainty that even though he can't pay, and no matter how much his existence is criminalized, he can never be homeless in Hawaiʻi. Because forever and always, home is ʻāina.

Work Cited

Affordable Rental Housing Report and Ten-Year Plan. Special Action Team on Affordable
    Rental Housing Report to the Hawai'i State Legislature, July 2018.

Tina Grandinetti is an Uchinanchu from Mililani, Hawai'i. She is a PhD candidate at RMIT
University and a lecturer at the University of Hawai'i at Manoā. Tina is an affiliate of the
Housing Justice in Unequal Cities Network.

No Kākou Ke Kuleana

The Responsibility Belongs to Us

Diane Paloma

Hulihia is the Hawaiian word for overturn, a complete change, an overthrow, with the sentiment of being turned upside-down. It is referenced in chants about Pele, the destructive lava flows that upheave forests. We witnessed this in 2018, when the flow overran a section in Puna on Hawai'i Island. However, the overturning of land from a lava flow also brings new life, regrowth, rebirth, and resilience. The duality of hulihia is that from the upheaval, new perspectives arise, while growth and expansion are encouraged.

For Lunalilo Home, COVID-19 has created a hulihia for how we conduct kupuna caregiving and necessitated new solutions. Lunalilo Home was established as a result of the Will and Codicil of King William Charles Lunalilo, who died in 1874. In 1883, Lunalilo Home was funded, built, and opened to Native Hawaiian elders. Originally located near present-day Roosevelt High School, and within a mile of the Queen's Hospital, Lunalilo Home was a sprawling care home before any formal healthcare infrastructure had been established. The political, economic, and business composition of Honolulu was changing dramatically, and in 1927, Lunalilo Home was moved to Maunalua, an area later renamed "Hawai'i Kai" after developer Henry Kaiser dredged the largest fishpond sanctuary in the islands. Today, 137 years later, Lunalilo Home continues to provide kupuna caregiving. Residential care, adult day care, and meal delivery are the three main programs servicing kūpuna, alongside respite care, counseling, and placement assistance.

Pre-pandemic, the elder care industry was challenging enough. With the increase in life expectancy, kūpuna experience the high cost of living in Hawai'i longer. Layer upon that their needed family support and prolonged chronic disease, the needs of kūpuna become overwhelming for both elders and their immediate family members—should kūpuna be fortunate enough to have them. Bed space is limited for the "silver tsunami," the surge of elders born into the generation known as "baby boomers." For those who can afford it, entry into Continuing Care Retirement Communities (CCRCs) involves a down payment equivalent to a Honolulu home, a multiyear wait list, and limited equity for future familial inheritances. There are not enough accessible resources for the number of kūpuna in the State of Hawai'i. Though we value the family caring for kūpuna well into their later years, in modern times this places an additional burden on an already struggling family unit.

King Lunalilo foresaw these problems, and deliberately affirmed the importance of our "hulu kūpuna," or esteemed and beloved elders. Kūpuna are revered around the world, and especially in Hawaiian society. They are the repositories of lived experiences and wisdom. They are the caregivers for parents who work long days. They are the ones to pass on vital knowledge, stories, and genealogies to the next generation. In that sense, it is no wonder that they are the pillars of society. The kūpuna living at Lunalilo Home today grew up in a Hawai'i that could be considered long gone. Kūpuna have shared that they recall gathering limu along the south shore of Waikīkī, the immense span of the fishpond in Hawai'i Kai, speaking Hawaiian to the dismay of their parents, and the "war time" with meals centered around canned meat. Without those stories, we would not know the Hawai'i of yesteryear, and it is a sad truth that we will never know the full extent of these recollections. Working with kūpuna provides for their physical needs, but we all need to focus on nurturing their mental and spiritual needs, which includes the transmission of knowledge to others. Our namesake King Lunalilo was a leader during another hulihia in Hawaiian history. While his reign was short, it left some pearls for us to acknowledge and learn from. I consider King William Charles Lunalilo the ultimate kupuna. He continues to care for the generations and teach us about how to thrive amongst the hulihia in the world today.

These three notable examples from Lunalilo's governance help me to understand how our ali'i adapted to the hulihia around them.

- The election on January 1, 1873, confirmed Lunalilo as the unanimous public choice, and the first elected ruler in the Kingdom of Hawai'i. At the time, there were laws mandating that *only* landowners would be able to cast a vote in the election. This is seen in the 1864 Constitution of the Hawaiian Kingdom: voters needed to generate an annual income of $75 ($1,226 in 2020) or own private property worth at least $150 ($2,452 in 2020). When Lunalilo assumed the throne, these financial requirements were removed during his thirteen-month reign. This significant change restored voting eligibility to an estimated two-thirds of the Native Hawaiian population, and affirmed Lunalilo as truly "the people's king." (Lee)
- In the time of lower-priced sugar and the recessive economy in 1873, members of King Lunalilo's cabinet suggested a treaty with the United States for the profitability of the agriculture economy—a treaty that would entail giving up Pearl River (now known as Pearl Harbor) to the US. Lunalilo ultimately decided to withdraw the offer after realizing that this would "stir strife and enmity between foreigners and natives." King Lunalilo's stance preserved Pearl River until the Bayonet Constitution under King Kalākaua. (Kuykendall; Inglis)
- In 1873, Hansen's disease (then known as leprosy) in the Hawaiian Kingdom had entered and infiltrated the community. King Lunalilo and his

ministers continued the 1865 decision to segregate those afflicted with the disease by sending them to Kalaupapa, Molokaʻi. Under this order, the Board of Health refused to let family and friends go with afflicted to Molokaʻi and aggressively enforced the segregation laws, causing severe social stress during Lunalilo's governance. (Daws)

The hulihia of 1873 offers parallel stories to current times. Does the uprising for racial justice represent the latest voice from the people? Does the fight for Mauna Kea revive the difficult debates around ceding Pearl River? Does the forced isolation of the Hansen's disease outbreak remind us of today, and raise questions around further separating the lāhui from its own future? If we see how the hulihia of today resonate with those within our history, can we break that upheaval cycle?

During this time of COVID-19, the hulihia to the kupuna care industry demonstrates how already vulnerable populations are made even more vulnerable. Elders have been identified to be the most susceptible to COVID-19 mortality. For those who live at Lunalilo Home, the "lockdown" and limitation of any visitors, including family members, resonates with the days of sending ʻohana to Kalaupapa. Now that the community is recognizing the vulnerability of our hulu kūpuna, we have progressed toward ways to collectively embrace these pillars of society. COVID-19 has highlighted the need to assemble and protect them from new and unknown diseases. Policy teams for kūpuna, coalitions for kupuna-focused food security, and services specific to kūpuna (i.e., special grocery and banking hours) have demonstrated a community approach to recognizing and caring for kūpuna in new ways. These small recognitions are part of a larger and needed transformation in how we view and care for all our kūpuna. How do we place them first and find new ways to honor their existence? This is the hulihia that King Lunalilo first introduced to us by leaving his estate and lands to the kūpuna of yesterday, today, and tomorrow. He innately understood the fragility of our eldercare infrastructure, and bequeathed his legacy to the health and well-being of our esteemed elders. The current strategic plan, Kauhale Kupuna, envisions a nurturing and vibrant community for all kūpuna. At our foundation, we need to move the community's perception of caring for kūpuna from a burden to a privilege.

My grandmothers passed early in my life, so I really only knew my grandfathers. While I cherished their affection, it was very different from the current pilina (connection) between my daughters and my mom. They are connected even more, now that Grandma has become their taxi driver, junk-food provider, and sometimes banker. I am grateful for the time they have with each other, learning about my mom in ways that I didn't know my grandmothers growing up. This is the value of kūpuna that King Lunalilo envisioned. Through our work in this hulihia, we build a community-minded approach to kupuna caregiving, learning from our history and ancestors. We can place them again as the respected hulu kūpuna of society—for now, and for whatever challenges lie ahead of us. OLA!

Works Cited

Daws, Gavan. *Holy Man: Father Damien of Molokai.* U of Hawai'i P, 1973.
Inglis, Kerri A. *Ma'i Lepera: Disease and Displacement in Nineteenth-Century Hawai'i.* U of Hawai'i P, 2013.
Kuykendall, Ralph S. *The Hawaiian Kingdom—Volume 2: Twenty Critical Years, 1854–1874.* U of Hawai'i P, 1953.
Lee, Anne Feder. *The Hawaii State Constitution: A Reference Guide.* Greenwood Press, 1993.

Dr. Diane Paloma is the CEO for the King Lunalilo Trust and Home. She is the former Director of The Queen's Health Systems, Native Hawaiian Health Program. She currently serves as 'alaka'i (hālau leader) for Ka Pā Hula O Ka Lei Lehua. Diane serves on various community boards and resides in Wailupe with her husband and three daughters.

Technology, Entrepreneurship, and Waiwai

Kelsey Amos and Donavan Kealoha

> Whatever is Hawaiian, support 'em full on.
>
> Israel Kamakawiwo'ole

Technology alone will not save us, but it can be a powerful part of the solution. What works in creating change is the power of convening diverse people to take innovative action based in kuleana to Hawai'i. When we pose questions, talk story, and investigate together, we build ideal conditions for cocreating the futures we want. True in the best of times, this is even more essential now, when global disaster and ineffectual or downright dangerous leadership lay bare the current system's inequalities, injustices, and dysfunctions.

Purple Mai'a started in 2013, when we saw a need for coding education for Hawai'i's youth. At that time, only three public high schools offered AP computer science—compared to thirty-three by 2018. We sourced our teachers and content from a community of local people who wanted to present technology in a relatable and culturally grounded way. Our students then felt empowered to learn and use technology for their own and their community's purposes.

We teach digital technology skills together with entrepreneurship because entrepreneurial action must complement progress in other arenas, such as policy, protest, and public education. If we don't pursue our own interests as Hawaiians and people of Hawai'i in technology and entrepreneurship spaces, no one else will—or worse, someone will seek to do it for us.

Innovate Technology by Grounding it in our own Community Needs and Cultural Wealth

We have a vision of culturally and community-grounded technologists and entrepreneurs. We're not the experts at loko i'a and language resurgence, but we can be the engineers and innovators who design the water sensors that track tides and nutrient levels in the fishpond, or create the Google Chrome extension that makes crowd-source translation and dubbing of Netflix content into 'Ōlelo Hawai'i possible. We can be up to date on machine learning, blockchain, robotics, augmented reality, and IoT, while staying grounded in local community needs and efforts.

In this moment of COVID-19, how as technologists and entrepreneurs do we innovate in this space? We can see some things immediately.

- Increasing demand for online learning and access to Honolulu-based programs can become more equitable for rural communities. We must also address unequal access to computers, smartphones, and broadband.
- Will we see a greater demand for technology that connects students with 'āina virtually, via technologies like virtual reality and augmented reality, in a post-COVID-19 world where we are more attuned to limited mobility?
- COVID-19 has pushed many employers to embrace employees working from home. Will this trend continue, granting Hawai'i's workforce access to national or even global employment opportunities remotely, earning enough to continue to live in the islands?

COVID-19 has taught us that the future is unpredictable. We need to keep fostering pilina, because those connected to community are best positioned to respond quickly to community needs in a crisis. We also need what we call "communities of practice" to innovate toward the future we want. Communities of practice are often thought of as groups of people in a similar profession—web developers who exchange ideas, for instance, shaping trends and progress in their field. We feel that while differing widely in individual skills and talents, a community of practice can also share a grounding in kuleana to a place, and to care for 'āina and people. We can lift each other up, creating an amplification effect.

One example of how technologists and entrepreneurs might contribute to 'āina-based communities of practice is ahupua'a restoration across the pae 'āina. The work in He'eia brings together education, conservation, resource management, research, biocultural restoration, regenerative farming, and economic development. Technologists and innovators could support what kia'i are doing, leveraging tech to amplify culture rather than leveraging culture for tech.

Innovate Business Models for Community Wealth

While solving problems locally, it's imperative to think globally, embracing opportunities to provide unique, homegrown, collaborative solutions to external markets, thereby realizing economic value that can be repatriated back to those communities who had a direct hand in birthing those ideas/solutions.

Many are already advocating for growing our technology and innovation industries, urging Hawai'i to become a model for sustainability and positive innovation. Having our tech industry bring in investment and high paying jobs is a worthy goal, but we must not forget that if we, as Hawaiians and people of Hawai'i, cannot shape how innovative solutions are created, marketed, distributed, and owned, we run the risk of settling for less—less value circulating in the economy with only low-wage or "service" technology jobs available, and tech that runs counter to our values. In response, we must build up our peoples' skills as we think about how Hawai'i benefits, who's leading, and whether we are just shifting around inequalities, or achieving a state of waiwai where less is actually more.

In her book *Kaiāulu*, Mehana Vaughan describes how in the recent past, people lived by becoming experts who managed their resources so well that they could always share. Her example is how lawai'a had to understand the fish and their environment, and learn how to mālama and manage them in order to have big catches, which would then be shared with everyone, without demanding immediate return. At the same time, people would receive what others shared from other resources.

The same should be true of building technology companies. We must become excellent entrepreneurs, while thinking creatively about how to structure companies seeking to make a profit (even if it's only one part of a triple bottom line), so that equity and ownership extend not only to all shareholders, but to stakeholders that include the organizations actually doing the work of biocultural resurgence, co-creating these market innovations with excellent entrepreneurs, and creating waiwai. To achieve our own purposes, we have to understand and innovate contemporary structures.

Shifted Energy is an enterprise with an innovative business structure that shares waiwai. The idea for this company originated in the work of local nonprofit Kanu Hawai'i to create a more compassionate and resilient Hawai'i. Shifted developed a way to use water heaters as batteries for renewable energy, allowing apartment dwellers, and not just homeowners, to benefit from shifting to clean energy. When Shifted established its own company, along with the founders and early employees, Kanu received a significant percentage of ownership. This differs from the typical Silicon Valley model, where the majority of a company is owned by its founders, with a smaller percentage set aside for employees. As investors put money into a company to help build it, they too claim significant ownership. Only rarely is anything given to community organizations. Founders usually wait until they get rich to become philanthropists, and this sharing usually represents a small percentage of the wealth claimed by founders and investors.

Why not build in the giveback from the beginning? A percentage of equity or ownership of Hawai'i tech companies could be allocated to a collective of community organizations. Then, if there is an exit or liquidation event, or revenues get to the point that dividends are available, the collective members would realize economic benefit. We could define the percentages for ourselves, in this way reimagining social safety nets. We would have to acknowledge that we're aiming to create technology businesses that are home runs. Not all of them will be, but if some do go big, that success will help everyone else.

So Hawai'i benefits—and if Hawaiians and people of Hawai'i are leading, they'll make the right decisions about what kinds of innovations to pursue, and how to share the results.

Innovate the Ways We Live

All this hoped-for economic growth from technology and innovation—funneled back into community and creating waiwai—must be paired with innovations in how we live. If we're all still pursuing a life of too much too fast, then success will come at the expense of someone else and their 'āina. But if 'āina and beloved community can meet people's needs, that is truly waiwai. Maybe we can live less individualistically, less dependent on markets, and with fewer material luxuries. And technology and entrepreneurship can help us shift to living in a (k)new way, where less is more.

Kelsey Amos is a new mom and has a PhD in English from the University of Hawai'i at Manoā. A co-founder of Purple Mai'a Foundation, she grew up in Waipi'o Uka, graduating from Mililani High School, and receiving her BA from NYU.

Donavan Kealoha is a father, husband, entrepreneur, venture capitalist, and co-founder and Executive Director of Purple Mai'a, a nonprofit technology education startup providing indigenized tech education to underserved, high opportunity youth across Hawai'i. A proud product of Hawai'i public education, Donavan graduated from Lāna'i High School, and holds a BA and JD/MBA from the University of Hawai'i at Manoā.

Ulu Kukui O Kaulike

Advancing Justice for Kānaka Maoli in One Generation Through Health Policy

Kealoha Fox

Valuing Our Ancestors

One hundred fifty years ago, Kahikina Kelekona, my kupuna kāne, wrote about maʻi pālahalaha (infectious diseases) at the intersection of land disposession, political shifts, discrimination, and industrialization. A journalist and editor of Hawaiian language newspapers, in *Ka Leo o ka Lahui* he referred to the spreading sickness of Hansen's disease, or leprosy as it was called then, as Maʻi Hoʻokaʻawale ʻOhana, the sickness that separates families. In 2020, with rising rates of COVID-19 and a weakened public health system, the testimonies of our kūpuna ask us what we will do to survive and thrive here with our family for another 150 years.

We can answer this call by applying cultural values, understood through the traditional metaphor of a kukui grove, to revitalize a Native Hawaiian culture of health that supports equity, justice, and self-determination in all health and social policies. The kukui, or candlenut tree, is deeply important culturally, functionally, and spiritually for Kānaka Maoli. Here, I refer to kukui as a healing agent. Ulu Kukui O Kaulike revitalizes an ancestral oil for movement. Like our kūpuna, we have the opportunity to light our collective torches, fueled by the assets and tools they left for us. This kukui grove will grow up to advance justice for Kānaka Maoli.

However, we remain subjected to a deep-rooted public health crisis marked by chronic and social conditions oppressing our well-being. Research and data point to non-clinical pathways for positive change. High quality education, for instance, affects someone's ability to live in safe and secure housing, which in turn improves life expectancy. During the coronavirus, the social determinants of health (SDOH) have been exposed around the world and here in Hawaiʻi. Food, a stable job, and a safe place to live have become the focus for recovery, as we move from inaction into response. But thus far, health policymakers have ignored how our culture, language, and traditional values can increase resilience as we recover. In our community, this is shocking, since it is the Kānaka Maoli who have applied ancestral wisdom to navigate health threats, have drawn positive cultural memory from trauma, and have survived many previous epidemics, despite devastating losses.

Ulu Kukui O Kaulike is a culturally-grounded policy strategy that envisions true vitality through a traditional Hawaiian framework of Mauli Ola, which balances physical, emotional, mental, environmental, and spiritual health. As of 2014, Hawai'i Revised Statutes 226–20 requires that state agencies use this framework to recognize health disparities when developing new plans, policies, or resource distribution, and to commit to the well-being of Native Hawaiians, Pacific Islanders, and Filipinos. Some of these agency departments do not always see their role as contributing positively to a healthy Hawai'i or to Native Hawaiian needs. But culturally-informed policymaking recognizes that our environment, social infrastructure, and social progress all help to create healthy people, places, and futures. Our goals and next steps should advance the past decade's actions while harnessing resources for turning points during the next.

Applying Our Values to Act

Like one in four residents in Hawai'i, members of my 'ohana rely on Medicaid (QUEST Integration) as a knot, along with SNAP/WIC, TANF, and SSI, in their life-saving safety net. Many families have jobs, but benefits still remain out of reach. Employer-based healthcare costs keep rising each year, even for those of us with stable full-time positions. At this moment, the coronavirus pandemic has collided with complicated health economics in Honolulu and Washington DC, requiring us to restructure the investments needed to address our people's health.

Medicaid plans provide insurance coverage to low-income people, people with disabilities and special healthcare needs, the homeless, pregnant women, and elderly adults. Constantly under attack from the Trump administration, Medicaid has been an important part of the history of national health reform. But every day, without interacting with the people most affected, political leaders and systems create obstacles to getting and staying healthy. Due to COVID-19 related job losses, since March 2020, the Hawai'i Department of Human Services' (DHS) Med-QUEST Division has enrolled tens of thousands of additional beneficiaries. Unfortunately, Medicaid coverage for COFA beneficiaries has not yet been restored, nor has Hawai'i dental coverage for adults, making access unequal and not comprehensive.

But progress toward advancing justice is possible. In 2019, AlohaCare became the first insurer in Hawai'i—or anywhere in the US—to make permanent commitments to Native Hawaiian members and our community. Understanding that Native Hawaiian health disparities continue because of SDOH, cultural and historical trauma, and a cultural disconnect between health and medical services, AlohaCare's new 2020 focus implements HRS § 226–20 by building from a cultural foundation that honors Hawai'i. Providing more culturally-responsive services by 2025 is a major target.

Now is the time to focus on what care coverage we want, to align health services with our community needs, and to realize unfulfilled promises. As AlohaCare has already done, some of Hawai'i's most esteemed companies must integrate a Native Hawaiian culture of health into their insurance plans and policies. It is the right thing to do and makes business sense. If we can do these things, thousands of people—many among those most oppressed by outdated systems and most impacted by COVID-19—will make huge gains toward improved health and well-being. What if every hospital, healthcare system, and community health center committed to prioritize our people over profits? Hawai'i can be a leader in creating healthy Pacific futures through bravery, rigor, local innovation, and a commitment to confront the challenges we are facing now.

Waiwai Ola

Imagine the progress we can make connecting our cultural values to SDOH in Hawai'i right now by shifting service delivery workflows toward culturally-responsive prevention programs. That opportunity will come in 2021, when DHS will begin investing $17 billion in Medicaid programs across all islands through to 2030. Emphasizing a process aligned with Indigenous innovation and the awakening of a Native Hawaiian culture of health, the next decade is ours for creating a world class healthcare industry and public health system that puts our values, community, and cultural expertise at its epicenter. Native Hawaiians can apply our cultural and ancestral resources as an antidote and an intervention into local challenges. Just like the kukui.

Within ten years I yearn to see cultural practitioners valued as part of an essential team-based care process. I want 'ai pono, lā'au lapa'au, ho'oponopono, hula, lomilomi, lua, and wāhine hāpai offered as community services underwritten by permanent funding mechanisms like Medicaid. By 2030, we will have decolonized institutions, and invested in community health hubs where resilience and healing are thriving in every island and district. Through a restitution process, legitimate and expert power can be returned to Kumu, Loea, 'Ōlohe, and Haku. Practitioners are already introducing traditional models into education, health, housing, and criminal justice reform, but to multipy these benefits to the mana lāhui, we need to invest deeply in good policy, solid practice, and long-term programming.

My hope is that 150 years from now, groves of medicinal trees will encircle our descendants as they reflect on how their ancestors (us) rose to meet our generation's greatest challenge. I imagine a spirited kūkākūkā, analyzing our intentions and discussing how we built back better, making systemic change in our favor possible—how we came together and protected the values of Hawai'i. I envision this new era we created as one in which reintegration came full circle, and this social safety net will be protected and strengthened by the practitioners of Mauli Ola who will flourish in 2170. Just as I seek out the voice of my kupuna in nūpepa to guide my own kuleana today, I have faith that our mo'opuna will look back on 2020, and recognize healing from disorder, because we translated a culture of health back into legacies of care across Hawai'i.

Ulu Kukui O Kaulike is a vision for a health policy that advances equity for Native Hawaiians, and eliminates health disparities within one generation. The growth of this kukui grove will represent an advance toward racial justice for Kānaka Maoli, as we return to healing in our families and across the lāhui, and back to the lands from which we grow. It's not just about getting back to where we were, but envisioning transformative and enduring change. The seeds have been planted, and the flame of systemic change has been lit, and will not be suffocated. May these kukui light the way ahead for all of us, and the important changes we seek.

Ka ipu kukui pio 'ole. *The light of justice that will not be extinguished.*

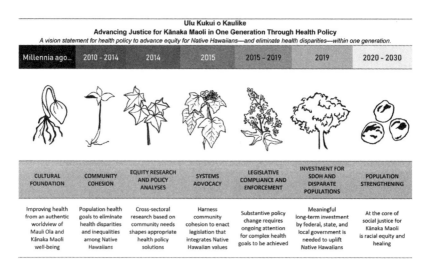

			Ulu Kukui o Kaulike			
			Advancing Justice for Kānaka Maoli in One Generation Through Health Policy			
			A vision statement for health policy to advance equity for Native Hawaiians—and eliminate health disparities—within one generation.			
Millennia ago...	2010 - 2014	2014	2015	2015 - 2019	2019	2020 - 2030
CULTURAL FOUNDATION	COMMUNITY COHESION	EQUITY RESEARCH AND POLICY ANALYSES	SYSTEMS ADVOCACY	LEGISLATIVE COMPLIANCE AND ENFORCEMENT	INVESTMENT FOR SDOH AND DISPARATE POPULATIONS	POPULATION STRENGTHENING
Improving health from an authentic worldview of Mauli Ola and Kānaka Maoli well-being	Population health goals to eliminate health disparities and inequalities among Native Hawaiians	Cross-sectoral research based on community needs shapes appropriate health policy solutions	Harness community cohesion to enact legislation that integrates Native Hawaiian values	Substantive policy change requires ongoing attention for complex health goals to be achieved	Meaningful long-term investment by federal, state, and local government is needed to uplift Native Hawaiians	At the core of social justice for Kānaka Maoli is racial equity and healing

Ulu Kukui o Kaulike: Kealoha Fox. Kukui art: Lisanne Paikai.

Dr. Kealoha Fox is a Native Hawaiian scientist, traditional practitioner, and advocate who practices a Social Determinants of Health model of care at AlohaCare, a nonprofit health plan in Hawai'i. Ulu Kukui O Kaulike was awarded the Snapshot of Innovation to Build a Culture of Health Award by the Robert Wood Johnson Foundation in March 2020.

Shine Your Light Wherever You Go

Shanty Sigrah Asher

> We cannot always build the future for our youth, but we can build our youth for the future.
>
> Franklin D. Roosevelt

Like many other Micronesians, my family and I are blessed we live Hawai'i. I dedicate this essay to our Micronesian youth. You are strong, beautiful, smart, and valued; never let anyone tell you otherwise.

I was once in your shoes. Let me tell you my story.

My home, Kosrae, is a forty-two square mile volcanic island in the Federated States of Micronesia (FSM), home to over 6,000 of the world's friendliest people. Then and now, the United States has been a big part of our livelihood and upbringing. We started learning the English language as early as pre-school. Our desire to know about America and her democracy was so strong that we learned more about it than about our own nation. A long-standing and steadfast relationship between FSM and the United States drives these desires, from the times of the Trust Territory of the Pacific Islands (TTPI) to the Compact of Free Association (COFA). Many of us take pride in this relationship, promised and built upon a mutual respect found nowhere else in the world.

In exchange for exclusive American control over FSM's water and air space, we can live and work in the US. This relationship opened up a door for me and countless others from FSM to enter visa-free, and gain access to the US's quality education system. After graduating from Malem Elementary School in 1996 and Kosrae High School in 1999, I enrolled at Chaminade University on O'ahu. The experience was exciting and terrifying. It was my first time living away from my family. Because I was one of a very few students who spoke English with a deep accent, my teachers and classmates found it hard to understand me. With no Facebook messenger, Zoom, or Skype to see family and friends, I was often homesick, and cried myself to sleep. On lucky weeks, I would buy a five-dollar phone card, and use the lobby payphone to talk to my family—for ten minutes. Life was arduous, but at eighteen, I learned to manage the little money I had.

In my second semester, I became less shy and more confident. I made friends and found my second Pacific Islander family—American and Western Sāmoans, Native Hawaiians, and Micronesians. Our values and struggles were similar. We all came from loving, caring, family-directed and oriented communities, so we took care of each other—sharing what we had, lifting each other up, and surviving financially and spiritually together. As Pacific Islanders, our bond made us stronger together. We knew that our ocean does not divide us, but unites us.

A feeling that seems almost nonexistent today.

After receiving my bachelor's and master's at Chaminade, I returned home to FSM. It was time to serve the country and people who had supported my education. My family of four moved to Pohnpei, the capital of FSM, where I spent five years as a Deputy Assistant Secretary of Pacific Affairs at Foreign Affairs. This chapter changed my life, offering me countless opportunities to serve, work alongside, and learn from admirable world leaders and diplomats and selfless community members.

A deeper and stronger desire to serve, and especially to protect citizens' rights enshrined in the Constitution, led me with my family to law school in August 2015, in "America's finest city," San Diego. Law school was frightening and surreal. As a child I had dreamed about becoming a lawyer, but when it was really happening, I started doubting myself. I was surrounded by incredibly strong, capable, and intelligent law students. The process was intimidating, but through determination, faith, and constant reminders of my family's and people's sacrifices, I told myself there was no room for failure—their sacrifices would not go unnoticed. I pushed through, juggling my responsibilities as a wife, mom, and law student. Thanks to my husband, our families, and our San Diegan friends and families, whom we love dearly and miss, we completed our mission. On May 12, 2018, I graduated with a Juris Doctor, and my little family returned to Hawai'i.

Being back in my second home was fulfilling yet heartbreaking—certainly a different story from when I first came. In 1999, not many people knew about "Micronesians." Not being very noticeable gave us peace and comfort. In 2020, however, "Micronesians" are noticed—and not in a good way. I now hear phrases like "Go back to your home country," or "You bunch of cockroaches." At school, amongst the hurtful comments thrown at our kids, my daughter was told, "You Micronesian? Nahhh, you too smart to be Micronesian." Over the past decade, this discrimination has become acceptable and constant in Hawai'i. Though efforts are made to tackle this injustice, these are troubling and challenging times for our kids, who are expected to cope and survive, as well as learn and dream about their futures—overwhelming responsibilities at such a young age.

I, like so many community members, did not want to lose hope. I did not want my daughters in Hawai'i to grow up with hate—it is "un-Pacific." A Pacific way is to treat everyone as family, with respect and compassion. Hawai'i is a Pacific neighbor.

Papa Mau Piailug taught Hawaiians the art of non-instrument navigation, uniting navigators and reawakening cultural pride and unity throughout Polynesia.

I am thankful to Pacific Resources for Education and Learning (PREL), my employer, for recruiting me to work with our communities on education and true Pacific values. Since my return, I have done a great deal of community outreach, assisting Micronesians one-on-one with REAL ID issues and unemployment, raising awareness about rights and responsibilities, and visiting schools to talk to students and educators about how we can better support our Micronesian students. If we can feel welcomed, appreciated and valued, cooperation and civic contributions will happen.

In February 2020, I was invited to talk to the principal and faculty at Kealakehe High School in Kailua-Kona about "Supporting Micronesian Students in Hawai'i Schools," part of Culturally Responsive Teaching training conducted by PREL. Because the presentation was in the afternoon, I arrived early to tour the school, and to meet and speak with teachers and our Micronesian students. It was a beautiful and memorable day, as I was embraced with the presence of over forty young, smart, and full-spirited Micronesian students, who forfeited their lunch break to talk story by the tree where they usually hung out. I told them about my journey; what it had been like coming to Hawai'i for school, and the challenges I endured and overcame. I felt they were inspired, because they asked me to return to help them with their financial aid applications, and to speak to them in a more organized setting about vocational training opportunities and career pathways. It was a fruitful day!

The same day, to inform and empower, in a history class I spoke to over twenty seniors, Micronesians and non-Micronesians, about the Compact of Free Association. Directing their attention to a big map, I pointed to the block of water belonging to COFA nations, and spoke briefly of what these three million square miles mean for national security and peace for the United States and Hawai'i. I also highlighted COFA's hope that FSM people will seek better opportunities, and be good ambassadors wherever our pursuits take us.

I strove for two things that day. For the non-Micronesian youth, to develop a deeper understanding, so that they could find in their hearts ways to look at and appreciate their peers and our community differently. For the Micronesian youth, to instill hope, self-worth, and a sense of responsibility. On that day, all the students were silent and attentive. I was certain something was learned.

My dream is that we can soon live in harmony—that our daughters can wear their skirts and dresses in public proudly, and that Micronesians are recognized for the good that we do. I have hopes, because on July 1, 2020, Governor David Ige nominated me, and the Hawai'i Senate confirmed me, to serve as a member of the Hawai'i Board of Education—the first Micronesian in this capacity. It's a historic decision, showing Hawai'i's commitment to become part of the solution.

To our Micronesian youth—be proud of who you are. You come from rich cultural backgrounds. Treasure your roots and identity. Your uncles, aunties, brothers, and sisters are fighting and sacrificing every day in the name of freedom. In return, be good ambassadors wherever you are. At school, follow rules and help your fellow students. At the public parks, respect the rules and leave the area better than you found it. Empower each other and always be respectful, remember where you come from, and always put God first in all you do.

May we continue to shine our lights wherever we go and whenever we can.

I am **Shanty Sigrah Asher**. Wife of Ronnie Asher, mother of Shanielyn, Ayorine, and Elmerlyn. Daughter of Deborah and Sankey Sigrah. Oldest of seven siblings: Darlene, Raleigh, Kathleen, Rebecca, Dessah, and Sihna. I am Kosraen, Pohnpeian, and a proud Micronesian.

Puʻuhonua o Puʻuhuluhulu University

He Kīpuka Aloha ʻĀina no ka ʻImi Naʻauao

Presley Keʻalaanuhea Ah Mook Sang

E ka mea heluhelu,

I have been requested to submit a paper on the radical emergence of Puʻuhuluhulu University, Maunakea, Hawaiʻi. In meeting this request, I have realized that the tenets supporting the radical conception and facilitation of Puʻuhuluhulu University were and are really grounded in the tenets defining my formative years in an intergenerational home. In this essay I share with you how Puʻuhuluhulu University transforms how we think of Indigenous education in a real-time Indigenous context, and how Puʻuhuluhulu University has emerged as a metaphor for my personal journey of transformation as a kanaka maoli, an Indigenous Hawaiian.

> Education either functions as an instrument which is used to facilitate integration of the younger generation into the logic of the present system and bring about conformity to it, or it becomes "the practice of freedom," the means by which men and women deal critically and creatively with reality and discover how to participate in the transformation of their world. (Shaull)

When I was young, it was emphasized to me by almost everyone in my ʻohana (family) that education is liberation. In my multigenerational home, however, the definition and understanding of what education entails varied from individual to individual. My Japanese mother focused on the importance of excelling in Western academia, while my Hawaiian father addressed the need to be cognizant of the space and place in which I reside—in his words, being "street-smart." There was an added layer of my English grandmother pressing the need to be articulate in a world filled with Pidgin jargon, and my Hawaiian grandfather's desire to transfer moʻolelo (stories and histories), so I could have a strong sense of identity and connection to my past, which is indeed my present and future. Because of all that, coupled with my own need to not only substantiate myself, but to make others around me proud, I've always felt like I was chasing approval and shifting my focus to accommodate whoever was taking notice. To validate myself as *educated* I felt I needed to exist and excel in these various roles; always trying, yet sometimes falling a little short. What

I didn't comprehend then was how these multifaceted perspectives on education privileged me to view education through various lenses, strengthening my openness and willingness to learn from anyone and anything with a lesson to be shared.

Although I was indeed privileged with these various views on education, I have been in the Western academic setting since I was four. After completing my compulsory education, I immediately enrolled in higher education, attaining both bachelor's and master's degrees in Hawaiian Studies and Hawaiian Language from the University of Hawai'i at Mānoa. While enrolled as a graduate student, I began teaching at the university at the age of twenty-two and have been an educator by those standards for the past eight years. Because of this, my life and understanding of nuances has in large part been confined by and tailored to theory and idealizing what is referred to as a decolonial existence.

But theory without praxis does nothing more than reinforce the colonial agenda. On July 13, 2019, I began what has been to date one of my boldest attempts at putting theory into praxis. Following a kāhea (call out) from aloha 'āina (patriotic) colleagues, I packed a bag and left for Hawai'i Island to stand in protection of Maunakea against its proposed desecration by TMT (formally known as the Thirty Meter Telescope). Following the arrests of thirty-eight kūpuna (elders) on July 17, the lāhui (nation) arrived at the Pu'uhonua o Pu'uhuluhulu en masse. We went from barely forty individuals to upwards of 7,000 in a matter of days. By the time the weekend approached, I had been holding space in the pu'uhonua for a week. I was exhausted, still fearing the arrival of law enforcement at any given time while trying to maintain my professionalism and conducting my online course for summer session. However, I felt a small sense of relief when I noticed how large our numbers had grown. So for a brief moment on that Saturday, I sat in my brother's 2004 Toyota Corolla and watched as hundreds upon hundreds of individuals made their way in and out of the pu'uhonua. After a few hours of sitting in solitude, I was approached with a request to schedule teach-ins, a common action in social movements. I realized then I had an opportunity to institute something I had only dreamed of. I was about to redefine education. It was then that I decided, with the help of some friends, to establish Pu'uhuluhulu University.

My intent was to educate the masses who showed up to practice aloha 'āina, and secondly, to prove that education is not confined within the walls of Western academia. We decided to claim this new institution as an actual place of Hawaiian learning, as opposed to the University of Hawai'i at Mānoa, which has publicly portrayed itself as an Indigenous space. It is my belief that an Indigenous education is fueled by community approval and acceptance. Unlike the current actions of the University of Hawai'i administration, Pu'uhuluhulu University therefore intentionally allowed and encouraged individuals of our kaiāulu (community) to take ownership of the 'ike (knowledge) they possess, and transfer those knowledge systems to the lāhui. Individuals from all backgrounds were welcomed to teach courses, from 'ōpio (youth) to kūpuna (elders), on any subject (language, history, science, health, etc.). The methodological approach of Pu'uhuluhulu University empowered all generations to learn from and transfer knowledge—a pedagogical approach similar to that of our kūpuna and the educational system they established in the mid-1800s.

After its inception, Pu'uhuluhulu University continued to offer free education to the community for eight months, until the demobilization of the kia'i (protectors) within the pu'uhonua due to COVID-19. Roughly one thousand different classes were offered by hundreds of educators of various backgrounds. These classes included, but were not limited to, History of the Hawaiian Language, Native Hawaiian Legal Rights, Mele Aloha 'Āina, Sea Level Rise, and Natural History. Following in the footsteps of Pu'uhuluhulu, other grassroots educational systems were created, including Hūnānāniho University, classes at Kahuku, and free online education and workshops provided by programs such as Kanaeokana.

To relate this back to my upbringing, Pu'uhuluhulu University mirrored what I have always innately wished education would look like, and helped me to realize why my formative years had waiwai (value). Through this endeavor, I began to understand that my desire to seek approval of others was actually an act of defining personal accountability to the collective. And indeed, that is exactly the reason why I decided to commit the amount of time and energy that I did to the movement. For the first time in my life, I felt an overwhelming sense of approval from my community, and I understood that Pu'uhuluhulu University gave others who have been seeking similar approval a space and place to find the same for themselves, either through teaching courses or absorbing the 'ike that was presented there.

Moving forward, it is my hope that Pu'uhuluhulu University can be used as a precedent for those who are equally eager to redefine education in this postcolonial era. Given the current situation regarding schooling during COVID-19, we have an opportunity to change drastically and quickly. Like the masses that showed up at Pu'uhuluhulu eager to join the aloha 'āina movement, there is a community of families who have an 'i'ini (desire) to help the 'ōpio of this generation receive the education they deserve without having to be afraid of the pandemic. Now is the time to dream and do. Now is the time to reclaim our ea (self-determination). Now is the time to a'a i ka hula a waiho ho'i i ka hilahila ma ka hale (step out and do without indifference). As it was expressed to me from a young age, the way of our future is through means of our past. I ka wā ma mua, i ka wā ma hope.

Work Cited

Shaull, Richard. Foreword. *Pedagogy of the Oppressed*, by Paulo Freire, translated by Myra Bergman Ramos, 1970, Bloomsbury, 2014.

Presley Ke'alaanuhea Ah Mook Sang is a kupa of Papakōlea, O'ahu, and an instructor of Hawaiian language at the University of Hawai'i at Mānoa. One of her most recent endeavors was the development and creation of Pu'uhuluhulu University at Maunakea, Hawai'i.

Haumāna

Jonathan Kay Kamakawiwoʻole Osorio

I have never doubted the value of the University of Hawaiʻi to the haumāna ʻeleu. I know how it transformed me from an aimless, cynical, and self-aggrandizing twenty-year-old into a being with a sense of purpose and value to others. And from the moment I began teaching for real at Kapiʻolani Community College with stories about human beings struggling to live good lives while caught in the wheels of imperial ambitions, racist and sexist bigotry and the laws that gave teeth to those bigotries, and money—always money everywhere beckoning the ambitious and the naive alike to forget about whatever ethics they were taught as children and take care of number one—I always sensed from my students both the struggle to understand, and a true delight in hearing an older adult reaffirm things that their own spirits found credible.

Now, after a twenty-five-year career in teaching and three years in administration, I can say without qualification that if anything defines the mana and extraordinary promise of the university, it is not the faculty or the chancellor. It is the student who defines and graces this place. I have worked with excellent faculty and there is real kinship among those of us who take this profession and its responsibilities seriously. But honestly, when I am remembering my life in this place, my mind goes immediately to haumāna, and while I could not possibly name them all here I will mention a small few who are part of a huge number of students who taught me.

Moon Kauakahi, Darlaine Māhealani Dudoit, Mamo Kim, John Kaʻimikaua, Noelani Goodyear-Kaʻōpua, Kahoʻonei Panoke, Micky Huihui, Tom Pōhaku Stone, Naʻalehu and Punihei Anthony, Pua Lincoln, Jocelyn Doane, Kamaoli Kuwada, Kamana Beamer, Aiko Yamashiro, ʻIlima Long, Andre Perez, Keala Francis, Julia Morgan, Willy Kauai, Joseph Salazar, Jesse Kahoʻonei, Logan Narikawa, Kawēlau Wright, Noʻeau Peralto, Justin Keliʻipaʻakaua, Mailelauliʻi Vickery, Heoli Osorio, Nanea Lo, Liʻi Nahiwa, Makana Kāne Kuahiwinui, Keʻalaanuhea Ah Mook Sang, and Kaipu Baker. What is remarkable about these people are the ways that they used their time as students to intervene in our society—to organize, teach, petition, and protest. They are heroic, because their faith in the things that we brought before them in this university caused them to act with courage and determination.

As faculty we intentionally disrupted their lives and left them with the responsibility of reconnecting themselves to ideals and values that we did not always understand ourselves. Unsheltered by resources, reputations, tenure, and academic freedom students have always done the hard work of unraveling the contradictions between what we teach and their own life experiences, and then making the heroic decisions to act upon what they had learned.

This is why the incredible activity on Mauna a Wākea this past year was such an historic and life-changing event for all of us in Hawai'i. For as spontaneous as those gatherings may have seemed, there was planning and logistics, fundraising, governance, social services, and public education everywhere you looked. And how could we from UH Mānoa not have been enthralled by the way that the kia'i, quite a number of them graduates and current students of our university, enabled people from everywhere to declare their love for the 'āina and defy the government, the intimidations of a militarized police, and the constant notifications from the press that we were a minority, holding up progress and development.

I was proud of the way most of us on the faculty and administration dealt with this protest 250 miles away and right outside of the offices of the UH President on Wise Field. I was impressed with how many faculty were willing to learn from our students, though that sentiment was anything but unanimous. It was interesting to me that when professors from the Physics Department were audio-taped making ad hominem and racist commentary about Hawaiians, the prevailing reactions from faculty and administrators was to be ashamed of those professors. That alone demonstrated that our haumāna in speaking to our better selves, even in the face of scorn, are changing our intellectual culture and ethics.

It would be sad indeed if a member of this faculty spent their career in this place with either a dim knowledge or a contempt for the ways that undergraduate and graduate students here have embraced and challenged the things we taught them, and insisted on applying them to their own lives, the lives of their families, home communities, and the larger society. It would be useful to recount a genealogy of student engagement with the University of Hawai'i, and with wealthy and powerful companies and even with the American military. In the 1960s, students and faculty from the newborn Ethnic Studies Program helped organize farmers in Kalama Valley, Waiāhole and Waikāne, Kahalu'u, and Ota Camp. In the late 70s, political science and law students joined Maui and Moloka'i community members to save Kaho'olawe from military bombing, and Hawaiian Studies haumāna marched in 1993 to remind the world that our nation was still alive, vitally alive.

From Kalama Valley and Waiāhole in the 1970s to Sherwoods and Kahuku in 2019, students have abruptly left the classroom and answered a call to bring their education to the assistance of others. In doing so, they are the ones to remind us that the purpose of this great academy of ours should be to address the needs of our society and our world, and to direct our best efforts to the places and lives most in need of our protection.

If we allow them, our haumāna will help this university train its attention and resources not on simply advancing science and technology, or studying the glorification of science and technology in the literature and histories of Europe and America, but attending to these islands, oceans, and the grand diversity of beings that live here. If we heed the haumāna, we might shift our ambitions from seizing the means of production and spending our lives growing wealth to sharing those means, while allowing ourselves to grow in generosity and compassion.

And could there be a more critical moment for a transformation in our sciences, our economies, and in our values than this moment, with the American ideological contradictions shaking that country to its core while a dangerous and as yet unpredictable virus exposes not just the weaknesses in American society but modernity itself? Perhaps now, in the shadow of this great pandemic that afflicts anyone but is lethal to the elderly and to the poor, undernourished, and unsheltered, does the actual proximity of mortality finally begin to demonstrate how thoroughly dependent we are on one another? Does this disease finally disclose what a waste our societies have made not merely of ecosystems and diverse species, but of people's lives, those who died in poverty and in wealth alike?

Indeed, we might ask ourselves, what ways of life to which we have become accustomed will not be changed, and changed utterly? And if we ask that question, should we not also ask, who is best suited to demonstrate and lead us to new ways of living, feeding, sheltering, and educating one another: a sixty-nine-year-old historian and university administrator, or a thirty-year-old graduate student who helped design and conduct a whole educational curriculum on the bare slopes of a mountain, with no money?

For those of us who are university faculty, professionals, and administrators, we must be prepared to acknowledge the need for change, massive change in this institution, and that this will require a tremendous negotiation of resources, directions, and methods with the communities we serve. That includes farmers in West Maui demanding the restoration of water to their streams, with unsheltered families in Wai'anae, and shopowners in Hilo, and also the bureaucrats at the State Capitol, who are somehow being expected to lead Hawai'i into an economy that does not require ten million tourists a year, or that must threaten the health of the aquifer at Moanalua because we are so dependent on US military spending.

But in the end, we must consult with our haumāna, because they have been the one consistent voice over a half a century calling to protect our working communities, to protect our forests, streams, and beaches, to sustain our cultural practices. They have been the ones who occupied Bachman Hall to protest a ruinous war in Vietnam, to restore Hawaiian language classes, and to disengage from military research and from patenting kalo and other life forms. They have sacrificed to protect a whole island and a sacred mountain. Students have been reminding Hawai'i of what is precious, over and over. And they have always been right.

Finally, we need to listen.

Jonathan Kay Kamakawiwoʻole Osorio is Professor of Hawaiian Studies and the Dean of the Hawaiʻinuiākea School of Hawaiian Knowledge at the University of Hawaiʻi at Mānoa. His published works include a history of the Hawaiian Kingdom and contemporary Hawaiian political issues, and he was co-editor of the first *Value of Hawaiʻi* volume. He composes and records Hawaiian music, and lives happily with wife and children in Wahiawā.

Ancient Is Modern—Transforming Public Education for Hawaiians

Kū Kahakalau

When it comes to education for Native Hawaiians, ancient is modern. Methods developed, tested, and employed by our ancestors to prepare future generations to thrive in our islands coincide with the latest in twenty-first century educational and neuroscience research. These methods are still the best for growing and maintaining a thriving lāhui.

With the dawn of a new era, tremendous opportunities present themselves to reimagine and redesign public education. In fact, we have entered a highly fortuitous time to operationalize a culturally-driven, family-oriented, and community-based Hawaiian system of public education. As early as 1997, such a system was recommended by the Native Hawaiian Education Council in their federal report. Over thirty years of Indigenous action research by me and others has confirmed that Hawaiian culturally-driven education truly works and positively impacts Hawaiian students on all levels.

Let's face it. The horse has been dead for decades. When I started my DOE career in 1985 as one of the first licensed secondary Hawaiian Language teachers, inequitable numbers of Native Hawaiian students were underperforming, not because they were stupid, lazy, or unmotivated—though that is what they were frequently told—but because the content, instructional methods, and assessments did not align with the needs and propensities of Hawai'i's largest public school ethnic group.

These inequities have not substantially changed over the decades. What has changed is that we know how to educate modern Hawaiians. Building on this research, we can now create a viable, decentralized Hawaiian system of education tailored to the needs, dispositions, and preferences of Hawai'i's host population. This system is currently being advanced by Kū-A-Kanaka, a social enterprise started by my family to revitalize Hawaiian language, culture, and traditions, Kanaeokana, a network of Kula Hawai'i that is strengthening the lāhui and nurturing the next generations of aloha 'āina leaders, and grassroots organizations throughout Hawai'i who are collaboratively growing a community-based education system built on strong Hawaiian language and culture foundations.

Research shows that Hawaiian students do not just prefer culturally-driven education. They *excel* when taught in an atmosphere of aloha, when the curriculum is relevant to the places they are born and raised in, and when assessments let them demonstrate what they have learned using their unique gifts and talents. I coined this ancient-yet-modern approach to learning: Pedagogy of Aloha, but it is also known as Education with Aloha (EA), Hawaiian Culture-Based Education (HCBE), 'Āina-based Education, and Hawaiian-focused education. Directly influenced by student feedback, this Pedagogy of Aloha has emerged over the past two decades, and positively impacted tens of thousands of Hawaiian learners of all ages.

Here I present my vision of a Hawaiian model of education called Kīnana Ho'ona'auao, which I translate as "place of attaining wisdom," as a prototype for intergenerational places of learning that should be established throughout Hawai'i, as independent components of a Hawaiian system of education, which advocates decision-making at a local level. This vision aligns with Article 14 of the United Nations Declaration on the Rights of Indigenous Peoples, which states that "Indigenous peoples have the right to establish and control their educational systems and institutions providing education in their own languages, in a manner appropriate to their cultural methods of teaching and learning."

Culturally-driven, family-oriented, and community-based, Kīnana Ho'ona'auao strives for contemporary and traditional rigor in theory and practice. It also helps learners to achieve island sustainability. As a community-based place of learning, Kīnana Ho'ona'auao is unique—molded by its place, history, and contemporary assets and challenges, and responsive to community wants, needs, and realities.

Kīnana Ho'ona'auao should be located in areas with high concentrations of Native Hawaiians, and grounded in our Pedagogy of Aloha, which can be described as Relations + Relevance + Responsibility = Rigor + Fun. Based on this formula, Kīnana Ho'ona'auao focuses on reciprocal relations not just among kānaka, but also with the 'āina and the spiritual world. Research confirms that in order to be effective, teaching and learning must take place in an atmosphere of aloha, where everyone feels cared for and supported. Utilizing traditional Hawaiian methods of conflict resolution designed to maintain harmonious relations, Kīnana Ho'ona'auao addresses issues expediently and assures that all feel safe and valued. Kīnana Ho'ona'auao is affiliation-oriented, with those involved in the educational process constituting an extended, intergenerational family of learners. Students are expected to greet adults and peers as they would family, using terms such as kupuna when talking to elders, and 'anakala and 'anakē when addressing teachers, administrators and other adults. Our kūpuna believed that mutual respect readies children for success. This aligns with our research, which confirms that social-emotional balance stimulates the mind and heart, teaches children how to engage in collaborative problem-solving and effective communication, and can reach even the most alienated learners.

Kīnana Ho'ona'auao curricula are relevant, culturally-driven, and place-based, starting in the community and radiating out in concentric circles. Hawaiian knowledge is the curricular foundation for all content areas, making the curriculum relevant and personal. Students conduct impactful research in and out of the classroom, and find real world applications for the content explored. For Hawaiians, nature has always been the principal source of knowledge, providing answers for the questions driving kānaka. At Kīnana Hoʻonaʻauao, all content is approached through a Hawaiian lens, because for Hawaiʻi's future generations to solve modern challenges, they must understand the dynamics of their place. Kīnana Hoʻonaʻauao helps students understand cause and effect within their unique island environment, and their responsibility to apply what they learn to generate positive impacts on a local and global level.

Kīnana Hoʻonaʻauao operates on a blended indoor-outdoor ratio, which gives students ample opportunities to develop reciprocal, familial relationships with the land, and prepares them to address modern environmental issues. Providing learners extensive place-based, project-based experiences teaches them how to take care of the land and fosters that deep love for the land known as aloha ʻāina.

Kīnana Hoʻonaʻauao is grounded in ancestral wisdom. In-depth knowledge of Hawaiʻi's host culture guides instruction, curriculum, and assessment, as well as behavioral expectations. Students learn by watching and listening when a teacher or master provides instructions and explanations while demonstrating specific tasks. By observing people and natural phenomena, students begin to understand the world around them and prepare to deal with complex ecological issues. Students learn by doing. Teachers introduce new concepts by engaging learners in hands-on application of new knowledge.

As they would be in an extended family, rather than being divided by grade levels, students are mixed together in a multi-age format, teaching each other and learning from one another. Giving older students responsibility to care for younger students lets them show that they can be trusted to mālama their kuleana. This is especially empowering for at-risk students.

Kīnana Hoʻonaʻauao values group success over individual achievement. Research confirms that students thrive in non-competitive settings. Moreover, encouraging collaboration prepares students for life at home, at work, and in the community, where such skills are indispensable. Kīnana Hoʻonaʻauao also integrates elders, family members, and community experts into the educational process, fostering long-lasting relationships with adults.

Kīnana Hoʻonaʻauao teachers have high expectations of their students and set high standards for growth on all levels. Moreover, teachers are extremely creative, making sure that students draw on their strengths and passions as they demonstrate their skills and growth through authentic demonstrations of knowledge, known in Hawaiian as hōʻike.

Kīnana Hoʻonaʻauao engages students in real world projects, including internships, service-learning, and mentorships providing authentic experiences. Exploring and solving relevant issues in their families, learning ʻohana, and communities stimulates students' creativity and innovation, critical thinking and problem-solving, and communication and collaboration. By giving students of all ages opportunities to solve real world problems in their communities, Kīnana Hoʻonaʻauao supports them as creators of information, particularly about Hawaiians and Hawaiʻi.

Kīnana Hoʻonaʻauao replaces quiet classrooms and lectures with an atmosphere of exuberant discovery, where students and adults are laughing, interacting joyfully, creating art, music, dance, and having fun. Neuroscience research suggests that when students feel minimal stress, information flows freely, assisting students in achieving higher levels of cognition, making connections, and experiencing "aha" moments. In addition, when classroom activities are pleasurable, the brain releases neurotransmitters that stimulate memory centers and increase focused attention.

At Kīnana Hoʻonaʻauao, learning is a dynamic, non-linear, spiraling process that builds on past experiences to seek solutions for the future. Employing both contemporary and traditional technologies, learning is practical, skill-oriented, and environmentally-aware, while reflecting, respecting, and embracing Hawaiian cultural values and philosophies that have guided our kūpuna for thousands of years. As an innovative, research-based twenty-first-century model of Hawaiian education, Kīnana Hoʻonaʻauao is ancient and modern, traditional and contemporary, providing learners with opportunities to walk successfully in multiple worlds.

Dr. Kū Kahakalau is a native Hawaiian educator, researcher, cultural practitioner, grassroots activist, and expert in Hawaiian language, history, and culture. After founding and directing the first Hawaiian-focused charter school and teacher licensing program, she is launching EA Ecoversity, Hawaiʻi's first sustainable higher education and career training program.

Writing in the Path of Our Ancestors

Ke Ea Hawaiʻi Student Council

Kauʻi McElroy

E iho ana o luna	*The high will be brought low*
E pii ana o lalo	*The low will be lifted up*
E hui ana na moku	*The islands will be united*
E ku ana ka paia	*The walls will stand upright*

Kapihe, 1814, at the birth of Kauikeaouli, Kamehameha III

It was a 6 a.m. wake-up call.

Nine students from nine Hawaiian schools prepared for sunrise protocol at Pōlolu Valley Lookout. ʻIwa birds greeted their voices, together chanting the sun above the clouds on the horizon. E Ala E. Then each student chanted alone, on behalf of a community, starting with Kumukahi and ending with Niʻihau. As their voices layered in the morning light, it was undeniable there were signs that these students were on the right path that their kūpuna intended them to be on. The hulihia was in motion.

I was one of those nine students. At that moment I felt like the hulihia was happening, and I was one of those lucky nine to be a part of it. I had a good feeling about what we were about to embark on, but even more so today, I see the value of why we started Ke Ea Hawaiʻi.

Ke Ea Hawaiʻi has grown to become an interscholastic student council composed of one elected representative from each of fifteen Hawaiian-focused charter schools across three islands: Hawaiʻi, Oʻahu, and Kauaʻi. This middle and high school council strives to be unlike an American student body government, which often replicates inequality, with a President, Vice President, Treasurer, and Secretary who plan social activities that boost school spirit. In Ke Ea, every school representative has an equal role. The council focuses on collective liberation through health, language, education, land, economic, and governmental initiatives.

Its mission is to give a voice to the unheard generation. It allows the youth who everyone talks about to sit at the table when we discuss Hawaiʻi's future, instead of having others decide for us, without us.

When we started Ke Ea Hawai'i in 2013, I was a junior at Samuel Mānaiakalani Kamakau Public Charter School. It was time to think about which college I would apply for and what career I wanted after high school. I had just gotten my first job working at a movie theater the previous year. It was exciting to taste what "adulting" was like, but that work was not aligning with my foundation of 'ike Hawai'i.

Ke Ea Hawai'i is what brought me back to my piko when I needed to reground myself and align with my kūpuna. At times, I would second guess myself and ask if I was holding too much on my plate with all the kuleana I had. But somehow I knew that it would be worth it in the end. I knew creating and nurturing Ke Ea was bigger than I could understand at that time.

Creating this council has opened the door and shown many Hawai'i leaders that young minds have valuable perspectives to offer. We have planned more than ten youth-led conferences and represented Hawai'i on the world stage at various times. Perhaps our largest contribution is still in its infancy.

The Hawaiian Kingdom Weekly and *Ke Aupuni Hawai'i* are student news shows in English and 'Ōlelo Hawai'i that synthesize and serialize important events each week. The project evolved out of our council's desire to hui ana nā moku, to unify our peers and communities, toward common goals through social media.

We felt that Facebook was underutilized as a place for consistent, reliable news. Social media posts are not fact-checked or archived the way newspapers once were. Meanwhile, we witnessed Hawai'i newspapers, radio, and television networks conglomerate under massive corporations run by stockholders. This is the opposite of the Hawaiian nūpepa era, when competition for power over mass media used to rival competition for public office. Newspaper scholar Dr. Rubellite Kawena Johnson captured this idea in the epigraph to one of her anthologies when she quoted former US President Thomas Jefferson, who said "were it left to me to decide whether we should have a government without newspapers, or newspapers without a government, I should not hesitate a moment to prefer the latter."

Our demand for sovereign government in Hawai'i must coincide with a demand for mass media control. We do not expect *The Hawaiian Kingdom Weekly* and *Ke Aupuni Hawai'i* to compete with Nexstar or Black Press. We foresee social media technology opening space for a healthy number of small-market news programs in Hawai'i similar to what we saw in the 1800s. Many weekly shows have indeed emerged in 2020 thanks to social media technology, including Nā'au News Now's *The Darkside of Hawaiian Politics*, Kanaeokana's *Lei Ānuenue*, and OHA's *Ola Ka Hāloa*. Our niche is youth and education.

The Hawaiian Kingdom Weekly and *Ke Aupuni Hawai'i* are produced by a team of ten students: news anchors, reporters, videographers, scriptwriters, and a social media team connecting viewers on Instagram, Facebook, and YouTube. Our intent is to provide our lāhui with updates on what is happening around the world from a Hawaiian kingdom perspective. So far, we've produced twenty-five episodes, one per week every week since January 2020.

Shows like these are crucial for our lāhui, considering the imbalance of information in the mass media and dominant society. Shows we produce ourselves help correct this imbalance, so we can decide what we should know, and can talk about issues the media corporations are not addressing. Social media has been an excellent platform for stories that news corporations do not cover. There is universal access to consume but also to produce news with the click of a "post" button.

Just as our kūpuna were excited about nūpepa, it is once again an exciting time for Hawai'i, as so many people can share news that travels instantly across the pae 'āina. No matter if it's good news, bad news, riddles, or funny stories, it belongs to us.

Being an alumna of a school whose namesake played a vital role in nūpepa for our lāhui, my appreciation continues to grow for what our kūpuna accomplished through newspapers. After reading S. M. Kamakau's stories from multiple angles, it is clear he was writing not just for the people of his time, but to preserve the past and the present for the future, so we have a solid source of information from someone's own eyes. Who are the modern-day historians who will document the stories in our time for posterity?

I think what we are creating is a part of the hulihia because we are making technology work for us, so future generations will have regular, consistent, reliable sources of news to look back on. Consider Mauna Kea. Despite the network news stations continuing to frame kia'i as "protestors," through social media many people were made aware of the desecration and disregard for law. Social media encourages other communities around the world to stand together in solidarity against irresponsible and illegal development projects that people are otherwise unaware of until they are completed. Mauna Kea organizers learned from previous movements, and then inspired other communities to stand up together for their 'āina and for one another, including Ihumātao in Aotearoa, Hong Kong, Wet'suwet'en, and Black Lives Matter.

I believe if we use social media for the right reasons it can really bring people around the world together to work hand-in-hand and change the structure of the broken systems around the world that were not made for us, but for a system built on racial hierarchy. I think media holds value that benefits all generations, old and young, and yet to come. Creating our shows, *The Hawaiian Kingdom Weekly* and *Ke Aupuni Hawai'i*, we usher in a new era of nūpepa, and we make our kūpuna proud.

Work Cited

Johnson, Rubellite Kinney, editor. *Kukini 'Aha'ilono (Carry on the News)*. Topgallant, 1976.

Kau'i McElroy was born and raised in Ko'olaupoko, O'ahu, and is a 2015 alumna of Ke Kula o Samuel M. Kamakau.

The Next Aloha ʻĀina

Mari Matsuda

> I hate the capitalist system
> I'll tell you the reason why
> They caused me so much suffering
> And my dearest friends to die.

So sang Sarah Gunning, a coal miner's daughter who grew up without books, TV, or radio. How did she come to bring political economy to traditional Appalachian a cappella, and why is her song in my head in Mānoa valley, as the breeze blows down from the hollow where Wilcox rebels hid after failing to restore their nation?

Sarah Gunning's baby died of starvation—her maternal wails, like Queen Emma's, heard by green hills.

A paddler said the canoe flies with equal application of strength. All resisters who watched beloveds die are paddling with us through history, applying their strength, as suddenly we fly over the crest, to the future.

I asked students, "After years of relative quiet, what brought thousands to the Mauna?" We talked. Here are my notes:

Pedagogy, intellectuals
Social media
Organizers
Culture/hālau
Hawaiian immersion schools
Intergenerational obligation
Material conditions
High quality media/design, "cool"
Historical timing
Experience in other struggles

"I learned from Kaleikoa Kaʻeo. He learned from Haunani-Kay Trask," one student said. Dr. Trask rests while she teaches through her students: an army of teachers, teaching an army of teachers the manaʻo of one who spoke of "colonialism," "imperialism," "racism," in explicating her first love and abiding passion, her nation, Hawaiʻi.

The ships of capitalism's ascendance were death ships. Conquistadors' galleons, bursting with soldiers sent to kill all standing in the way of conquest. Slave ships, floating torture chambers. Three-masters bringing Cook, the whalers, the plagues, the bible, the laws that turned life-giving ʻāina into private feeholds. As ships were christened for plunder, mill-soot darkened cities and children set spindles for cotton grown on land cleared by genocide, grown by labor toiling under the lash. In Hawaiʻi, too, the lash.[1]

Some decry applying current judgment to the past, yet there were sailors on the slave ship, also under the lash, who turned away in horror when human cargo was jettisoned in a storm. Lonely priests charged blasphemy when, in God's name, genocide followed the conquistadors. The Kānaka Maoli never stopped recording, in mele and writings, love of their land, and grief at its theft. They lost loved ones until only one in ten remained. They pledged their hearts "until the very last aloha ʻāina."

Auwē!

The slaves rebelled. The coal miners went on strike. While the sugar barons imposed a bayonet constitution, giving votes to rich haole but not to makaʻāinana, they acted against the record of thousands of Chartists who fought in England for the right of the unpropertied to vote. The system of the few denying democracy to the many was condemned at every step. The fortunes built by breaking the hearts of grieving mothers were built without permission.

We walk daily over ground marking the fight-back. At Hilo Bay, workers were shot organizing for fair wages. On every island, organizers spoke against the Big Five in multiple languages. At our University, generations of students fought for a pono world. Hawaiʻi Youth for Democracy was called a "communist front" for fighting fascism and worker exploitation in the forties. Takeovers have regularly graced Bachman Hall—against the war in Vietnam, for Ethnic Studies, to divest from apartheid South Africa, to ban classified research, for the Mauna. Students cozied into sleeping bags and dined on donated bento, imprinting resistance.

In 1976, I was a law student helping progressive undergraduates who took over ASUH, using activity funds to fly in Angela Davis. Dr. Davis quickly recognized her comrades: the Protect Kahoʻolawe ʻOhana, and the tenants struggling at Waiāhole-Waikāne. She cited them by name at a mass meeting overflowing the Campus Center Ballroom.

"Wouldn't you be more effective," a woman asked, "if you didn't call yourself a communist?"

"No," Dr. Davis explained, "in many places I go, especially in the South, people remember communist organizers as the only ones who came to their community to help people in their struggles."

* * *

Sarah Gunning, coal miner's daughter, one of fifteen siblings, grew up barefoot and Kentucky poor. She met communist organizers of the National Miners Union who came when children were hungry. She learned of a system responsible for her suffering, to name it and fight it.

My mother also grew up barefoot and poor, one of ten children raised on a sugar plantation at Makaweli, Kaua'i. Communist organizers fanned out to every camp, and workers who knew in their weary bones what it felt like to work, as we still sing at bon dances, "one dolla day," were ready to huli.

The Hawai'i Seven were tried under the Smith Act for advocating the violent overthrow of the United States. The actual plan was more democratic and therefore more dangerous. The Seven wanted workers to control the conditions of their lives, and keep the benefits of their labors. They were not violent. You could not meet more gentle, kind women than the Nisei put on trial.

Aiko Reinecke. Rachel Saiki. Eileen Fujimoto. They were my mother's friends, and like her, their experience with racism and poverty made them lifelong advocates for labor rights, peace, and justice. They were sweet, smart women who would not let you go hungry on their watch. "Have you eaten?" was their greeting. If I had the time, I could write a book about each of these people, each of these struggles, so rich with life lessons.

The story of resistance to the stealing of a nation by the sugar barons and self-described "mission boys" is well-documented by Dr. Silva, Dr. Osorio, and others. Nothing ever done by the roaring machine of profit and exploitation that smashed across modernity happened with the consent of the people whose lives were destroyed by it. Certainly not in Hawai'i Nei. Songs of resistance play daily on the radio—some with a reggae or rap beat, some written by ali'i over a hundred years ago, still sung today, telling the story of a people who love this land.

The story is rewritten—in a play in 'ōlelo Hawai'i that sells out every night at Kennedy Theatre and travels to New York, with Jon Osorio playing himself, honoring the memory of George Helm and the struggle to save Kaho'olawe. A PKO veteran jumps up from the audience to join the cast in a spontaneous hula. The audience weeps.

And then, the mountain. I honor and do not presume to tell each protector's precious story of their personal call to Mauna a Wākea. Each individual's act connects to the arc of history that Dr. King called us to bend toward justice.

In the summer of 2019, Hawaiians said "enough, 'a'ole." The following summer, Black Lives Matter led an entire nation to that same place on the question of police killings. In every state in the US and in Hawai'i, mass protests filled the streets, as pandemic threatened the lives and livelihoods of millions. Crisis piled upon crisis, revealing the utter unsustainability of a system based on selfish individualism and endless profit-seeking. Kentucky coal miners and Mauna Kea kia'i hollered "Black Lives Matter," as tributaries of struggle converged.

It is midnight on the clock of the Anthropocene. The smash, grab, take machine has taken so much that we will perish unless it stops. ʻAʻole. Every resister, ever, stands behind us as we seek a better way.

We can choose to love the land and all that comes from it. We can take one another into sacred bonds of mutual care. We will not let you fall, you are not alone.

What do you want? I know what you want.

Safety

Beauty

Joy

Love

Meaning

How do I know you want it? Because I do. So desperately. Enough to link arms with you and face down men with guns.

I know how much good is possible because I have seen it with my kin in struggle. I know how much beauty is possible because I write with green mountains over my shoulder, and I will die with a hundred songs in my head.

It's connected. Black citizens murdered for just trying to live their lives, calls to let the virus "kill the weak," our tolerance of mass shootings, of the old woman sleeping on pavement. Incapacity of empathy cascades from history, back to the cargo hold of the slave ship.

But you, who feel kinship with a mountain, you who feel pain when any other human is in pain, you are the one we are waiting for. Your paddle slices cleanly into the ocean, your strength matched equally by so many others. Welcome, to the new world you are making. You will love it. It will love you back. I promise.

Note

1. A plantation worker beaten and flogged to death, reported in *Republic of Hawaiʻi v. Hickey*, 11 Haw. 314 (1898).

Mari Matsuda is a professor at the William S. Richardson School of Law and an artist, www.marimatsudapeaceorchestra.com.

Hāmākua 2120

A Moʻolelo of Abundance from a Future

No'eau Peralto

A century has passed since the Great Hulihia of the 2020s, when the former State of Hawai'i took its final breaths during the global COVID-19 pandemic crisis. The pandemic was indeed a "portal, a gateway between one world and the next," as Indian author-activist Arundhati Roy suggested in her 2020 essay, providing an opportunity for our kūpuna to imagine another world—one vastly different from the one they had inhabited. In the midst of a global pandemic, they imagined—or perhaps it was a combination of their courageous imaginings and enactings—a world that stitched the rupture between their future and a more distant past.

Today, we know this vision as a moʻolelo of abundance. In fact, our kūpuna created the conditions for us to live the moʻolelo of abundance that we all know and love. Perhaps this world of ours looks a lot more like the Hawai'i centuries prior to the COVID-19 virus. Perhaps our early twenty-first-century kūpuna never thought it possible before the pandemic. Perhaps we have not yet reached the nuʻu that they strived for. After all, the future is created every day, through our actions and inactions.

For generations now in Hāmākua, we have lived on the precipice of complete autonomy from the rest of our island and world—not disconnected, but merely lawa, satisfied and fulfilled by the abundance that we have cultivated on our 'āina and in our community. It has not come without struggle. Every meal we can now provide for our 'ohana has come at the cost of immense sacrifice. When I think about the time of the Great Hulihia that set us on this path, I think of our courageous ancestors who changed the course of our history. I think of the ones who emerged out of the time of sugar plantations, who saw past the towering stands of eucalyptus plantations, and who acted with bold conviction to return our hands to the land, and to transform *land* into *'āina* again.

For us in Hāmākua Hikina, it started in Koholālele with Hui Mālama i ke Ala 'Ūlili (huiMAU). Driven by a mission to reestablish the systems that sustain our community, huiMAU turned three hundred acres of eucalyptus-covered land into food-bearing 'āina within ten years of the onset of COVID-19. As it had been eighteen generations prior to the Great Hulihia—in the time of our great ali'i mahi'ai, 'Umi-a-Līloa—Koholālele again became a piko of resurgence for regenerating aloha ʻāina in our moku. After huiMAU established the Kulāiwi Koholālele Hālau for ʻŌiwi Excellence, it was not long before a new generation of aloha ʻāina was born, establishing kīpuka aloha ʻāina in ahupuaʻa throughout Hāmākua, from Kaʻula to Honokeʻā. Koholālele became a model for twenty-first century ahupuaʻa-based governance, where mahiʻai limalau (collective cultivation) became a common practice again in Hāmākua. When the pandemic forced governments to prioritize genuine homeland security over militarization, hunger and famine became our collective adversary, as it had in generations prior—

> me he mea ala e hoouka ana imua o kekahi kahua kaua, me ke alualu aku i ka enemi kipi o ka aina, oia hoi ka wi o na kau i hala ae, me ka hoopuehu aku ia ia a lilo i mea ole, me he opalaʻla i mua o ka makani. ("Mahiai limalau")

Within two generations, mono-cropped fields of sugarcane and eucalyptus overgrown with guinea grass became one of Hawaiʻi's most famous groves of ʻulu—affectionately known as Ka Maha ʻUlu o Koholālele. It is beloved today not because it is where everyone in our community goes to work, but because it is where everyone goes to ʻai, to eat of the ʻāina. Organizing with local mahiʻai to replace outdated zoning regulations with new aloha ʻāina-centered policies, huiMAU created Ka Maha ʻUlu o Koholālele as a residential maha ʻulu (cultivated ʻulu grove). This regenerative space provides ʻohana with kuleana ʻāina—a place where they can noho papa, subsist and thrive, be born and be buried, and to which they are ultimately accountable. It is reminiscent of the community created by ʻUmi and Kaleiokū in Waipunalei during their wā hulihia—kahi hānai kānaka o ʻUmi—

> O ka hanai no ia i kanaka, a piha ua halau a piha ua halau . . . . aia na kanaka a pau o ka mahiai ka hana nui . . . he malama i ke kanaka nui i ke kanaka iki, i ka elemakule, i ka luahine i ke keiki, i ka ilihune i ka mea mai. Hookahi hana nui o ka hanai i ke kanaka. (Kamakau)

As the maha ʻulu grew, so too did the mahiʻai. And as the mahiʻai cultivated ʻai, so too was our capacity cultivated to ai, to love ourselves and each other intimately, and to ʻai, to govern ourselves.

Our local economy is now a circular one, founded upon aloha ʻāina and centered around community care and sharing. In the wake of the Black Lives Matter movement, funding for policing and prisons in Hawaiʻi was gradually reinvested in hoʻoponopono, healthcare, and education. The department of education was decentralized in favor of community-based hālau designed to create educational pathways for specialization in life-sustaining and innovative technologies and practices, with a particular focus in Hāmākua on the "four M's"—moʻolelo (storytelling and creative arts), mahiʻai (food cultivation and weather forecasting), mālama ʻāina (ʻāina regeneration), and mālama kaiāulu (community care). In 2020, most adults worked in the tourism and construction industries. Now over 90 percent of us work right here in our Community Hālau, which provides educational programs and physical and mental healthcare services for all ages: in Ka Maha 'Ulu, which provides 100 percent of our food resources, from 'āina to 'ōpū via the Hāmākua food hub network; in the Hui Mālama 'Āina, which stewards our moku's watersheds, forests, streams, springs, and fisheries, and oversees development projects, waste management, and all pathways of travel; and in a variety of 'ohana- and community-owned enterprises that provide other essential services related to energy, repair, recycling, and self-care.

Our kūpuna in Hāmākua weren't the only ones creating this hulihia. Post-COVID-19, kīpuka aloha 'āina emerged and erupted in every corner and crevice of this pae 'āina. From the depths of our deepest despair emerged ea—a new Hawai'i, breathing free of the chains of imperialism. Following the collapse of the United States of America ushered in by the Trump administration, Hawai'i quickly reassumed its position as an independent country and a leader among a constellation of deoccupied and demilitarized island nations in Oceania. This political autonomy was not given; it was the result of an intergenerational struggle to reestablish ea. The organizing and collective action of po'e aloha 'āina in kīpuka

A vision map for a future Hāmākua. Haley Kailiehu, 2020.

aloha ʻāina reignited our critical Hawaiian national consciousness around social justice, food sovereignty, and community-based governance.

In Hāmākua, this means that decisions about our ʻāina, kai, and kaiāulu are now made at the scale of kalana (sub-districts) by an ʻaha (council) of knowledgable, kuleana-driven representatives from each of the three Hāmākua kalana. Within these ʻAha ʻAi Kalana, kuleana for decision-making is weighted in relation to each person's physical and intellectual proximity to the people, places, and/or practices at the core of each decision. Matters of moku-scale importance are vetted by ʻAha ʻAi Moku, and matters of mokupuni importance are decided by ʻAha ʻAi Mokupuni. Matters of pae ʻāina-scale importance are vetted by the ʻAha Kuapapa—a decentralized assembly of representatives from each moku of each mokupuni. This structure of governance has empowered communities in Hawaiʻi to ea, to excel in fulfilling their kuleana, and to come together as an aupuni kuapapa when necessary. For example, the ʻAha Kuapapa supported the perpetual designation of Maunakea and the Kaʻohe aquifer as a national wahi kapu, free of industrial development and militarization, protected to fulfill their life-giving functions for natural and cultural regeneration.

The COVID-19 pandemic did not create the Great Hulihia. It was merely the portal—the piko—into which our kūpuna courageously entered and emerged anew. Here in Hāmākua of 2120 we recall this as our moʻolelo of abundance.

And so the questions I pose to you:

What world did the kūpuna of your ʻāina imagine?

What world did they fight for?

What world did they birth into existence for you?

Works Cited

Kamakau, S. M. "Ka Moolelo Hawaii." *Ke Au Okoa*, 17 Now. 1870, ʻaoʻao 1.

"Mahiai limalau ma Ahualoa, Hamakua, Hawaii." *Ka Nupepa Kuokoa*, 5 Malaki 1864, ʻaoʻao 3.

Roy, Arundhati. "The pandemic is a portal." *Financial Times*, 3 Apr. 2020, https://www.ft.com/content/10d8f5e8-74eb-11ea-95fe-fcd274e920ca.

Noʻeau Peralto was born and raised in Waiākea Uka, Hilo, Hawaiʻi, and is a proud descendant of kūpuna from Koholālele, Hāmākua, Hawaiʻi, where he now resides. He holds a PhD in Indigenous Politics from the University of Hawaiʻi at Mānoa. His dissertation research explored the continuity of aloha ʻāina praxis in his home community of Hāmākua Hikina through the ʻāina- and story-based resurgence work of Hui Mālama i ke Ala ʻŪlili—a grassroots, ʻŌiwi-led nonprofit organization of which he is a founding member and the current Executive Director. Noʻeau is a community organizer, educator, and a cultivator of seeds and stories.

Dear Reader

Making the Value of Hawai'i Together

Aiko Yamashiro

> In the end the value of Hawai'i cannot be determined by one person alone. Here I can only share what it means to me, and that I want to sit and hear you share what it means to you. If we do that over and over again with many people, maybe then we'll know.
>
> Dawn Mahi, "Kalihi Calls"
> *The Value of Hawai'i 2: Ancestral Roots, Oceanic Visions*

Dear Reader,

I want you to know that this book was hard to write. Some of the essays we were hoping for could not be written, because the world was too fast and loud and sad to get words down. Some of the essays in here almost did not get written because these days some of us find it difficult to get out of bed, and some of us find it difficult to stop moving long enough to write.

As an editor, I have had the privilege of being invited into the writing of many of these essays, and I got to learn where the ideas in this book come from. While sitting alone in my one bedroom in Ka'alaea, while working on this book late at night with many of the authors, I have visited hot humid valleys and wide bays. Experienced songs and languages and dances I don't know. Felt red dirt and cool fishpond waters, and cold hospital rooms. I have met grandparents, children, 'āina, ancestors passed. I have met many of these authors' *why*.

Sometimes we think that writing happens in isolation, in silence and concentration. Or that ideas and visions come out whole and fully formed. As an editor I want to make sure to tell you that the essays here about the value of Hawai'i come from being together. From laughing and playing and crying and trying and struggling and living together—with other people and with 'āina we love.

Each essay is full of voices, stories, and homes. They were written in response to and written with community. These essays were never meant to sit quietly in a book. They are an offering to us to move and share and create.

How can we make the value of Hawaiʻi, together?

Writing and sharing poetry in group settings has taught me the power of saying words we mean, and really listening to each other. I have had the privilege of teaching poetry at UH Mānoa, in community settings, and at an after-school club at Castle High School, my alma mater. For teenagers, young adults, aunties, and uncles, poetry can be a way to express the worries we have about being a good friend or sibling or parent or partner. The dreams for our lives that excite us, and make us afraid too. The grief we feel when losing a loved one.

I have heard the tremble in a voice when saying something important out loud for the first time. I have experienced the absolute silence of a circle of people listening, who understand the weight of such a gift. When we say words we truly mean and listen to each other. When we can be vulnerable and open our whole souls. I think that is how we build trust, understanding, and stronger community together.

How can we make the value of Hawaiʻi, together?

As artists, when we come together to create collaboratively, we must come without a clear end in sight. Not without purpose, but without a set answer. We must come a little open. Ready to learn, or change. This is the same way we come together to mālama ʻāina, or to fish or to make lei. This is the same way we go to visit a tūtū. Show up. Bring yourself, your gratitude, and a snack to share. We come to share our lives. We come ready for a genuine conversation.

I believe that genuine conversation can build community. I currently work at the Hawaiʻi Council for the Humanities, a nonprofit with a commitment to creating public humanities programs—programs where we bring the powers of literature, culture, history, philosophy, and other human insights to bear upon and explore complicated and important questions about our lives. What do we value, and why? What does it mean to call Hawaiʻi home? What futures can we dream of and create together?

Our mission is to connect people with ideas that enrich lives, broaden perspectives, and strengthen communities. One way we've been doing this is by holding community conversations called Try Think, a program that began as a humanities class in the Oʻahu correctional facilities. Some of its central beliefs are that *everyone matters, but not everyone feels they matter,* and *valuing our differences is what creates true safety.* We believe in creating spaces to connect with each other that are not spaces of debate or winning. Instead, we practice together how to listen and open ourselves to perspectives and experiences that are not our own. Creating a culture of genuine conversation—where every voice can be heard and considered—can lead to transformation. As a friend, poet, and former student reminded me recently, we can do great things once we trust ourselves and each other.

Being a good editor is about being a good listener. Completely opening to someone else's story, and working with them to help them tell it in the clearest and most powerful way. As one of four co-editors, I got to struggle deep in the stories of some of these authors, helping to shape them for this publication. One completely rewrote her piece after realizing who it was she really wanted to talk to. Not *about* them, but *to* them. Another told me he was too depressed to write anything, and then managed to tell a story that made me cry—with the force of not just his spirit, but all the people he wrote about, who he carries, who help support him.

Listening to these amazing authors and community members has reminded me that we are made in all our interactions, relationships, in our kuleana we have chosen and that have chosen us. We come to what we love and commit to, with our best talents. We come with all who have made us.

How can we make the value of Hawai'i, together?

It is the start of obon season as I write this—a time when the ancestors are visiting us to dance and eat and sing and remember together. Last night, I attended an online obon musical program put on by Ukwanshin Kabudan, along with ninety other people of different generations. The presenters play old songs that open up memories in everyone. Normally at this time, I would be following a bon dance circuit, going to different temples every weekend to eat fried noodles and musubi, and follow behind Japanese and Okinawan grandmas who remind me of mine who have passed. They shine in kimono and hapi coats decorated with leaves and flowers. My hands follow their hands—planting seeds, tilling soil, rounding the moon.

Norman Kaneshiro sensei is talking about the linguistic and cultural differences between the Okinawan word "chibariyo" and the Japanese word "ganbare." *Ganbare* is about trying hard to overcome some external hardship, he explains. Of not yielding, even in intense difficulty. *Chibariyo* is different. It is about reaching deep inside to muster all that you are—your experiences, your culture, your ancestors, everything they taught you. This is a source of tremendous strength and energy in times of struggle. As the sanshin plays and the voices climb and fall, I think about what it means to stay open to the tremendous universe we each carry.

Dear Reader, thank you for listening to me. I want to hear you too. I will bring all of myself to this.

Let's make the value of Hawai'i together.

Aiko Yamashiro was raised in Kāne'ohe, O'ahu, and is lucky to live near enough to see her mother Aileen, brother Daniel, sister Amy, niyok, kalo, ha'u'oi, and the Ko'olau mountains almost every day. She is also lucky during this lockdown to sometimes get to visit Okinawa, Guåhan, and other loved ones in her dreams. Aiko writes and shares poetry, admires her friends, and is thankful for song in times of joy and grief. She is the executive director of the Hawai'i Council for the Humanities.